On Intellectual Activism

PATRICIA HILL COLLINS

On Intellectual Activism

TEMPLE UNIVERSITY PRESS  PHILADELPHIA

TEMPLE UNIVERSITY PRESS
Philadelphia, Pennsylvania 19122
www.temple.edu/tempress

Library of Congress Cataloging-in-Publication Data

Hill Collins, Patricia.
  On intellectual activism / Patricia Hill Collins.
    p. cm.
  Includes bibliographical references and index.
  ISBN 978-1-4399-0960-7 (cloth : alk. paper) — ISBN 978-1-4399-0961-4
(pbk. : alk. paper) — ISBN 978-1-4399-0962-1 (e-book) 1. Womanism.
2. Racism—United States. 3. African American intellectuals. I. Title.
  HQ1197.C65 2013
  305.48'896073—dc23
                                                    2012015151

♾The paper used in this publication meets the requirements of the
American National Standard for Information Sciences—Permanence
of Paper for Printed Library Materials, ANSI Z39.48-1992

Printed in the United States of America

6 8 9 7 5

Contents

Acknowledgments

THIS BOOK REPRESENTS the collective voice of conversations large and small that I have had over three decades with people from all walks of life. It is impossible to acknowledge each conversation individually. Instead, I send out a thank you to each of you who use my work in your classrooms, term papers, and scholarship. I am grateful to those of you who hosted my visits on your campuses, in your classrooms, or with your community groups.

I want to thank some of the many individuals whose contributions were important to the preparation and production of this book. The research and editorial assistance provided by a broad group of students over the past two decades not only influenced my thinking about themes in this volume but also helped me get the work done. University of Cincinnati graduate students Tamika Odum, Julie Hilvers, and Vallarie Henderson provided invaluable support during the early stages of this project. They transcribed talks, edited essays, and helped me manage an unwieldy set of notes from public lectures. Special thanks also go out to Quay Martin, a gifted Africana Studies major at the University of Cincinnati, who conducted a lengthy interview with me about my life's work. The transcript she provided from that interview has been invaluable. I'd like to thank University of Maryland sociology graduate students David Strohecker, Kathryn Buford, Valerie Chepp, Kendra Barber, William Yagatich, Anya Galli, Michelle Beadle, and Tony Hatch, who provided research and editorial support for various essays in this book. Special thanks to my wonderful T3 education graduate students Laura Yee, Rob Carey, and Wyletta Gamble whose passion for equity in education reminded me of the importance of critical pedagogy to intellectual activism.

This book could not have been completed without the invaluable assistance of Margaret Austin Smith, a sociology graduate student at the University of

Maryland, and the primary research and editorial assistant for this project. Meg tirelessly read various drafts of all of the essays and edited the manuscript in its entirety. Her incisive mind and excellent organizational skills made this book much stronger than if I had done it on my own. She has a promising future and I look forward to having her as colleague.

This project also benefited from the institutional support that I received from the University of Maryland. Being granted a sabbatical for 2011–2012 enabled me to finish this book on schedule. Special thanks to Bill Falk and Reeve Vanneman, former chairs of the Department of Sociology, for their continued support for my work. I would also like to thank the Department of Sociology's administrative staff, Patty Bernales, Mini Rajan Geraldine Todd, and Karina Havrilla, whose professionalism and ability to get things done continues to amaze me. I am also very grateful for the ongoing support that I have received as a Distinguished University Professor. It has been invaluable in my finding time to devote to this project for a public readership.

This book has benefited from the expertise provided by a wonderful team of people at Temple University Press. Micah Kleit, my editor, has been a source of support throughout this project. I am also grateful to the entire production team, with special thanks to Nancy Lombardi for her expert oversight as the production editor, Gary Kramer for his marketing acumen, and Kate Nichols for her supervision of cover design. Special thanks to Karla Schroeder for expert copyediting of my manuscript.

My family and friends continue to encourage me and provide much needed support. Roger Collins my spouse, Valerie Collins my daughter, and Lauren Pruitt my daughter-in-law, each in their own special way, inspire me to keep going with this difficult work. Special thanks to family members Marilyn and Bill Lewis and Taryn Carter for being so welcoming to a prodigal daughter who is returning to the family fold. Colleagues and friends old and new also contributed to the completion of this project—special thanks to Beth Perry, Linda Riggins, Pauline Schwartz, Wendy Gillenson, Wayne Taylor, Bobbie Knable, Maggie Andersen, Bonnie Dill, Elizabeth Higginbotham, Patrice Dickerson, Dee Irby, Tina Merriweather, Angelene Jamison-Hall, Michelle Burstion, Pauline Smolin, and Kelly Leon.

Finally, I dedicate this book to the memory of my father, Albert Hill, a tireless drum major for social justice.

Introduction

Speak the truth to the people
Talk sense to the people
Free them with reason
Free them with honesty
Free the people with Love and Courage and Care for their Being
     —MARI EVANS, from *I Am a Black Woman* (1970)

MARI EVANS' POEM "Speak the Truth to the People" invokes the social and political upheaval of the Civil Rights and Black Power movements of 1960s and 1970s. As an African American poet influenced by the Black Arts Movement, Evans' poetry aimed to speak the truth to the public about issues as diverse as racism, poverty, domestic violence, and the power of love as an antidote to oppression. Her 1970 volume *I Am a Black Woman* constituted one voice in a groundswell of Black feminist intellectual production that saw speaking the truth to African American women as its special mission. This same era produced a broad array of artists and intellectuals from diverse racial, ethnic, class, gender, and sexual backgrounds who, through their scholarship, art, and political activism, questioned prevailing power arrangements. Their creative work contributed to social movements against racism, sexism, militarism, homophobia, age discrimination, and class exploitation. Collectively, their work exemplifies traditions of *intellectual activism*: namely, the myriad ways that people place the power of their ideas in service to social justice.

Just as the themes of intellectual activism are far-reaching, the mechanisms that people use to engage in intellectual activism are similarly broad. Evans, for example, studied fashion design at the University of Toledo, but like others of her generation, rejected the imposed separation between scholarship and activism, school and society, thinking and doing. Refusing these binaries created space for new forms of creativity. Evans' chosen terrain of intellectual activism consisted of writing poems, plays, children's books, and a musical adaptation of Zora Neale Hurston's *Their Eyes Were Watching God,* activities quite far afield from her formal field of study. Significantly, by writing and directing *The Black Experience,* a television program that aired from 1968 to 1973 in Indianapolis, Evans foreshadowed the current impetus toward using mass media venues to educate the public. Through visual arts, music, poetry, fiction, essays, journal articles, nonfiction, books, and videography, like Evans, many artists, intellectuals, activists, and everyday people have recognized the necessity of multiple expressions of intellectual activism for social change.

Today, we face equally important social issues—environmental degradation, terrorism, poverty, violence against women, government indifference, racism, and youth disenfranchisement permeate the news. We forget what it was like for youth of Evans' generation. They faced an array of social injustices against women, African Americans, Latinos, poor people, and lesbian, gay, bisexual, and transgendered people that uncovered stark contradictions between the American Dream and its actualization. Their social movements and their signature intellectual activism reflected these broader social concerns. In their intellectual activism, the youth of Evans' generation could stand on the shoulders of their parents, who faced similar challenges a generation earlier. Drawing on the educational opportunities that their parents struggled to provide for them, Evans' generation changed the terms of discourse and social practices concerning race, gender, class, and sexuality in the United States. Despite the unfinished promise of social justice practices in the contemporary period, their legacy to us has been a social justice agenda in the United States that can serve as a beacon for those who wish to support it.

Given this history, I wonder how effectively today's scholars and public intellectuals speak the truth to the people about contemporary social issues. For prior generations, media access was more carefully rationed and controlled, making it difficult to find others of like mind and to educate the public about important social issues. Face-to-face interaction and landline telephones were necessary for community organizing. Now, however, new technologies have opened up formerly unimaginable ways for us to talk to one another. We are swimming in information, but how much of that information moves us closer to the truths that will sustain us? For example, in 2011, sharing information via cell phones and the Internet, youth in the Arab world sparked democracy movements with global impact. Yet without careful cultivation, these high-tech versions of grassroots politics may be drowned out by the voices of pundits that blast forth from countless cable television stations, from satellite radio, and by the trivialities of podcasts gone viral. Individuals can now see themselves on YouTube and post their ideas on blogs with blinding speed. Yet for all this talk and noise, what are we saying that is of value? Where are the conversations that will spur contemporary intellectual activism?

Believing in the possibility of intellectual activism is one thing—figuring out how to do it within contemporary politics of knowledge production is another. During the social movements of the mid- to late twentieth century, people like Evans who engaged in intellectual activism were more closely tied to social movement politics. African Americans, Latinos, women, and working-class whites were excluded from the classrooms, faculty meetings, editorial meetings, publishing houses, and media venues of knowledge production. Their social position as outsiders shaped their perception of how their intellectual activism might bring about change. They saw power from afar, typically imagining its organization and envisioning what they would do differently once they gained access to it in business, government, and academia. In contrast, within increasingly corporate colleges and universities and monopolistic mainstream media, in the early twenty-first century, we confront a contradictory politics of inclusion and exclusion. Some individuals from formerly excluded groups now occupy positions of power and authority inside the social institutions that formerly excluded them, with many of these insiders engaged in intellectual work. At the same time, as the lyrics of global hip hop remind us, far too many others remain just as firmly excluded as before. Across the globe, youth, women, people of color, religious and sexual minorities, and the disabled bear the brunt of contemporary social issues. Where is their intellectual activism? What does it mean to harness the power of ideas for social justice within these constraints? What does intellectual activism mean in the context of an inclusionary politics of the early twenty-first century that manages to produce exclusionary outcomes?

Speaking the Truth to Power, Speaking the Truth to the People

As individuals, each of us occupies a dual location: included in some groups, yet excluded from others. The issue for most of us lies less in being a pure insider or outsider than in the terms of our participation within all of the venues to which we belong. For example, as an American citizen, an African American woman from a working-class background, and an academic who has experienced considerable upward social mobility, I have consistently grappled with this theme of being simultaneously an insider and an outsider. Throughout my professional career, I have struggled to gain clarity concerning how ever-shifting patterns of belonging and exclusion have shaped the contours of my intellectual activism.

Negotiating the contemporary politics of knowledge production from "outsider within" social locations raises some fundamental dilemmas. In a misguided effort to protect standards, many of my academic colleagues within colleges and universities derogate any work that they see as being too "popular" as less rigorous and scholarly than other work. Worse yet, having one's work deemed "political" demotes it to the realm of the nonacademic. These norms suppress the kind of engaged scholarship that interests me and that is fundamental for intellectual activism. Significantly, higher education claims that it has a monopoly on knowledge production and that scholarly knowledge occupies the pinnacle of excellence. In addition, my activist colleagues working outside colleges and universities see my decision to work within the academy as a default position. They often view professors as people who are either too timid or are not sufficiently committed to the front lines of whatever political or social movement preoccupies them. Because they are outsiders, they can misrecognize academic politics as real politics. They too can cede the power that is attached to knowledge production to people with advanced degrees or stellar careers within higher education. Further, most members of the general public are also outsiders to the legitimated mechanisms of knowledge production in colleges and universities, but they are also major stakeholders in what happens there. Typically unaware of this border warfare between academic insiders and outsiders, members of the general public view higher education as an ivory tower where one can wait out the latest economic downturn.

This perspective that sees intellectual work as occurring primarily within academic settings, populated by pampered teachers and scholars, and political or activist work as situated in the so-called real world, filled with activists and members of the general public, severs ideas from power relations. This basic binary worldview obscures the complexities of engaging in intellectual activism in both social locations as well as the connections between them. Seeing only two choices limits our choices. Rather, because ideas and politics are everywhere, the potential for intellectual activism is also possible everywhere.

In this context, I see two primary strategies that underpin contemporary intellectual activism, both of which constitute legacies of late-twentieth-century social movements. One form of intellectual activism aims to speak the truth to power. This form of truth-telling harnesses the power of ideas toward the specific goal of confronting existing power relations. On a metaphorical level, speaking the truth to power invokes images of changing the very foundations of social hierarchy where the less powerful take on the ideas and practices of the powerful, often armed solely with their ideas. One can imagine this process through the David and Goliath story of the weak standing up to the strong, armed only with a slingshot (as relying solely on the power of one's ideas seems to be). A Google search of the phrase "speak the truth to power" uncovers numerous hits seemingly focused on confronting those who wield power within existing social institutions.

My lengthy educational training was designed to equip me to wield the language of power to serve the interests of the gatekeepers who granted me legitimacy. My teachers did not consider that I might choose to use those same weapons to challenge much of what I learned, at least not as deeply as I have actually done. While we may think of our educations as our individual intellectual property, we quickly find out that powerful groups expect us to place our fancy degrees in service to conservative political agendas. Power routinely claims that it has a monopoly on the truth. Yet my education revealed multiple truths, most of which were co-opted and repackaged to suit the vested interests of the more powerful. The richness of alternative points of view remained ignored, neglected, ridiculed, and/or persecuted out of existence.

Much of my academic writing strives to speak the truth to power, namely, to develop alternative analyses about social injustices that scholarly audiences will find credible. For example, my book *Fighting Words: Black Women and the Search for Justice* (1998) speaks directly to scholarly audiences. In that volume, I present a complex argument, in often dense prose, with the goal of speaking the truth to power. To write it, I mastered the language of abstract social theory, with an eye toward unsettling the very same academic power relations that ironically would be used to legitimate the book itself. Because *Fighting Words* required years of diligent study and endless revisions, many see my efforts to write books like this as removing me from the more important realm of everyday political life. I see it differently. Speaking the truth to power in ways that undermine and challenge that power can often best be done as an insider. Some changes are best initiated from within the belly of the beast. Standing outside, throwing stones at the beast, and calling it names won't change much, except perhaps, to make the beast more dangerous because now it no longer believes that its underlings love it. Challenging power structures from the inside, working the cracks within the system, however, requires learning to speak multiple languages of power convincingly.

A second strategy of intellectual activism aims to speak the truth directly to the people. In contrast to directing energy to those in power, a focus that inadvertently bolsters the belief that elites are the only social actors who count, those who speak the truth to the people talk directly to the masses. The distinction here is critical. It's the difference between producing a memo that documents the many cases of a boss's bad behavior and beseeches him or her to change his or her ways and having a meeting with the staff to strategize ways that they, individually and collectively, might deal with the boss *and* the lines of authority that put them in the situation to begin with. The former strategy speaks the truth to power—the latter strategy speaks the truth to the people.

Mari Evans' poem invokes this second form of truth-telling. Evans demands much from intellectual activists by arguing that ordinary, everyday people need truthful ideas that will assist them in their everyday lives. Such truth-telling requires talking, reason, honesty, love, courage, and care. For academics whose horizons have been narrowed to preparing for the next reappointment, promotion, and tenure committee meeting or their lecture for the huge introductory sociology class that meets at 9:00 a.m. three days a week like clockwork, this conception of truth-telling constitutes a luxury that may be reserved for only the most privileged faculty members. Who has time to talk with every student, reason with the students, give them an honest assessment of the required textbook, love them in ways that empower and not demean, show the courage to try something radically different, and express a level of basic care? Moreover, intellectual activists who do devote their attention to the public can pay a high price. In the United States, scholars and activists who place their education in service to their local publics are routinely passed over for cushy jobs, fat salaries, and the chance to appear on NPR. In some areas of the globe, speaking the truth to the people lands you not on cable television but under house arrest, in jail, or killed. Contemporary American intellectuals must remember that, when it comes to our ability to claim the power of ideas, we are the fortunate ones. For our parents, friends, relatives, and neighbors who lack literacy, work long hours, and/or consume seemingly endless doses of so-called reality television, the excitement of hearing new ideas that challenge social inequalities can be a rarity.

I am an intellectual whose scholarly work aspires to speak the truth to power. Yet a sizable portion of my intellectual work has also aimed to speak the truth to the people. Both forms of truth-telling are intertwined throughout my intellectual career, with my books, journal articles, and essays arrayed along a continuum with speaking the truth to power and speaking the truth to the people on either end. For example, the *Handbook of Race and Ethnic Studies* (2010) that I edited with John Solomos explicitly endeavors to speak the truth to power. As a reference work that is written for scholarly audiences, this volume aims to raise new and provocative questions that will enable scholars of race and ethnic studies to speak the truth to power in this field of study. In contrast, the focus of *Race, Class and Gender: An Anthology* (1992–2012) that I edited with Margaret Andersen aims to speak the truth to the people. Not only does this edited volume strive to advance our knowledge of race, class, and gender, it also targets undergraduate students as an important part of the public. Both works explore similar ideas, yet with very different audiences in mind.

Engaging these two forms of truth-telling within a singular work is challenging and, if skillfully achieved, may not be recognized as dual forms of truth-telling at all. For example, *Black Feminist Thought: Knowledge, Consciousness and the Politics of Empowerment* (1990, 2000, 2009) is written in multiple registers, one targeted toward scholarly audiences and the other aimed at a more general readership of African American women. I faced a difficult challenge in crafting this book—how could I write a book about African American women's intellectual production that would be accepted by scholarly audiences that had long excluded and derogated this group? Conversely, how might I write a book that spoke directly to African American women that they would find truthful, yet avoid the risk of being dismissed by scholarly audiences (who controlled publishing resources)? I had to find ways to examine the everyday creativity and resistance of African American women within the constraints of an academic discourse that would not be seen by scholars as being too popular or political. I also had to consider how my arguments in *Black Feminist Thought* would be recognizable to and useful for African American women.

The response lay in sharpening my skills of translation, carefully attending to how the ideas in *Black Feminist Thought* traveled in both directions. Because the material at that time was so new and I was an unknown scholar, I knew that my publisher would recruit scholarly reviewers to give my manuscript a thorough assessment. Yet to shield my book from the power relations that made African American women objects of scholarly knowledge, I also developed ways of including African American women as reviewers of my material. For example, I invited a few African American women undergraduates from my University of Cincinnati Africana Studies courses to serve as readers for chapters of my manuscript. My students were bright, energetic, primarily working-class students whose childhoods in the Cincinnati metropolitan areas had provided them broad, heterogeneous networks of African American friends, neighbors, and relatives. I was not interested in my students' ability to correct my English (the copyeditor's job) or to inform me of how my book might benefit from additional citations from the top scholarly journals. Instead, I asked them to tell me what thoughts and emotions the ideas in my book raised for them. Did the ideas in *Black Feminist Thought* "ring true" for them? Could they think of examples from their own experiences that illustrated and/or contradicted the book's main ideas? As I wrote and revised my manuscript, I tried to incorporate both forms of truth-telling into this one volume.

Black Feminist Thought became an award-winning book, with a "classic" edition released in 2009. Its subject matter is certainly important to its readers, but I think that one fundamental reason for the success of *Black Feminist Thought* has been its ability to engage in dual forms of truth-telling. The format of the book enables undergraduate and entering graduate students to access the challenging concepts that they need to speak the truth to power in the academy. To assist in their translation of social theory, I chose to use theoretical language in the volume, yet I also included a glossary of terms that would encourage my readers to tackle difficult ideas. Graduate students and scholars can access more theoretical arguments about how oppressed groups can produce oppositional knowledge that assists in their survival. *Black Feminist Thought* also serves as a point of entry for readers who are interested in intersectional scholarship on race, class, gender, and sexuality. Over the years, I have come to appreciate how people apply the general arguments raised by the experiences of African American women to their own situations. Overall, *Black Feminist Thought* provides its readers with a shared space that validates what each one brings to the table, yet enables them to gain access to the knowledge of the other. It shows that, via processes of translation, it is possible to bring these two seemingly antithetical traditions of truth-telling closer together.

Content and Organization of *On Intellectual Activism*

On Intellectual Activism has two specific goals. First, drawing on my experiences with these dual forms of truth-telling, the speeches, essays, and interviews in *On Intellectual Activism* explore selected core ideas associated with intellectual activism. At its heart, this volume explores intellectual activism as a multifaceted phenomenon that links content and process, ideas and actions, and oppression and resistance. Here I use my own scholarship as one site for examining this construct, yet the core ideas go beyond my own experiences. The contradictions of doing this kind of work should be visible, as should its rewards.

Second, this book also introduces important themes from my own intellectual activism: (1) Black feminism and its emphasis on experiential knowing, intersecting systems of power, and the importance of social justice: (2) the sociology of knowledge and its analysis of how power relations shape knowledge of domination and resistance; (3) critical education, or the necessity of developing a more robust understanding of teaching and learning as central to all intellectual production; (4) racial politics in the United States as a way of understanding social hierarchies in general; and (5) the necessity of building self-reflexivity into intellectual activism itself. Here I include accessible discussions of topics from my scholarship from the 1980s to the present, much of it designed to speak the truth to power. Because the majority of the writings included here consist of revised versions of unpublished speeches and interviews, this book documents the trajectory of my intellectual activism, where I aimed to speak the truth to heterogeneous groups of people. By presenting ideas that were developed in large part in conversation with audiences large and small, as a volume, *On Intellectual Activism* engages in this second form of truth-telling.

On Intellectual Activism is organized into five parts that illustrate important conceptual anchors for my intellectual work. Each essay is edited to stand on its own, yet complement others in its section and in the volume overall. Although the book is best read sequentially, because the essays could also be organized in different ways, you can read them in any order.

The essays in Part I, "Black Feminism," draw on my grounding in the ideas and experiences of African American women, the group that has most preoccupied me during my scholarly career. This focus on African American women has anchored a core theme of my scholarship, namely, my longstanding project to understand oppression, a multifaceted project that has taken many forms. Two main ideas are at work here, both of which focus on social structural sources of power. First introduced in *Black Feminist Thought,* and developed throughout my scholarship, I have used the thesis of *intersectionality* and the idea of the *matrix of domination* as interrelated constructs to describe social structures of domination. Intersectional thinking suggests that race, class, gender, nation, sexuality, ethnicity, age, and other forms of social hierarchy structure one another. My goal has been to conceptualize intersectionality and study its manifestations in a matrix of domination from one social setting to the next.

The essays in Part I introduce selected important concepts where I was trying to translate ideas in conversation with different audiences. Introducing standpoint epistemology and its significance for understanding the worldviews of oppressed peoples plays a prominent part here. For example, in *Black Feminist Thought,* I introduced the idea of oppositional knowledge and argued that people's experiences within intersecting systems of race, class, and gender shaped their views of the world and their knowledge. In *Fighting Words* (1998), I engaged the question of how to sustain oppositional knowledge in the face of continual pressures to quit. The essays in this section also map my engagement with Black feminism as a social justice project, a concept that is reflected through my consistent attention to issues of power and politics. *Black Sexual Politics: African Americans, Gender and the New Racism* (2004) marked a more explicit shift to politics themselves, adding the additional system of sexuality to rethink gender, with an eye toward stimulating a different politics among African Americans in response to the new racism. *From Black Power to Hip Hop: Essays on Racism, Nationalism and Feminism* (2006) took this interest in politics one step further to examine nationalism and feminism as important social justice projects that affect African American women. Collectively, the essays trace themes through their earlier expression to engage the question of future directions for Black feminism itself.

The essays in Part II, "Sociology of Knowledge," stem from my position as a visible public intellectual within the field of sociology. It also describes the kind of sociology that I take into other fields as well as the kind of intellectual production that I share with the general public. "Public sociology" is a relatively recent term that describes a certain segment of sociology as a field of study, although it is not a term that I have used exclusively to describe my work until now. My approach to public sociology is to examine how it feels to do this kind of work, versus speculating about how it might be done or passing moral judgments on how it should be done. Because doing public sociology is engaging in intellectual activism, the costs and benefits attached to this kind of work become more apparent.

Not all public sociology sees itself in these terms. However, the recent rediscovery of public sociology in the United States has provided institutional support, or at least a vocabulary, for talking about issues of intellectual activism. In the current climate of academic sociology, this idea of public sociology has been elevated to a level of increased visibility that has given it some legitimacy. Public sociology speaks to the desire that many sociologists have to talk with and educate the public.

While related, public sociology and critical education are not the same. Critical education encourages people to think about the hard questions, the questions for which there may not be answers, and then helps them to become much better at crafting their own questions. Critical education constitutes another conceptual anchor of my work. The essays in Part III, "Critical Education," examine the interconnections of my use of critical pedagogy, teaching, and scholarship. On the one hand, I think of my publications as pedagogical tools—my dedication to clear prose within my writings on social theory reflects this commitment. I approach my classroom teaching experiences and public speaking engagements as oral arenas for constructing knowledge with my students and audiences. My conception of critical education is situated within this recursive relationship between scholarship and teaching—scholarship and teaching are both required to engage in the public conversations that accompany dual forms of truth-telling.

I see my own work as one of engaging in intellectual activism within a context of critical education, broadly defined, that in turn incorporates an expansive array of projects. School sites have been my primary location, but families, neighborhoods, religious institutions, and media are also important social locations for the kind of critical education discussed here. Fields as diverse as women's studies, Latino studies, cultural studies, American studies, subaltern studies, and postcolonial studies often have a strong critical education component at their core, a factor that distinguishes them from traditional academic disciplines. For me, the fields of Africana studies (formerly African American or Black studies), women's studies, and sociology have been my primary sites of practice within this broader framework of schooling in the United States. These three fields of study have provided me with distinctive sets of pedagogical and scholarly tools that have been significant for truth-telling.

Over the corpus of my work, I have focused on anti-racist discourse and practice that might catalyze people to think about their worlds differently and, as a result, act differently within them. My work constitutes theoretical interventions in what counts as truth about race and racism. The essays in Part IV, "Racial Politics," continue along this path by opening up space to discuss some of the most persistent questions about race in the United States, catalyzed by massive social changes of the late twentieth and early twenty-first centuries. This is a difficult time to talk overtly about race, leaving many American citizens believing that we are living in a post-racial world. The 2008 election of Barack Obama to the American presidency has simultaneously highlighted the visibility of race and the difficulties of talking about it. In this context, terms like "family," "community," "post-racial society," and "color blindness" are invoked by thinkers on both the left and the right sides of the political spectrum, with racial subtexts carried within what appears to be a newfound unity across the historically divisive categories of race and gender. Yet what are the policies and practices attached to these terms? What conversations does the use of these terms facilitate and close off?

Recognizing the continued need for a language to conceptualize social injustice and a politics to work for social justice is an important first step in intellectual activism. Yet doing the work to breathe life into ideas requires working across differences and building communities in which dialogue is possible. The essays in Part V, "Intellectual Activism Revisited," address different components of the work of building diverse intellectual and political communities—for example, the need for a vision that will sustain the arduous practices of resisting oppression based on race, class, and gender; the need for that vision to resonate across many social locations; and the need for practices that can sustain differences of ideas.

This section addresses the need for intellectual activism to be self-reflexive. In Part V, I revisit "Toward a New Vision: Race, Class, and Gender as Categories of Analysis and Connection," a widely reprinted speech that I initially delivered in the mid-1980s. I include the original version here because I want to see how different the essay feels to me after more than 25 years of work in this field. Keeping with the theme of self-reflexivity, I revisit the core questions and concerns of "Toward a New Vision" in "Where Do We Go from Here?" In this essay, I cast a critical eye on my original essay's promise and its unfinished potential. I also draw together ideas about Black feminism, critical education, race in U.S. society, and themes explored in *On Intellectual Activism*. This theme of self-reflexivity permeates the book, with each individual essay introduced by a short reflexive statement. This is the spirit of Part V, looking backward in order to figure out how to move forward with speaking the truth both to power and to people.

On Intellectual Activism, Truth-Telling, and the Spoken Word

My writings in *On Intellectual Activism* reflect not only the *content* of the corpus of my ideas about intellectual activism but also my choices concerning the *process* of engaging in this kind of work. In heterogeneous democratic societies, finding ways to share important ideas with diverse groups of people is a necessity. In essence, I have tried to make the main ideas of my intellectual work accessible to nontechnical, broad audiences both inside and outside academia. My goal has been academic rigor and accessibility.

I have found that my analyses of important social issues, especially if I want my ideas to be clear, are strengthened when I engage in dialogues, namely, when I speak *with* people and not *at* them. Within African American culture, the spoken word is highly valued, and as a result, Black oratorical traditions shape autobiographies, fiction, essays, and other dimensions of Black American literary traditions. Many of the most powerful African American leaders have been preachers, a field where thought and talking suggests a unique praxis. My choices have often centered on the power of the spoken word, a standpoint that I learned from African American oratorical traditions as diverse as the African American preaching style of Martin Luther King, Jr., and Malcolm X, Black kids "playing the dozens" on the streets of Philadelphia, the toasts of Black popular culture, and the poetry slams and open mic nights of spoken poetry. Such traditions view voice and movement as crucial to communicating meaning, if not more important than written text. Oral traditions appreciate that knowledge is created in specific times and places, primarily by engaging with an audience that brings its own distinctive rules about what it deems credible in assessing the value of truth. For a speaker like myself, there is a difference between actually engaging an audience in a public conversation of knowledge creation and giving a convincing performance as a bona fide Black feminist scholar.

Regardless of content, in my case, Black feminism or racial politics, I see conversations with multiple publics as a foundational and necessary component of intellectual activism. When it comes to the spoken word, making meaning is more than just delivering words. In brief, *process* matters. Speeches and the spoken word not only report the findings of something that has already been discovered but also create knowledge in the moment of communication. Not to be confused with the performances of professional public intellectuals, the kind of engaged truth-telling I recount here can be unfinished, ragged, speculative, boring, and/or all aspects of being "in the moment" for whoever is at the podium, holds the microphone, or has the floor. If one cannot "speak the truth to the people" and listen for dissent and/or the affirming "amen" or "got that right," then how valuable are written words that remain unspoken?

African American oral traditions often are organized via a call-and-response format, one where African American members of an audience bear witness to what the person who holds the floor is saying or doing. Bearing witness is one way to be an active participant in knowledge creation. I often invoke this sensibility in my speeches. Delivering speeches is different than writing for a nameless, faceless, silent readership. Because each speech aims to make meaning *with* a particular audience, it must be crafted for that group and it evolves in the process of delivery. In the United States and abroad, I have delivered countless speeches on college campuses, at conferences, for community groups, and for corporate and civic organizations, taking with me the call-and-response ethos of African American oratorical traditions. Each situation is unique, and no two speeches, even if read from the same text, have *ever* been the same.

Public lectures, for example, are always altered not only by the demographics of the audience but also by the themes raised in question-and-answer periods and in ensuing one-on-one discussions with audience members. Even if I am the only one speaking, I am always in a public conversation with the listeners in attendance. One size does not fit all for speeches. Even the same speech reads differently for different audiences. Sometimes the audience will be highly homogeneous and, if so, I can make certain assumptions and proceed accordingly. For example, speaking to an audience of professional sociologists is markedly different than addressing an audience of Black folks at the local public library. If I know the rules, social norms, and issues of importance for each group, I adjust the content and form accordingly.

Giving speeches that draw on the spoken words ethos of Black oratorical traditions has increased my sensitivity to key elements of speaking to different groups of people. Delivering a successful speech (or writing a successful article, organizing a successful book, or having a successful classroom session, course, and/or curriculum) involves bringing four elements into balance. First, what is the *purpose* of the speech? Why give this speech at all? What is the core question/big idea that everyone in the audience shares, regardless of heterogeneity? Second, who is the intended *audience*? Who is this speech for? What are the concerns of the people in the room? Third, what specific *content* will I share in the speech? What are the main ideas of the presentation? How effectively and efficiently can I communicate these ideas with the audience? Finally, what is the overall *form* of the speech? How can I best explore and present the main ideas of the talk? What is the best way to get the content to the audience?

These four elements of purpose, audience, content, and form typically work together differently in an academic book that aims to speak the truth to power and in a speech as a spoken word event whose purpose is to speak the truth to the people. Each form of truth-telling requires its own distinctive balance among these four elements. When it comes to speaking the truth to power, writing for nameless, faceless readers who can pause, look up footnotes, and reflect on specific points at their convenience and on their own terms may vary from one field to the next, yet the author still controls the written text (but not its interpretation). Presenting the same ideas in person is riskier because it highlights the vulnerabilities of the speaker regarding purpose, audience, content, and form.

When it comes to speaking the truth to the people, giving an effective speech requires creating an instant community. For me, the greatest challenge has been speaking the truth to heterogeneous groups of people. Many people shy away from the task of speaking the truth to the people different from themselves, choosing instead to speak only with people who share their rules, even if the audience may disagree with the content of the talk itself. For academics, figuring out what is important to say to heterogeneous audiences not only is difficult but also typically is not valued by tenure committees and other academic gatekeepers. Academics know that the test of so-called truth is in its "telling"; yet when we present our ideas, in writing or orally, to small groups of homogeneous practitioners within our disciplines, we limit our truth-telling. We often do not speak the truth to power, but rather collude with existing power relations.

Editing my speeches and other spoken word experiences for *On Intellectual Activism* meant recording on paper ideas and arguments that typically occurred in conversation. Literal transcripts just cannot capture the meanings created in a one-time event. Here I assemble the richness of ideas gleaned from multiple conversations in a format that returns to you, as a readership, a text that I hope you can use. Some essays evolved from my handwritten notes prepared for 5- to 10-minute panel presentations and were not given as speeches at all. In contrast, other essays resulted from synthesizing multiple versions of speeches delivered for different audiences. Still others evolved as each new dialogue shaped the text. Just as I have engaged others in preparing these ideas, I strive to engage you in dialogue with this text: I introduce each essay with a brief reflexive statement describing how the essay came about and how I approached its content in that context. For selected essays, I also provide a short list of readily available additional resources.

Those of us who participate in intellectual activism must do a better job of engaging the public. How differently our ideas about families, schooling, immigration, and government would be if we presented them not just at academic conferences but also at neighborhood public libraries, to groups of college students, to returning students, at parent education classes, or even to our own families. In this spirit, the essays in *On Intellectual Activism* illustrate different strategies for engaging diverse publics by attending to distinctive constellations of purpose, audience, content, and form. As you read, I encourage you to pay attention not just to the thematic content but also to how I say what I say in each essay. When it comes to intellectual activism, content and process both matter.

Note on Usage

I REMIND READERS THAT a major struggle within African American history occurred in the early twentieth century, when African Americans fought for the right to capitalize the word *Negro*, then a more derogatory lower-case word *negro*. The term "Negro" was a self-defined identification and African Americans demanded the use of a capital "N" when referring to themselves. Similar still unresolved controversies surround the capitalization of the term "Black." In this book, I use the terms *Blacks*, *African Americans*, *Black Americans*, and *U.S. Blacks* interchangeably when these terms are nouns that refer to this specific historic and cultural group. I think it is important to respect the terms that Black Americans use as terms of self-identification and group solidarity. These terms refer to an historically constituted, ethnic group originating in American slavery that has incorporated earlier waves of immigrants of African descent who could not become white. I distinguish African Americans/Black Americans/U.S. Blacks/Black people/Blacks from contemporary immigrants of African descent from the Caribbean and continental Africa. Although this volume speaks to the racial politics that affect people of African descent, incorporating a more comprehensive analysis that recognizes the politics of ethnicity and nation is beyond the scope of this project. While less clear-cut, I also capitalize these terms when they are used as adjectives with direct connection to an African American population (e.g., Black people, Black feminism). I use lower-case "black" and "white" as descriptions for systems of ideas, ideologies, or any construct that does not explicitly refer to African Americans as a historically constituted collectivity or that has direct connections to ideologies of white supremacy (e.g., "black masculinity," "white culture"). Finally, because whites as a social group routinely reject whiteness as a term of racial self-identification that describes their history as a dominant racial group in the

United States, I do not capitalize the term "white." Because the essays were written at different times and for diverse audiences, the capitalization issue may not be entirely consistent. I also realize that there are differences of opinion on this issue of capitalization.

I

Black Feminism

Why *Black Feminist Thought?*

REFLEXIVE ESSAY: *I first delivered this speech in the early 1990s as an in-troduction to* Black Feminist Thought. *Because I developed the basic ar-gument prior to the advent of new communications technologies, I could not rely on PowerPoint and other visual media to assist me in summa-rizing the book's complicated ideas. Instead, I use the spoken word tech-nique of storytelling to engage my audience. This revised essay includes a succinct summary of the origins of the book, its intentions, and its po-tential significance. In revising this essay, I see the effects of writing in a segregated world that, in the 1980s and 1990s, continued to privilege the ideas and experiences of the West. Since that time, the world appears to be much more multi-cultural, multi-ethnic and accepting of diversity, yet I ask you to consider how much the basic power relations that catalyzed this essay have changed.*

I MAGINE YOURSELF in a theater, getting ready to see the rehearsal of a play. If you are lucky, your imagined theater is on Broadway and the production promises to have a lush set, a large cast, skilled lighting, and professional actors. If you are less fortunate, maybe you are imagining the last rehearsal of a community theater event in your local town or supper club, complete with last-minute snafus. Or perhaps because your actual theater experiences have been limited to the small stages of elementary or high school auditoriums, your imagined play is populated by your eighth-grade classmates, with costumes and settings to match. Never mind how you imagine the theater and the play.

Earlier versions of this talk were delivered at the University of Maryland–College Park, Indi-ana University–Bloomington, the University of Kentucky, and the Illinois Sociological Asso-ciation 1991–1993.

Whatever the location, and even though their scripts may differ, the stories of the plays are often the same.

There in the middle of the stage stands a young, blonde, attractive, virile, white American male, script in hand, eloquently reciting his lines. A spotlight follows his every move, an unspoken technical mechanism that lets us know that he is the star of the drama. Strangely, even though we may show up at different theaters in search of different plays, they all seem curiously the same. Our star, and those who resemble him, seems to occupy the middle of every single story, even when he is not on stage. All stories are his story. It's as if no other story ever happened.

In some versions of the play, our star is a good guy. Because he's a nice guy, he sees himself as universal, an everyman whose story somehow represents everyone's story. Stories where our star is a hero are designed to show his positive features—his bravery, his heroism, his intelligence, his leadership abilities, his imagination, his rationality, his creativity, and his inventions. In other versions, our star is a villain. Believing that he is better than everyone else, he pushes to the head of the line, complaining when he has to wait; he demands the biggest piece of meat, leaving others to go hungry; he drives the biggest car, not caring much about the actual costs of his transportation. He insists that everyone tell him how smart and wonderful he truly is. Whether hero or villain, our star is always the hero of the story. Because he's the center of every story and in the center of every stage, it becomes hard to imagine a play where he is not there.

Our star is rarely alone on the stage because he requires a series of props to help him tell his story. The props look like people, but from the point of view of our star, they are not fully human. They neither talk nor move, unless directed to do so by the play's director and as described in the play's script. Their purpose is to enhance, or "prop up," the star power of the play via their relationship with the star. Some of his props are beautiful objects to be admired, collected, and enjoyed. Their exotic colors and bodies so fascinate our star, whether hero or villain, that he often can't stop thinking about them. Other props simply do our star's dirty work—they provide for his physical needs, typically without being asked, thanked, or paid. Regardless of their appearance or function, we only see and/or hear from these props via their roles in our star's story. Star power requires that props have to participate in the star's drama, his knowledge.

The props are vital in telling our star story. For any given play, stagehands wheel out a specific set of props to make the drama come alive. For example, the story of the taming of the Wild West to make room for the founding of America requires bloodthirsty, savage Indian props. Typically one-dimensional cardboard cutouts of people with red skins, who wield tomahawks and have a predilection for scalping hard-working pioneers, these Indian props make our star into a bona fide hero. Within this play, pioneers who conquered the West (and who resemble John Wayne) did us all a service by killing all the Indians and making America safe to settle. Indian props apparently have very little to say about this genocidal history—"ugh," "how," and "kemosabe" seemingly exhaust their vocabulary. Our hero may need Indian props for this particular story of the taming of the West, yet when that story is over, stagehands wheel the Indian props backstage. There they remain, gathering dust until they're needed again.

When the story of race in America is scheduled for production, stagehands wheel out a different set of props. Although the light continues to shine on our hero, smiling cardboard cutouts of Uncle Ben, Uncle Tom, Aunt Jemima, and Sapphire appear close by. The servant props, especially the mammy prop of Aunt Jemima, don't seem to mind their positions as "the help." These servants are so good that, despite a history of slavery and servitude, they smile and seemingly harbor little resentment. Unlike Indian props, which seem frozen in a nineteenth-century time warp, and because they are in closer proximity to white people, black props get better dramatic roles. Black props are known for laughing, smiling, and occasionally breaking into song and dance—they are so happy to be near the star. What fabulous entertainer props they are.

Just as the Indian props and the black props appear in different stories, so too do a host of other props that "prop up" the star power of different plays. Stagehands have an arsenal of props waiting in the wings to play all kinds of roles. They bring out white women props, for example, to show off the star's masculinity and ability to attract, keep, and marry beautiful and desirable women. White women props also appear as the star's mother, a heroic figure who sacrifices everything for him as her fair-haired child. Our star may be a rugged individualist, yet his ability to star in a subplot of the Western family drama also enhances his star power.

One day, an amazing thing happened on stage—the props began to move! The uppity ones had the nerve to occupy center stage, pushing the star out of the limelight. Some props that had been waiting in the wings to make cameo appearances—the Indian prop that was scheduled to walk on stage, be killed, and then be carried off—stormed the stage and refused to leave. The stage became increasingly crowded by an array of props, many of which saw one another for the first time. Aunt Jemima didn't know that there was a Suzy Wong prop that shared much with her sister Jezebel. The shadowy Muslim North African terrorist prop realized with a start that he looked like his U.S. Latino brother prop. Different languages, similar props—did Arabic and Spanish have a connection?

Things went from bad to worse on the increasingly crowded stage. Some props refused to recite their lines, broke character, and began to talk back to the hero. Some said, "Wait a minute, I don't want to be your prop. What about my story? There's something wrong with plays that only present one point of view—yours." Others just got to the point: "Your play stinks. I've hated it for years, and I won't be in it anymore!" Some props had the nerve to talk to each other, ignoring the poor star altogether. For example, the Suzy Wong and hot-blooded Latina props started a heated conversation with the Jezebel prop about race, gender, and sexual exploitation. Not to be outdone, the poor white trash props pointed out that they were not nearly as racist as they were purported to be. Even more remarkably, some props began to shout, "We're here; we're queer; get used to it!"

You might imagine the star's response to this topsy-turvy disruption of tradition. He was dumbfounded. It was almost as if the chair that you're sitting on now yelled, "Get your behind off of me!" and ran out of the room. Wouldn't you be shocked if an object that you completely took for granted, a prop that made your life comfortable, turned out to be a living, breathing being with free will that did not bend to your own?

To be fair to this particular white, elite, male, heterosexual star on the stage of a U.S. drama, we're all guilty to some degree of our own version of hero worship. Each of us typically objectifies some other group of people as props in our lives, with ourselves in the center. Men are encouraged to see women as props, as whites are taught to view Black people through stereotypes that objectify them. Rich people often cannot see the poor as equal in any way, while many Christians, Jews, and Muslims understand their own religion as superior and that of the others as lesser. As Muslims who travel from Turkey to Germany or from Algeria to France know all too well, a star in one setting can become a prop in another. People with less power across an array of categories that vary from one setting to the next (e.g., race, class, gender, sexuality, ethnicity, age, and ability) can be objectified as having no will of their own—no intellect, no thought, no point of view—no worthwhile knowledge. But if those props began to move and talk, can you imagine what a shock that would be to the heroes of those different categories? You'd be disoriented because your world would have been turned upside down.

American society is currently at a critical juncture because people who were formerly objectified as props not only are moving and talking but also saying some things that are difficult for many of us to hear. Since the social movements of the 1950s to 1970s, native people, women, African Americans, working-class people, Latinos/as, immigrant groups, and lesbian, gay, bisexual, and transgendered people, among others, have all challenged America's stories of its own exploits. Typically, these groups reject their particular history of objectification and subordination as props, instead choosing to tell their own stories from their own point of view. Many of these groups have proposed alternative interpretations of Western intellectual dramas that refute taken-for-granted stock stories of America's greatness. Star power is not what it used to be in defending systems of privilege. The plethora of new stories challenge not just the truthfulness of stories that turned these groups into props but also the process of knowledge production that made the star's stories seem natural, normal, and inevitable.

Why *Black Feminist Thought*?

Black Feminist Thought, my first book, illustrates my efforts to examine African American women's ideas and experiences within this broader political and intellectual context. African American women's distinctive history on the stage of U.S. politics has simultaneously rendered us props for other people's stories, yet positioned us to work for social justice. Because of this social location, U.S. Black women have made distinctive contributions to a broader social justice project of rejecting an array of stories of race, class, gender, sexuality, age, and ability that have objectified many groups and turned them into props. My intellectual work participates in this larger process of challenging prevailing stories of Western societies that have long stood as universal, unquestioned truths.

Please note that the story of "The Day the Props Began to Move" describes the politics of doing intellectual work, not simply the ideas themselves. *Black Feminist Thought* is not simply an academic project for me, something I wrote because it was chic to do so or because it advanced my scholarly career. Instead, I wrote *Black Feminist Thought* to provide an interpretive context for many of the experiences that I encountered as an African American woman. Being treated as a prop is not simply a convenient metaphor. For me, as is the case for many African American women and all others who are treated as props, this treatment has tangible, palpable effects.

In the 1970s, I began to question the persistent invisibility of material on African American women that characterized my elementary, high school, and college experiences. By then, it was becoming clearer to me that bodies were differently valued and had differential sets of expectations attached to them. No matter how talented or motivated you are as an individual, social scripts that are the legacy of racism, sexism, class exploitation, and heterosexism assign categories of superiority and inferiority. I resented the social scripts that I encountered in school or on television that depicted Black women as servants, bad mothers, or sluts. Were Black women really as debased as we had been made out to be? Whose "truth" was this? It certainly wasn't mine.

My schooling played a major part in constructing the social scripts that objectified and derogated African American women. My formal public school education aimed to get me to see myself, at best, as a prop for the exploits of more important groups and, at worst, as a danger to myself and to others. If I failed to embrace my objectification as a mammy-in-training, I could be cast as a dangerous, crazy Black woman who was ripe for punishment. Not only was I encouraged to accept my assigned place as "the help," but I was also supposed to believe that this was my rightful place in the world. By the time I graduated from high school, I had endured a sustained effort to foster self-doubt about my authentic, original voice. I was supposed to doubt what I saw, especially my own lived experiences as a young Black woman. I was encouraged to distrust both my own experiences and my own interpretations of the world. Moreover, I was supposed to replace the collective standpoint shared by my mother, my aunts, and the women in my African American, working-class neighborhood with the hero's view of the world that was taught in school. Taking on the hero's standpoint, not only of the world but also of myself, would make me a successful prop. When I arrived at school each day, I held my breath, knowing that the price of success would be delivering a command performance as a prop. I might gain a part on the stage near the hero and maybe, just maybe, if I were good enough, I'd get a small speaking part. I lived William E. B. Du Bois's social script of double consciousness, of always having to see myself through the eyes of white teachers and classmates. Leaving school each day allowed me to exhale and leave that script behind.

Many of the themes in *Black Feminist Thought* reflect my sustained effort to reconcile my independent view of the world with my devalued place in it. Although I could not see it at the time, that reconciliation would require me to try to figure out how race, class, and gender as systems of power operated in my everyday life. Because I grew up in racially segregated neighborhoods, understanding racism was high on my list. Race was clearly an important theme in my life, yet in Philadelphia public schools, struggles for African American empowerment, including those of the Civil Rights Movement that was in full swing, were missing from the standard curriculum. I can recall only one mention of race in my public school education, when we studied slavery in a sixth-grade American history class. To my surprise, our textbook found a way to discuss slavery without paying serious attention to African Americans as people. Black people were reduced to a few lines: "The slaves were happy because they sang all the time."

That book made no sense to me. Growing up, I had attended numerous events with African American relatives, friends, and neighbors of various genders and hues. Because U.S. society was so racially segregated, especially in Northern cities, I had grown up immersed in everyday Black culture. I was surrounded by Black people who loved to sing, on the porch across the street and on the corner at night in ways that distracted me from studying chemistry, as well as the musicians within my own family. I did not know what kind of Black people were included in my textbook. I could not imagine how any Black person I knew would *ever* be so happy about being enslaved that he or she would sing about it in a state of contentment. My textbook celebrated stories of elite, white, male heroes, tales that were designed to make me doubt my view of the world that was grounded in the truthfulness of my own childhood experiences. In my reality, people grappling with racism did not sing and dance because they loved being exploited and disempowered.

My growing racial awareness influenced *Black Feminist Thought*, primarily because my childhood experiences made racism so difficult to ignore. Yet social class was another category that I was encouraged to ignore in the face of my objectification as a prop in someone else's story. During my childhood, I certainly was aware of class differences, yet like so many other Americans, I saw race as a master frame and social class as a category of individual expression. While I disbelieved the myth that race didn't matter in America, I uncritically absorbed the myth that America was a classless society. Apparently, social class was missing from the public school curriculum as well, but I could see neither its absence nor the significance of that omission until I went away to college.

My college classmates came from fairly well-off families, yet they didn't seem to flaunt their wealth or to care about it very much. In contrast, I thought about money all the time. A quarter to them was nothing. Not so for me. I was perpetually annoyed at their cavalier attitude toward borrowing money from me to do their laundry and never paying it back.

College opened my eyes to the vast social class differences in the United States. I got an up-close-and-personal look at wealth and how my life was very different from those of my classmates. A good friend of mine invited me to her home for Thanksgiving, and when we pulled up in front of what appeared to me to be a mansion on Long Island, my jaw dropped. I love my friend to this day, but I recognized that it was far easier for her to get to college and stay in college than it was for me. College also exposed me to the similarities linking working-class individuals across differences of race and ethnicity. White students on scholarship seemed to have less money than I did. Removed from our racially and class-segregated neighborhoods, we got along well as individuals. Yet they seemed to have greater difficulty than I did in reconciling the vast differences in wealth between our respective communities and those of our well-off classmates.

During this same period, I became increasingly aware that gender also mattered in ways that intersected with race and class. Gender constitutes yet another system of power that ultimately became central within *Black Feminist Thought.* Once I started looking for gender, it seemed to be everywhere. I became a mother, an experience that catalyzed my analyses of motherhood and family. Gender rules typically remain invisible until someone violates them. Because I attended an all-girls high school, I didn't learn the gender rules concerning what was appropriate for girls. In my high school, girls studied physics, played all the parts in all of the drama productions, played all of the instruments in the band and orchestra (not just the "girlie" ones), and were rewarded for being smart.

Of all of my transgressions of gender rules (which also can tie closely with those of race and class), my favorite example comes from a conference on the history of the study of technology. As a newly minted assistant professor, I attended the conference to present material from my dissertation and perhaps to meet some new colleagues. I dressed carefully in all of my high-authority clothing: my "dress-for-success" blue suit and an attaché case that screamed competence. I was the ultimate oxymoron—an African American woman in white male drag. The conference went smoothly until I went to lunch. What an ordeal. When I walked into the room, I felt transported back to my first day in junior high. Where would I sit? I searched in vain for other African American conference attendees. There were none. The few Black people who were in the room were not eating lunch; they were *serving* it. More to the point, this also appeared to be an all-male space. I searched for women. There were very few, and most of them either ignored me or stared at me with puzzled looks that said,

"Who let her in?" There was no escape—I was pinned on stage by the spotlight cast on my visible race and gender.

Realizing that lunch would be no fun, I sat down at a table with one of the few women in attendance. In contrast to my high-authority clothing, her flowing skirts and colorful top screamed "hippie." How bad could she be, I wondered. I soon found out. My new friend began to babble uncontrollably, one question spilling out after the next, none waiting for an answer: "I know I've never seen you before. I come every year and I know that I would remember you if you'd been here before. Who are you? Why are you here? I know I've never seen you before. Who are you?" She couldn't help herself. I felt assaulted, yet I was also fascinated. My luncheon companion had seemingly carved out her own provisional niche at the conference, one where her gender was unimportant. She was the hero of her own stage, albeit the small one of her luncheon table, and I was an interloper. While all this was going on, the men at the table stopped talking, kept eating, and watched this drama of the two of us putting on a show for them. Heroes often love nothing better than a good prop fight. Talk about naive. Had one of the other few female conference attendees not pulled me aside later in the day and told me that the conference was euphemistically referred to as the "boys and toys" conference, I would not have talked to one person all day long. I left that conference with a sense of gratitude and relief for my sociology doctorate that shielded me from conferences like that one.

Collectively, these experiences made getting to the point of being able to write *Black Feminist Thought* a struggle. My entire academic career has been characterized by numerous examples of my objectification and silencing that made certain experiences, such as the erasure of African Americans in my sixth-grade textbook, learning about the vast differences in wealth and poverty by traveling into unfamiliar college territory, and enduring hypervisibility created by the babbling woman at the "boys and toys" conference, pale in comparison. I could have internalized race, class, and gender norms that said at each step along the way, "Don't listen to yourself; stay focused on the hero." I certainly have had my share of colleagues and students who keep their heads down and their eyes focused on emulating the heroes to recognize the seductions and penalties of playing by the rules.

Instead, like many other African American women, my survival depended on my ability to question this entire endeavor. I needed to find appropriate language to analyze my own personal alienation in school and workplace settings. While often helpful in providing puzzle pieces, the academic literature that I consulted proved inadequate for explaining my experiences. Talk of insiders, outsiders, and marginal men came close, but something was missing. Eventually, I chose the term "outsider within" because it seemed to be an apt description of individuals like myself who were caught between groups of unequal power. Whether the differences in power stemmed from hierarchies of race, class, gender or, in my case, the interaction of all three, the social location of being on the edge mattered. Whether we are included yet ignored (my sixth-grade textbook), welcomed with open arms (my college experiences), or barely tolerated (my stint at the "boys and toys" conference), our very presence often violates the rules.

More importantly, I began to see that what I had originally perceived as an *individual* issue might be part of a larger, *collective* issue that affected many people. Over time, what began as a personal search to come to terms with my own *individual* experiences of disempowerment within intersecting power relations of race, social class, and gender led me to wonder whether African American women as a group occupied a comparable *collective* social location. I saw my story neither as "representing" all Black women nor as an "example" to refute the theories advanced by our hero about the alleged inferiority of Black people, poor people, and women. Instead, I realized that what I was experiencing as one lone person, in fact, might help me develop a more comprehensive analysis to understand and challenge the treatment of African American women as props. What I decided to do was move from a position of being silenced, to questioning the social dynamics of race, class, and gender in my everyday life, to taking action: in my case, writing *Black Feminist Thought*. Stated differently, writing and giving talks became my chosen terrain of intellectual activism.

My experiences convinced me of the importance of seeking out interpretations of African American women's reality by those who lived it. In *Black Feminist Thought* I argue that power relations shape Black women's standpoint on the world and that, conversely, this consciousness catalyzes their actions in the world. Stated differently, how did African American women who had been treated as props on the American stage experience, think about, and act in their worlds? In what ways, if any, did their views resemble and/or differ from the legitimated knowledge about Black women that was designed to render them props?

Looking Inward: Studying a Black Women's Standpoint

Black Feminist Thought investigates these questions via two main areas of emphasis. First, the book aims to document internal discourses among African American women: our experiences within race, class, and gender as systems of power and our interpretations of our own social worlds. What were African American women saying to each other about what it meant to be a Black woman? What were Black women actually doing? Much of *Black Feminist Thought* strives to identify key components of Black women's standpoint on our own experiences. We know much about how society views Black women, specifically, the hero's version of the story of the props. But we know far less about how African American women would tell our stories if we were the subjects in the story instead of the objects.

Take, for example, U.S. Black women's interpretations of motherhood and African American family life. During my freshman year, I read *The Negro Family: The Case for National Action*, usually referred to as the "Moynihan Report." This was my first encounter with the so-called black matriarchy thesis that presented African American women as domineering, emasculating matriarchs within African American families. The ideas in the report were familiar. I had uncritically laughed at comedy shows that depicted Black women in this fashion, for example, *Amos and Andy,* which ran from the 1920s through the 1950s on both radio and television. Yet when I encountered the same ideas in legitimated scholarship, they weren't nearly as funny. We may laugh about these ideas within popular culture, yet this theory and others like it become serious business when they shape public policy.

There had to be another point of view. As I began to look at what Black women were saying, both as individuals whom I knew personally and through the burgeoning literature of Black women's studies, I discovered an amazing and highly affirming array of alternative interpretations of U.S. Black motherhood and African American family life. Black women talked about motherhood and acknowledged their strength within their families. Yet none blamed their mothers for social problems within African American communities and instead often depicted their mothers as the backbones of African American community life.

This perspective, apparently common knowledge among African American women, seemingly escaped the authors of the Moynihan Report. Within African American communities, Black people at that time expressed a deep admiration for the Black women in their lives. For example, when I taught my first-ever class on Black women's studies to an unruly class of eighth-grade, inner city, African American girls, I asked the following question: "Who is the person that you most admire in your life?" I expected my students to name famous African American women, or if they couldn't think of any, famous African Americans. Their answers surprised me. One by one, their answers were the same: "my mother" or "my grandmother." When I asked why they picked these particular people, these African American girls said, "because they can take care of themselves, because they're teaching us to be independent, because we see their contributions to our families." An alternative view of the world was hidden in plain sight—I simply had to ask different questions and listen.

Experiences such as these led me to examine all the different ways that Black women's knowledge had been distorted or omitted. I began to wonder what we would find if we aimed to interpret the world from the standpoint of African American women. Motherhood constituted only one such topic in building this self-defined standpoint—there were many more. Work, the sexual politics of Black womanhood, the depiction of Black women in the media, and characteristic patterns of Black women's activism all lent themselves to this archeological task, themes that appear as chapters in *Black Feminist Thought.*

Moreover, as was the case with motherhood, explicating this Black women's standpoint began to yield different interpretations of what was accepted as truth—interpretations that often differed dramatically from the elite, heterosexual, American white male hero-worship of Western scholarship. Take, for example, African American women's ideas about education. Black women educators apparently saw education for African Americans as providing far more than just technical skills. They advocated a different model of education. If you're a slave, do you want a model of education that's going to teach you to be a better slave? Who wants to be a more technically literate slave whose skills better equip them to play prop roles with grace and skill? Black women educators certainly wanted their students to acquire the technical skills they needed for survival, but they also valued the critical thinking skills required to challenge that system of slavery. They offered a critical education. Because Black women educators had historically played a very important role in African American communities, their actions as educators suggested a different understanding of Black women's politics in the United States. Historically, African American women had been quite politically active through their roles as mothers and educators, even though prevailing wisdom failed to view their actions within this framework.

Looking Outward: Black Feminist Analyses of Race, Class, and Gender

A second area of emphasis within *Black Feminist Thought* consists of balancing the inward-looking focus on African American women's experiences with an outward-looking analysis of intersecting power relations in the United States. Many people think that studying African American women means talking only about Black women's experiences. To counteract this belief, *Black Feminist Thought* investigates Black feminist analyses of the arguments advanced by many social groups, most notably, white men, white women, and African American men, as well as offering alternative analyses of society overall. It turns out that African American women have long been challenging the knowledge claims of many social groups. Until recently, however, few people in positions of power and authority appeared to be listening.

Black women had repeatedly challenged white male interpretations of history, namely, the stock stories of American history. Black women intellectuals provide many examples of how African American women challenged theoretical and empirical knowledge shaped by elite, white male assumptions. Take, for example, how anti-lynching activist Ida B. Wells-Barnett advanced an alternative analysis of lynching that prefigures contemporary arguments about race, gender, and sexuality. When she was a journalist in Memphis, Tennessee, two of her African American male friends were lynched, not because they sought white women as sexual partners, but instead because their businesses competed with those owned by whites. Unlike all of the other newspaper reports that claimed the Black men were lynched because they raped or lusted after white women, Wells-Barnett knew that the prevailing wisdom was a lie. Her response? She researched lynching and advanced one of the first intersectional analyses of race, class, gender, and sexuality in the United States, identifying sexual violence as a mechanism for maintaining existing power relations. Wells-Barnett paid for her boldness. When she published her findings, the white citizens of Memphis, Tennessee, burned the African American newspaper that had published her work to the ground. They also threatened that if she ever came back to Memphis, they would lynch her too. Wells-Barnett broke her silence as a prop in order to present a different interpretation of race, gender, class, and sexuality than the generally accepted wisdom. Wells-Barnett is one of many African American women who advance similar claims. Anna Julia Cooper, Mary McLeod Bethune, Zora Neale Hurston, Pauli Murray, Angela Davis, Alice Walker, Audre Lorde, June Jordan, and other well-known African American women thinkers have advanced similar arguments about how race, gender, class, and sexuality intersect within American society.

For African American women, challenging our allies has been more difficult, but no less important than critiquing white male power. Black women have launched some harsh critiques of white women and the feminist politics they allegedly espouse. The relationship between African American and white women emerged as an important theme within American feminism in the 1970s and 1980s. When white feminists used terms such as "woman" or "women," African American women often replied, "Exactly which women do you mean?" Much important work has resulted from Black women's challenges to legitimated feminist theory and practice. One especially contentious point concerned the ways in which white women have benefited from U.S. Black women's disadvantage, a theme that permeates Black feminist scholarship on domestic work. This frame of domestic work has provided a rich template for examining the relationships among women in the United States.

Challenging Black men to become better allies with Black women has also been an important part of looking beyond a Black women's community. Whereas the ways in which racism privileged white women and penalized African American women were evident, gender privileges and penalties flowing from sexism were often treated as family matters within African American communities. Building alliances with Black men that took the intersections of race, class, and gender into account revealed the importance of replacing an either/or view of the world (one is either white or black, or male or female) with a both/and perspective that encouraged Black men to see themselves as having both a race and a gender. All sorts of categories yield to this both/and thinking. Black feminist thought challenges prevailing tendencies to categorize everyone in either/or boxes of being either oppressors or oppressed. Everybody wants to be on the good side. No one wants to self-identify as an oppressor. We certainly do not want to be victimized and to be perceived as weak, but at the same time, we want to be on the right side and champion the cause of the victimized. In everyday life, negotiating these boundaries is virtually impossible because most of us experience contradictory positions. We are oppressed by someone, and then we oppress someone else. This is what happens with African American men, who clearly experience racial oppression but who also enjoy a degree of gender privilege, especially in the home. They may be oppressed by their race, but privileged by their gender. In this way, *Black Feminist Thought* identifies important themes that need to be addressed.

The Day the Props Began to Move Revisited

Where are we now? There is no scripted ending to this story because it is our story in the making. Individually and collectively, we are all involved in writing the next chapter in this drama, each from a different vantage point. I see several possible chapter outlines for the next phase of the script, some of which seem more in tune with early-twenty-first-century realities than others. Perhaps you can generate more.

In the first scenario, the star eliminates all the props that are too noisy, troublesome, or bothersome. Alternately, the hero visibly punishes some of the props to scare the others into submission. Fear has been a prominent feature of the post-911 environment in the United States. Events such as the 2003 declaration of war on Iraq to search for mythical weapons of mass destruction, the ambiguous, color-coded warnings from the Department of Homeland Security that cautioned Americans to be on alert for suspicious behavior, and the detention of unprecedented numbers of young African American and Latino men for reasons of public safety all illustrate the ability of fear to shape behavior. Eliminating and neutralizing the props that aim to share center stage is certainly one possible scenario if the hero refuses to share power.

A second scenario finds the hero diffusing the challenges raised by props by accepting some token props to keep everybody else in line. Instead of punishing a few props as an object lesson, the hero rewards a few token props to achieve the same outcome. Tokenizing a few props allows the hero to say to the rest, "Your failures are your own fault. The system is fair—see, token X has made it, so why can't you?" Under this strategy, only a few props make it onto the stage, and because the hero's story has changed, token props play different parts than the props of the past. Token props are needed for the hero's play to be plausible, to show that colorblindness, gender-neutrality, and economic opportunities are available to all. Visible token props enable the play to continue. This decision to reward tokens can also be a very effective way of dividing the props to better control them all.

A third scenario seemingly provides space for something different. In this version, an extended period of upheaval renders unworkable the former stories that created the categories of heroes and props. The world is forever changed, and everyone knows it. The children of heroes and props alike come to understand their different histories as well their interconnectedness on a global stage. We now are in that place. Yet the former stars and props of global drama come to understand this interconnectedness in different ways. Raising hopes and then dashing them catalyzes conditions for a global drama where the props rise up with an eye toward eliminating their particular stars and all that they represent. Revolution, insurgency, and mass protest are real possibilities.

The bottom line is that, whether we fight to hold on to threadbare stories of heroes and props or strive to write new, more socially just stories, ordinary people hold the power for change. Individual Black women resisted their place as objectified props and aimed to tell their own stories. In doing so, they crafted the dynamic, collective voice of Black feminist thought. I encourage each of you to write, edit, and rewrite your own stories until they ring true for you. Armed with thoughtful interpretations of our lived experiences we can collectively craft new interpretations of our shared realities. Imagine the possibilities for our world if we do.

ADDITIONAL RESOURCES

Bambara, Toni C., ed. 1970. *The Black Woman: An Anthology.* New York: Signet.
Giddings, Paula. 1984. *When and Where I Enter: The Impact of Black Women on Race and Sex in America.* New York: William Morrow.
Goffman, Erving. 1990. *The Presentation of Self in Everyday Life.* New York: Penguin.
Morrison, Toni. *The Bluest Eye.* 1970. New York: Holt, Rinehart and Winston.
Rollins, Judith. 1985. *Between Women: Domestics and Their Employers.* Philadelphia: Temple University Press.

Fighting Words . . . or Yet Another Version of "The Emperor's New Clothes"

REFLEXIVE ESSAY: Fighting Words *uses Black feminist thought as a touchstone for examining oppositional or critical social theory. Because* Fighting Words *is written for a scholarly audience, making its main ideas accessible to multiple audiences presented a greater problem for me than my other works. Narrative traditions, especially storytelling, poetry, folklore, and song, have long been teaching tools for ordinary people. In this speech, I use the familiar story of "The Emperor's New Clothes" to introduce core concepts in the sociology of knowledge, namely how power relations shape the contours of knowledge. The metaphor of the crowd standing in different power relations to the emperor introduces the theme of the significance of social hierarchy for understanding knowledge. My retelling of the story also illustrates how centering on African American women's experiences can produce new truths. This short narrative enabled me to introduce some core ideas concerning epistemology, such as standpoint, the nature of credible evidence, and the role of intellectuals in speaking the truth to power and to the public.*

I originally presented a version of this essay as part of a keynote address at the 1991 statewide conference of the New Jersey Curriculum Transformation Project and gave versions of it before *Fighting Words* was published in 1998. Most recently, I revised the essay for a public lecture at Mississippi State University in 2012.

FIGHTING WORDS: *African American Women and the Search for Justice* examines the connections between power relations and the processes of knowledge production that are needed to uphold them. One important idea in the book is that unjust power relations and knowledge are linked and that, when it comes to social inequalities, one cannot operate without the other. Despite the significance of my thesis, *Fighting Words* is a difficult book to discuss, not only because its arguments are complex but also because accessing them requires technical language that many of my students, let alone everyday people, do not possess. Grounding the core ideas of *Fighting Words* in an updated version of a familiar story should give you a feel for the main ideas in the book.

Hans Christian Andersen's children's story "The Emperor's New Clothes" may be a classic, but I would like to give it a new twist. This story is a metaphor for how knowledge works to uphold and/or challenge power relations. In my version of the story, the emperor symbolizes powerful groups and their interests, and his clothes represent the many types of dominant knowledge that uphold unjust social inequalities that flow from those power relations. Dominant knowledge carries many names. For example, the traditional public school curriculum, with its standard textbooks, scripted lesson plans, and standardized testing, is a good example of such knowledge, but other types of knowledge work just as well. Traditional academic disciplines such as biology, psychology, history, and sociology all produce bodies of knowledge. Similarly, theories such as poststructuralism, postmodernism, and queer theory constitute bodies of knowledge with their own framing assumptions and sets of practitioners. Today, mass media and the Internet are important sites for knowledge production. Across all of these sites, knowledge need not reflect the interests of more powerful individuals and groups—knowledge can be oppositional as well. The important point of the story is that dominant knowledge, the kind that represents the emperor's interests, can be challenged from below, often from unexpected sources.

Another Version of "The Emperor's New Clothes"

Imagine a beautiful sunny day, with thousands of people milling around a large plaza in a major urban area. People in the crowd seem festive, and the scene is similar to New Year's Eve celebrations in New York's Times Square. Because this is a "back in the day" or "old school" event, members of the crowd do not have smart phones to tweet one another or iPod Touches to snap each other's pictures. Instead, they spontaneously break out into praise songs for the emperor and show each other the latest dance steps. Everyone seems to be in a good mood. It's a big emperor party, and almost everybody has the day off.

At first glance, the crowd seems to be an undifferentiated mass of people, all equal in their celebration of the emperor's magnificence, if only in their imaginations. On closer inspection, however, in this particular empire, as in empires in general, the crowd is arrayed on a series of stair steps, with those closer to the emperor gaining better views, with some even having seats. Because the emperor is the center of the empire, his platform towers above all others, with all stair steps leading in his direction. Because he is closest to God, or Science, or Truth, or whatever is worshipped in his particular empire, the emperor looks down from his throne, casting an all-seeing eye on his subjects. His word is all-powerful—what he says goes.

Because the emperor's subjects believe that he is the center of the universe, they measure their status based on their proximity to him. Some subjects share the top platform with him and are very close to him. This inner circle of subjects surround the emperor, looking both ways, first to the crowd and then to the emperor, all designed to ensure his protection. They see the vastness of the masses stretching out below and feel grateful that they are not among them. Those in the emperor's inner circle have a clear view of him and, for the most part, they look like him. Those who most closely resemble the emperor use that similarity to convince others with a more obstructed view that, as mini-emperors, they too represent the emperor's glory and should be worshipped as well.

Other subjects of the empire who are further away from the emperor stand on lower platforms that are still raised above the masses. Some desperately try to move up the stair steps leading to the emperor, hoping to better their status. They jump, crawl, and often frantically try to heave themselves up onto higher stair steps so that they too can look down on the crowd below. Sociologists call this phenomenon *social mobility*. Many in this group will do anything to be near the emperor and out of the crowd. Others are far more ambivalent.

Still other subjects of the empire are a little further out, hemmed in and/or kept out by legalities of zoning ordinances, white-only bathroom signs, citizenship papers, and policing that is devoted to protecting the borders. Increasingly, invisible fences that resemble those designed to keep dogs in yards are the border patrol tool of choice. Few crowd members living in the emperor's colonies, neo-colonies, ghettos, barrios, and reservations have met the emperor in person, but most of his subjects know far more about his celebrated exploits than he knows about their everyday lives. In this emperor-centric society, textbooks, pictures, television shows, videos, newspapers, and books written and circulated by the emperor's lookalikes keep all eyes focused on his exploits. Some hope to catch glimpses of the emperor; yet even though they were required to attend the boring parade, most are happy to get the day off from their jobs at Walmart and privatized prisons, the biggest employers in the empire.

There's more to this story than the big picture. How does the emperor convince his subjects that the empire is a good idea? Here, clothing matters. Clothing hides the emperor's imperfections—his spreading paunch, his balding head, and the fact that he may not be that bright. Just as long as he looks grand, he need not be grand. Clothing is the emperor's knowledge that makes him look good to himself and others. You've heard the expression, "Clothes make the man."

Yet the emperor neither created nor spread his knowledge by himself. He's not that smart. His brilliance, however, lies in his ability to find extremely loyal subjects who defend his territory as if it were their own, especially if their actions work against their own best interests. When it comes to this knowledge-clothing, *scholars* tailor clothes that fit the emperor to highlight his good features and hide the bad ones. His scholar-tailors must be vigilant because just as styles change, so must the knowledge that defends the emperor's power. Without careful attention, his threads can go out of style quickly. Here the scholar-tailors step in to help, bringing an arsenal of specialized skills to keep the emperor's wardrobe looking spiffy and fresh. Many scholar-tailors base their careers on specializing in emperor cuffs, pants, shirts, or the more intimate area of emperor underwear. We call the resulting clothing *academic disciplines.*

Scholar-tailors cannot do everything. Some of the emperor's messengers descend the stair steps into the crowd, proclaiming, "Here ye, here ye, behold the emperor's glory. The emperor is all-knowing and all-powerful. Bow down to him, and give him your allegiance and your taxes." We call these people *teachers,* and more recently, *media pundits.* In this knowledge production process, it is important to remember that, even though the faces of those who tailor the emperor's clothes and spread his message may change, his power remains intact. The emperor may need to change his scholar-tailors, teachers, and media pundits to make sure that his wardrobe is hip and up to date. The clothes may change, yet once an emperor, always an emperor.

In the original story, the emperor was actually naked. Yet despite this obvious fact, none of his loyal subjects challenged the knowledge that proclaimed his grandeur. In the original story, one child who got a good look at the emperor cried out, "The Emperor has no clothes!" How shocking. Simply stating the truth created an entirely new reality. One by one, people in the crowd proclaimed the emperor's nakedness. In the original story, speaking the truth to the empire's people was a route to speaking the truth to the emperor's power. A little child revealed truth.

Let me tell you why this story is a fairy tale. In Anderson's version, people actually listened to children. Not so in our society. Let's look at what might happen in contemporary U.S. society. Here's my version, now retitled, "Keisha Spots a Naked White Man."

In my version, the child is not a boy, but instead is a sassy little Black girl named Keisha—not Jennifer, Morgan, Jordan, Melanie, Buffy, Candi, or Princess—simply Keisha. Because Keisha's mother miraculously got a day off from both of her jobs, Keisha is standing in the crowd next to her mother, excited to be attending such an important event. Not being one of the chosen ones, Keisha is so far from the emperor's platform that she can't see much at all (this version happened before the advent of Jumbotron screens, which change the details but not the substance of the story). From where Keisha stands, she can barely distinguish the emperor from the inner circle of people surrounding him. Because her neighborhood has no white residents, all white people look alike to her—she can't tell them apart. Keisha also can't see through the backs of all of the grown-ups in the crowd who, from time to time, turn back to look at her and yell out what they see. Some of them also proclaim the emperor's glory, while others remain curiously silent, even sullen. Most don't seem to care—they're happy not to be at work. Yet for a moment, the crowd parts, and Keisha gets a clear view of the emperor. What a shock! He's naked! She turns to her mother and blurts out in amazement, "Ma—that white man is naked! Is *that* the emperor?"

We must recognize that in real life, a sassy, self-defining, self-reliant little Black girl like Keisha would have received a very different response than the child in Anderson's original version. Keisha is unlikely to be taken seriously. Who ever listens to little Black girls? You may disagree, but this is my story, and I'll tell it the way I want.

Keisha's mother was shocked. She realized how dangerous it can be for little Black girls, or for Black women, for that matter, to speak out. Keisha was going to be an embarrassment if she kept saying such outrageous things. Initially, Keisha might have been ignored, in the hopes that she might shut up on her own. Depending on Keisha's track record as an uppity little Black girl, her mother might have tried to silence her: "She's just a child—don't listen to her." Despite her mother's efforts, Keisha pushed on. If she couldn't be shushed, she might have been belittled or demeaned, either by nearby members of the crowd, by some of the emperor's "teachers" who lived among the marginalized, and/or sadly, by her own mother. "She's just a little Black girl—what does she know," a chorus of voices proclaim. Worse yet, if Keisha kept up her outrageous ways, she might have been eligible for something we call *counseling*. "Let's see if we can *help* her speak standard American English, drop the 'angry Black girl' attitude, and behave a little better," her therapist suggested. What an elegant loop—belittle her, point out how she needs counseling, and then "help" her fit in.

Our honest little Black girl may not have been so lucky. She may have been locked up as one of those so-called crazy women that are legendary in the essays and fiction of Alice Walker, June Jordan, Gayle Jones, Toni Cade Bambara, and Ntozake Shange, to name a few. Alternately, after enough incidents of shushing, Keisha may have turned her ideas inward and kept them to herself. Slow suicide through addiction happens to so many creative and talented Black women when their ideas are suppressed and they are beaten down. Sadly, perhaps she would have been killed and no one would have cared, or perhaps even noticed. Just another inconsequential little Black girl—who cares that her spirit, if not her actual body, was murdered?

Knowledge/Power Relations: *Black Feminist Thought* and *Fighting Words*

"Fighting the words" of dominant discourse that encouraged Keisha to see the emperor as all-powerful and herself as a person of little value put her at risk. In the United States, although the First Amendment to the Constitution is designed to protect political speech of all types, bomb threats, incitements to riot, obscene phone calls, "fighting words," and all speech that infringes on public order can be prohibited in the interests of the common good. Speech turns out to be far more regulated than imagined. Within the American legal system, the "fighting words" doctrine constitutes insults of such magnitude that, because they incite people to violence, can be censured. Keisha's words were not intended to incite people to violence, but her words so challenged the social order that they easily could be treated as "fighting words." In this context, a good deal of oppositional speech finds itself in a similar situation to Keisha's—pressured to capitulate to prevailing standards. Speaking the truth both to power and to the people can be redefined as "fighting words" and punished.

Black feminist thought is but one expression of the many self-defined standpoints produced by people whose location within intersecting power relations of race, class, gender, sexuality, age, and religion mandate that they glorify their respective emperors. Black feminist thought is the type of knowledge produced by all of the Keishas who collectively live in a very different world than the emperor and his friends, and who, as a result of these experiences, see the world from the distinctive vantage point of being on the bottom.

Very simply, Black feminist thought in the United States is the compilation of worldviews of many little Black girls and the women they grow up to be. It is the knowledge that they create, based on their own experiences, and with their own minds. Like Keisha, many African American women have disbelieved the emperor's view of themselves as small and insignificant. Instead, many claim their voices and empower themselves by naming reality as they see it. Like Keisha, many African American women have experiences that provide them with specific angles of vision on their experiences. Their point of view, if uncensored, provides fresh, albeit potentially dangerous, ideas. Keisha models this new standpoint on knowledge and power. The power to define new ideas that potentially catalyze new actions lies at the heart of Black feminist thought. From wherever we are in the emperor's crowd, if we continue to respond to the same old questions, if we continue to bounce off of the emperor's knowledge and structure our thinking in terms of his interpretive frameworks, we are perpetually reactive. We lose the ability to speak the truths of our lives.

In *Black Feminist Thought*, I claim that African American women's migration experiences as workers between two different communities, paid domestic work within white households and unpaid domestic work within their families and communities, generated a potentially distinctive angle of vision, or standpoint on the world. I explore how a collective perspective on race, class, and gender relations that formed the basis for a Black feminist standpoint ostensibly accompanied these shared experiences. Although I drew from social theory prepared by the scholar-tailors of my discipline, I grounded my analysis in the experiences of African American women themselves and what they said about their own point of view on the world. I tried to hear from the Keishas of the world.

Historically, because so many African American women workers were so heavily concentrated in private domestic work, they encountered two types of knowledge. On the one hand, as full insiders within African American communities, they received and shaped knowledge largely hidden from white people. Such women were often quite powerful within African American communities, especially in Black churches and other institutions of African American civil society. Because they were members of a subordinated group that had to remain vigilant about resisting racial oppression, Black women actively participated in resistance traditions. Whether small-scale and hidden, through traditional Black women's community work, or as participants and leaders in social movements, many African American women have been change agents. At the same time, African American women who worked this triple shift of unpaid family employment, low-paid domestic work, and Black community service often did so at substantial cost to their own well-being.

Black women who came into contact with white families via their forays into the private spaces of white households also were exposed to another type of insider knowledge typically hidden from public view. Working in domestic service showed them the most intimate details of their employers' lives, an experience that often sparked remarkable insights about the everyday lives and thoughts of white people. Stated differently, those coming out of the crowd to clean up after emperors, mini-emperors, scholar-tailors, and the like understood power in ways that eluded these same groups. Black women knew that white supremacist ideology was just that—knowledge produced by members of an elite group and circulated by that group to justify and obscure unjust power relations. Such women routinely returned to their African American families with stories of how ordinary, both good and bad, white people actually were. Even though their white employers may have treated them well, even at times imagining their domestic workers to be "like one of the family," Black women knew that they could never be full family members. Despite their grasp of insider knowledge, they could never gain the full insider power afforded white family members unless the very terms of family membership changed.

Black women in domestic work thus had access to what James Scott calls the "hidden transcripts" of *both* African American and white households and communities. In this case, Black women had access to the knowledge produced in private that groups unequal in power wanted to conceal from one another. However, Black women could only exercise power from positions of authority in their families and neighborhoods and not in social spaces controlled by whites, namely, within white families or social institutions of government, corporations, and the media. The knowledge generated while sitting around the kitchen table, waiting at the bus stop, planning church dinners, or working in other safe spaces within African American civil society thus reflected characteristic themes central to Black women's survival in the outsider within locations that they occupied when working for their white "families" as well as the distinctive worldview that they crafted within African American civil society.

Fighting Words builds on this analysis by examining the kind of knowledge and power relations that create the different views of the world of the emperor and the little Black girl in the crowd. Stated differently, *Fighting Words* investigates the standards we use to assess what we know and/or why we believe what we believe. Why did so many people in the story believe the emperor? What made his standpoint so compelling? Why might so many people routinely disbelieve legions of Keishas who advance a different point of view? How do power relationships shape who is believed, who is disbelieved, and why? These questions lie at the heart of *epistemology*, a theory of knowledge that examines the standards used to assess what we know or why we believe what we believe. In much of my work, I use Black feminist thought as one specific location to examine these more general issues of epistemology. Helping people survive and cope with harsh conditions is a far cry from trying to change those conditions. What works in one time or place may not work in others. The social conditions that generated the particular expression of Black feminist thought in the 1950s and 1960s—U.S. Black women restricted to domestic work, living in racially segregated neighborhoods relatively untouched by drugs and crime—no longer exist. Just because Black feminist thought contributed to *past* political struggles does not mean that *contemporary* Black feminist thought can do the same. Moreover, tactics for legitimating knowledge also change. Current challenges lie in developing ideas that respond to current social conditions. Because the social structures of Black women's work and family experiences have changed, so too must Black feminist thought. But in what direction?

Remaining Oppositional

Black women's struggles to get Black feminist thought taken seriously are profoundly shaped by existing knowledge and power relations. If only social change were as simple as adding Black women into existing textbooks, academic journals, and books and stirring them into existing knowledge, things would be simple. All Keisha needed to do was join the collective praise song for the emperor, and most likely she would have been left alone. Yet that praise song was predicated on compromising her own authentic voice, a place where she might survive but surely could never thrive.

Surviving requires an expansive repertoire of scholarly and political skills that not only protects but also nurtures Black women's intellectual activism. Black feminist knowledge that challenges the standpoint of more powerful groups is likely to be silenced, ridiculed, reformed as the price of fitting in, and/ or ghettoized. Black women are typically not seen as theorists, and our work is not deemed theoretical unless we produce theory in ways comparable to those of highly educated white men. This presents a real dilemma for Black women intellectuals. If we criticize elite discourse using its terms, we gain legitimacy for our work by traditional standards. But by doing so, we may simultaneously delegitimize our own authentic point of view in our own eyes and the eyes of those closest to us. Are we fitting in, or selling out?

Fighting Words takes on one important epistemological theme, namely, how does a discourse remain oppositional? Contemporary Black feminist thought must constantly ask itself whether it remains oppositional, whether it retains the standpoint of the Keishas who can tell the truth of their own experience and act on it. Many aspiring and established Black women intellectuals now create ideas for dissertation committees, tenure committees, journals, and the popular press—all targeted to a liberal white public segmented into constituencies most receptive to the given intellectual. Writing to mainstream audiences to gain access to the public that one truly wants to reach is important and, far too often, necessary. However, as Zora Neale Hurston's continual struggles with her white patrons illustrates, visibility can extract high costs. Moreover, in a context of heightened social media, who speaks to African American women these days? Are the blogs, tweets, and song lyrics of Black women popular singers up to the task of remaining oppositional? Can poetry slams fill the void left by the departure of Black women's fiction?

When it comes to questions of intellectual activism generally, or Black feminist thought as oppositional knowledge that participates in Black women's traditions of intellectual activism, I find it useful to focus on Keisha. Just as Keisha may have faced formidable obstacles in getting her ideas heard and taken seriously, current power relations of race, gender, class, sexuality, and nation present similar challenges for African American women and similarly oppressed groups. As times change, standards for who is believed and why change along with them. What steps would Keisha need to take to ensure that her knowledge remained oppositional? How can we protect her and, in doing so, ensure our own survival?

As the early twenty-first century unfolds, Black feminist thought and other sites of intellectual activism stand at a crucial crossroads where centers of all sorts, imperial and otherwise, are up for grabs. Understanding knowledge and power relations through metaphors of centers and margins, colonial powers and their colonies, the emperor's platform and the territorial hinterlands of the crowd is giving way to multiple centers, nodes within interdependent social networks. In the United States, the very meaning of "American" is contested both within the U.S. borders and in a global context. Where do African American women fit within this mosaic of change? The social conditions that shaped African American women's communities from which Black women thinkers drew inspiration and in which they lived are markedly different now. What issues does Black feminist thought confront in a changing political climate?

Three questions might help us navigate new paths for engaged scholarship such as Black feminist thought. First, does engaged scholarship like Black feminist thought speak the truth to people about the reality of their lives? We might ask whether the knowledge that we want Keisha to learn about the world is truthful in relation to what she experiences. It didn't matter how many people told her that the emperor was wearing fine clothes. She knew he was naked. She trusted her own eyes, her own experiences, over the words of others. Patterns of whose knowledge counts, whose is discredited, and which standards are used to determine the difference encompass much more than logical consistency or empirical verification. Because reason and truth have so long been coded as white and male, it is difficult to accept truth coming from new sources. Who are the "experts"? Why do we believe what these experts say? Who decides what counts as knowledge? Keisha's words remind us that we need new mechanisms of validating truth that take into account how power relations legitimate what counts as truth.

Second, does engaged scholarship like Black feminist thought equip people to resist oppression? Is it functional as a tool for social change? Keisha is a sassy little Black girl. She may not have time for "knowledge for knowledge's sake." These questions ask whether knowledge is functional for her, whether it has pragmatic utility in helping her solve the problems in her life. All social theories, whether critical or not, have an explicit or implicit theory of freedom and resistance embedded in them. After all, freedom constitutes, in one sense, the opposite of oppression. For me, a social theory's ability to prepare people to resist oppression constitutes a measure of its worth.

Finally, does engaged scholarship move people to struggle in favor of social justice? Here Keisha could be very useful. If the Keishas of the world are not *moved* by ideas, how can they be moved to take action? For oppressed groups, this question concerns how effectively critical social theory provides moral authority to struggles for self-definition and self-determination. The necessity of an ethical foundation as the vision for a critical social theory like Black feminist thought becomes increasingly important in an era where power relations themselves are being so dramatically reformulated. The search for justice is an ongoing, principled struggle that resists disciplinary power relations and gives meaning to everyday life.

ADDITIONAL RESOURCES

Guy-Sheftall, Beverly, ed. 1995. *Words of Fire: An Anthology of African-American Feminist Thought.* New York: New Press.

Jordan, June. 2002. *Some of Us Did Not Die.* New York: Basic/Civitas.

Matsuda, Mari J., Charles Lawrence III, Richard Delgado, and Kimberlé Crenshaw. 1993. *Words That Wound: Critical Race Theory, Assaultive Speech, and the First Amendment.* Boulder, Colo.: Westview Press.

Shange, Ntozake. 1975. *For Colored Girls Who Have Considered Suicide/When the Rainbow Is Enuf.* New York: Macmillan.

Smith, Barbara. 1998. *The Truth That Never Hurts: Writings on Race, Gender, and Freedom.* New Brunswick, N.J.: Rutgers University Press.

Walker, Alice. 1983. *In Search of Our Mothers' Gardens: Womanist Prose.* New York: Harcourt Brace.

Black Sexual Politics 101

REFLEXIVE ESSAY: *When* Black Sexual Politics *was first published, I was a guest on several Black talk radio programs. These public conversations with largely African American listeners sharpened my skills of translation. After each radio interview, I took notes on the topics and themes that had generated the most heated debates. Working from my memory and my notes, I revised this essay several times to incorporate the ideas of Black radio listeners. Translating the main ideas that I treat at length in* Black Sexual Politics *into a form that was accessible to the callers helped me identify terms like "gender outlaws" and "sexual deviants" that resonated with callers. Ironically, the three core ideas of this essay do not appear in this form in* Black Sexual Politics, *thus illustrating the challenges that face public intellectuals of speaking the truth to people.*

M Y PRESENTATION TODAY is designed to introduce you to some of the main ideas in *Black Sexual Politics: African Americans, Gender and the New Racism.* In *Black Sexual Politics,* I argue that all people who are interested in social justice need a new anti-racist politics to deal with racism and a new conceptual framework to analyze it. *Black Sexual Politics* uses the experiences of African Americans, a group with much at stake in this project,

---

I first delivered a version of the speech published here in 2004, using an accompanying Power-Point, to a wonderful African American community group at a branch of the Tulsa Public Library. From there, I moved on to deliver different variations at Rutgers University, the University of California at Santa Barbara, George Mason University, Pennsylvania State University–Abington, the University of Michigan–Flint, and the University of Richmond, college campuses with markedly different populations. This version distills the conversations from those diverse venues.

to examine the contradictions and tensions that surround both new forms of racism and anti-racist politics. I focus on racism and anti-racism, primarily through the experiences of African Americans and during the important period of the post–Civil Rights era. However, the analysis that I present touches far more people and is certainly about more than race.

Let me say a bit more about the origins of this particular project. When I finished *Black Feminist Thought* (1990), I realized that many people still saw feminism and gender analysis as applying primarily to women. If women were in the room, then gender was represented. This kind of thinking also guided racial analysis—if Black people are in the classroom, then somehow race is represented. Black feminism took aim at these assumptions, arguing that race, gender, class, and sexuality intersect in the lives of African American women. I wanted to take this main idea of *Black Feminist Thought,* namely, the need for intersectional analyses of everyone's experiences, and apply the tools of Black feminist thought to analyze Black men's experiences and black masculinity. Not only were Black men affected by race and class but their experiences also reflected intersections of gender and sexuality.

I spent over a decade after the initial publication of *Black Feminist Thought* in 1990 and its revision in 2000 developing an analysis of how intersectional power relations shape ideas about femininity and masculinity. *Black Sexual Politics* is the product of those years. Here is my definition of Black sexual politics: Black sexual politics consists of a set of ideas and social practices shaped by gender, race, class, and sexuality that frame the way that African American men and women treat one another as well as how other people perceive and treat them. Such politics lie at the heart of beliefs about black masculinity and black femininity, gender-specific experiences of African Americans, and the forms that racial politics take in the post–Civil Rights era.

When *Black Sexual Politics* was published, I faced the task of figuring out how to explain its main ideas to the very same populations whose lives I aimed to reach with my analysis. I knew that the media had grown in importance in the time between the publication of *Black Feminist Thought* in 1990 and the publication of *Black Sexual Politics* in 2004. One glaring difference concerned the growing significance of popular culture within American culture. My undergraduate students who were enrolled in "Contemporary Black Women," the benchmark course that I used while writing *Black Feminist Thought,* were willing to read works of fiction and develop their ideas using these sources. A decade later, my undergraduate students who were enrolled in "Introduction to Black Gender Studies," the course I used while writing *Black Sexual Politics,* were deeply immersed in popular culture. For *Black Sexual Politics,* I knew that I had to make extensive use of Black popular culture, or my students could not make sense of my arguments. I thought that I was ready—I had included carefully chosen, popular culture examples in *Black Sexual Politics.*

None of this prepared me for my first foray into Black talk radio. My topic of "Black sexual politics" was certainly provocative, yet the first call-in question gave me a sense of what lay in store. "I want to know what you think about all these Black men running around after white women," the first caller asked. "What can we do about that!" The next caller followed in kind: "I'm a Black woman who wants to marry a Black man. But all the Black men are in jail or, worse yet, they're gay. Do you have any advice for me on how I can find a good Black man?" By this time, I saw where the conversation was headed. Ironically, *Black Sexual Politics* was written to address some of the very questions that the callers were asking, yet, according to my analysis, the callers were asking the wrong questions. Their questions "got in the way" of their ability to grasp an analysis of the social conditions that were creating the issues they identified.

I clearly needed another line of approach. How might I translate the main ideas of my book in ways that would be most meaningful for my callers? Starting with interracial dating or gay Black men would be too inflammatory—the callers would simply take sides and shout at each other across preconceived and often deeply entrenched points of view. Instead, I needed to present the main ideas in *Black Sexual Politics* in a form that my callers could hear and, from that starting place, lead them to consider unfamiliar arguments about familiar realities.

Three main ideas drawn from *Black Sexual Politics* helped me to explain my book. But these three ideas do not appear in the book exactly as they do here; rather, they are the outcome of many public conversations about these ideas.

First, viewing African Americans as gender outlaws and sexual deviants has long been a fundamental pillar of racism in the United States. I think we are all familiar with how tightly bundled together race and class have been in producing patterns of wealth and poverty, power and political disenfranchisement in the U.S. context. This intersectional relationship of race and class or, more accurately, racism and class exploitation, is what made Barack Obama's election so noteworthy. Yet it is equally important to stress that American racism works not only in conjunction with class politics but also through gender and sexuality. This is a major idea of *Black Sexual Politics,* and my goal in this book is to develop an argument that makes it virtually impossible to analyze racism without also talking about sexism and heterosexism.

A second main idea of *Black Sexual Politics* is that a powerful mass media has repackaged and sold these ideas about Black people as gender outlaws and sexual deviants. Long effective under prior racial formations of slavery and Jim Crow racism, contemporary repackaging is vital to a new "colorblind racism" that masks the workings of the social class system. Simultaneously domestic and global in scope, this colorblind racism travels via the Internet and similar new communication technologies. Music videos, movies, television shows, YouTube, Netflix, and Facebook celebrate and/or derogate elements of African American culture that make Black youth culture simultaneously visible and often misunderstood.

The third main idea of *Black Sexual Politics* is that African Americans must develop a more progressive Black sexual politics that takes gender and sexuality into account. Failing to do so will hamper African Americans' ability to solve social problems such as school achievement, violence, high rates of HIV/AIDS, and similar issues. Because these social problems are not unique to African Americans but take special form in Black populations, developing a progressive sexual politics for African Americans means seeing how other groups might engage in similar projects.

Gender Outlaws, Sexual Deviants, and Racialized Gender Ideology

Few of us realize how dependent gender ideology in the United States is on ideas about race and sexuality. Most fundamentally, so-called normal gender ideology contains beliefs about ostensibly normal masculinity and femininity. "Real men" are supposed to be dominant (in charge), smart, virile, and strong. Similarly, "ideal women" are supposed to be subordinate, emotional, ornamental (sexually alluring), and weak. In this gender ideology, masculinity requires a comparable set of beliefs about femininity and vice versa to give each construct meaning. These ideological gender constructions of "strong men and weak women" produce social scripts that tell each of us how we "should" think and behave.

African American experience points to the ways that this gender normality is also racialized. The assumed gender normality of real men and ideal women gains meaning only in contrast to groups that are clustered at the ostensibly abnormal end of the gender spectrum. There one finds Black people stigmatized as gender outlaws, primarily because they are allegedly saddled with a reverse and thereby deviant gender ideology of "weak men and strong women." This depiction of Black men and women as gender outlaws because of ostensibly weak men and strong women constitutes a linchpin of gender ideology overall.

I cannot tell you how often this particular ideology of the seemingly weak Black man and the allegedly strong Black woman reappears in scholarship and popular culture. From the 1965 Moynihan Report to now, this ideology has influenced social science research and public policy on African American families. Worries about preserving Black men's "manhood" seem ever-present. Within African American communities, debates have waged about the meaning of this depiction in popular culture, for example, debates about the depiction of African American men in films such as *The Color Purple,* or ongoing debates centering on filmmaker Tyler Perry's character Madea as a strong Black woman who is played by Tyler Perry, an African American man in drag. Please feel free to suggest your own contemporary examples from scholarship and popular culture. They are easy to find if you look for them.

Public policy and media depictions are bad enough, but when African Americans also believe that men are too weak and women are too strong, this gender ideology affects relationships among U.S. Black people. Take the example of how the belief in the so-called weak Black man, combined with the shortage of Black male college students, shapes relations on college campuses. There one hears talented Black women say, "Oh, we have got to let the men run the meetings because so few have made it to college. If they're weak, we're just going to have to put up with it and not hold them responsible." Conversely, perfectly capable Black men say, "Baby, can you type my paper? You know how hard it is for us Black men!"

In addition to being depicted as gender outlaws, African Americans have also been depicted as sexual deviants. As was the case with gender ideology, here too ideas about "normal sexuality" as heterosexual and/or married rely on a parallel set of ideas about "deviant sexuality" as homosexual and/or unmarried for meaning. Within this dominant sexual ideology, Black people occupy the "deviant" end of the sexual spectrum. Black people are depicted as *naturally* hyper-heterosexual, in other words, having an *excess* of heterosexual energy that, if left untamed by Western civilization, would express itself in endless sex acts. This rampant hyper-heterosexuality seemingly constitutes one reason why Black people have so much sex outside of marriage, why so many African American children are born outside of marriage, and why African Americans constitute a problem for society.

When coupled with the gender ideology depicting African Americans as gender outlaws for having "weak men and strong women," this gender ideology gets mapped onto a hyper-heterosexuality that produces gender outlaws and sexual deviants. For example, Black women are accused of being willing to have sex without inhibitions, of failing to commit to male partners, of being too strong in bed and scaring away male partners, and of having lots of babies as a result of their unrestrained "fucking." Similarly, Black men's alleged weakness as fathers and thinkers becomes an excuse for celebrating and fearing their alleged sexual prowess. Within this logic, myths of oversized Black male penises and, taken to its extreme, violent rapists who cannot control their sexual natures permeate popular culture and political campaigns alike.

Western sexual ideologies may stigmatize U.S. Blacks as sexually deviant, but African Americans are not the only group to receive this treatment. Lesbian, gay, bisexual, and transgendered (LGBT) people occupy the ostensibly abnormal end of the sexual continuum, serving as the ultimate anchor for heterosexuality's normality. LGBT people are categorized on the deviant end of the normal/deviant sexuality continuum, so goes dominant logic, because they engage in *unnatural* sexual acts. In essence, homosexuality becomes defined as the *absence* of heterosexual desire. If Black people represent an *excess* of heterosexual desire, their sexual practices constitute a natural, albeit deviant, form of heterosexuality. Thus, African Americans and LGBT people are *both* relegated to the deviant end of the normal/deviant sexuality continuum, yet for different reasons concerning the presence or absence of heterosexual desire, and the inherent naturalness or unnaturalness of their sexual behavior.

The reasoning here is curious—if all of the Blacks are heterosexual, then a natural heterosexuality become a fundamental characteristic of African American identity as well as an essential feature of Blacks as a race. This logic renders LGBT Black people less authentically Black. Moreover, if heterosexuality constitutes the natural state of Black people, then homosexuality has no place among Black people. By default, all of the (normal!) homosexuals become white. Within this ideology, Black people (imagined to be naturally heterosexual) become privileged by their sexuality and penalized by their race. In contrast, homosexuals (imagined to be white) become privileged by their race and penalized by their sexuality. In this sense, homosexuality is implicated in upholding not just heterosexism but a *racialized* heterosexism that positions Black people as deviant heterosexuals. Normal sexuality, now redefined as simultaneously white and straight, is positioned in relation to these *two* sites of seeming deviancy. In other words, sexuality is evaluated as normal if it is *neither* the allegedly animalistic, naturally heterosexual practices attributed to Black people *nor* the ostensibly unnatural sexual practices routinely attributed to LGBT white people.

Keep in mind that what I am examining here are links between *ideologies* and not truths of gender and sexuality that in turn link with *ideologies* and not truths of race. These are ideas that people can choose to believe or disbelieve. By themselves, ideas can be benign. However, when linked to systems of power, ideas about Black people as gender outlaws and sexual deviants permeate the social structure and can become hegemonic. Hegemonic ideas are so taken for granted that they are rarely questioned because we believe that they describe things that are natural, normal, and inevitable. In essence, this racialized gender ideology helps to uphold specific racial formations of slavery, Jim Crow, urban ghettoization and, most recently, colorblind racism in the post–Civil Rights period. They may have taken different forms during prior periods, but because they are hegemonic and deeply woven into the fabric of American understandings of race, gender, and sexuality, their effects persist today.

Let me conclude this first core theme of *Black Sexual Politics* by giving more background on how these ideas about Black people as gender outlaws and sexual deviants work together. In essence, American racism works with and through ideologies of gender and sexuality by creating a series of sexual stereotypes for all who participate in U.S. society, not just Black people. In this case, African American men have had a series of controlling images applied to them. In prior historical periods, U.S. Black men were depicted as the "buck," the "brute," "Uncle Tom," and "Uncle Ben," sexual stereotypes that pivoted on ideas about their ostensibly natural hyper-heterosexuality. Representations of the "buck" and the "brute" also depicted sexualized Black men as violent, an image that morphed into the ever-present thug within gangsta rap. In contrast, "Uncle Tom" and "Uncle Ben" constitute nonviolent, asexual representations. Uncle Tom and Uncle Ben represent safely tamed, acceptable, ostensibly weak African American men who are content to serve their masters, and who become sidekicks and apologists for the system.

Ideologies of African Americans as gender outlaws and sexual deviants generated a parallel set of controlling images for African American women. Depicting Black women as the "mule," the "breeder woman," the "jezebel," and the "mammy" or "Aunt Jemima" served diverse purposes in different historical eras. Again, assumptions of Black women's natural, albeit deviant, female strength, coupled with an alleged hyper-heterosexuality, constituted a significant part of these sexual stereotypes. The "breeder woman" and the "jezebel" are sexualized images of Black women that find contemporary expression in the "welfare queen" or the ubiquitous prostitute, or "ho." In contrast, the "mule" and the "mammy" are asexual, tireless workers, an interpretive context that makes "Aunt Jemima" figures ever-popular with the white public. How else might we understand the long-suffering yet heroic Black women figures depicted in *The Help*, a successful book-turned-movie phenomenon? These historic images also foreshadow contemporary images of hard-working, middle-class women whose devotion to their universities and corporations transcends that granted to their families. Because they are women and controlling their sexuality can be used as a mechanism of taming, they too become more acceptable when they serve.

Colorblind Racism, Racialized Gender Ideology, and the Mass Media

What is the new racism? I use this phrase to describe new racial formations that arose in the post–Civil Rights era, typically after the Civil Rights victories of the 1950s and 1960s. I pay special attention to the period from the 1980s to the present, a time of concerted backlash against the victories of many social movements. The new racism of the post–Civil Rights era does not constitute an abrupt break from the past, as in "old" forms of racism no longer exist. Rather, "old" practices and "new" strategies become bundled together in new ways.

The "old" racism relied on laws and social relations of strict racial segregation. From the late nineteenth century to the mid-twentieth century, the United States set out to institutionalize segregation in all aspects of American society, not just race. This logic of segregation says: Separate people into boxes (e.g., categories of race, gender, class, and sexuality), keep the boxes separate from one another, and rank each box's worth. Racial segregation is the most visible, yet it is only the tip of the iceberg. The logic of segregation affects all aspects of U.S. society and global politics that carve up the world's people into nation-states. The whole notion of borders, boundaries, and segregation has been a very important cognitive frame for American perceptions of its peoples and the world. During the Jim Crow era, the logic of segregation catalyzed ideologies that explained social practices that separated people from one another and discriminated against some of them. For example, the old racism said that one drop of black blood made you African American. Theories of racial purity (e.g., pure white, pure black, pure this, and pure that) emerge within assumptions of segregation. Science, religion, and social policy converged.

In contrast to the logic of racial segregation, the new racism of the post–Civil Rights era endorses an ideology of racial integration that many describe as "colorblind racism." Many of you grew up during this new racism that strives to convince you that passing a few laws in the 1950s and 1960s did away with the institutional effects of more than 350 years of racially discriminatory practices. "The old racism," you may argue, "that's over, done, had it—it is so twentieth century." People do not realize how segregated this country still is. One distinguishing feature of the new racism is how it continues to rely on a logic of segregation that remains powerful yet masks its own operation. Neighborhoods, cities, regions, job categories, public schools, and colleges and universities all demonstrate persistent racial segregation: not the stark either/or kind of the past, with its clear, inviolable boundaries, but a more genteel version coded through euphemisms of "good" and "bad" neighborhoods or "gifted" and "at-risk" students. In *American Apartheid,* sociologists Nancy Denton and Douglas Massey point out the growing hyper-ghettoization of U.S. Blacks. In contrast to the block-by-block and neighborhood racial segregation within cities of the past, entire cities are divided by racial segregation.

In the post–Civil Rights era, the commitment to racial integration that began with such enthusiasm, vision, and hope has settled into an imperfect desegregation with rapidly dwindling public support. Take, for example, the status of African American youth, where the combination of housing and schooling speaks to the seriousness of this new racism. As many scholars report, when it comes to African Americans, housing segregation is alive and well. "Location, location, location"—you've heard the mantra of the real estate industry. Where one lives in America still decides so much about each child's life chances, especially schooling. More than fifty years after *Brown v. Board of Education,* African American students continue to attend predominantly minority (Black and Latino) public schools. The Civil Rights Project at UCLA reports some alarming resegregation trends within U.S. public schools. In 1968–1969, 77 percent of African American students were in predominantly minority schools—that mostly meant Black schools then. By 1980–1981, this number had dropped to 63 percent, a positive direction. By 1998–1999, the trend began to reverse—70 percent of African American children attended predominantly minority schools. This phenomenon of resegregation of poor and working-class African American youth in particular seems to be coming in under the radar in the United States. However, the entire notion of resegregation constitutes an important part of the new racism.

Given the visibility of trends such as African American hyper-ghettoization in cities and the racial resegregation of American public schools, I wonder how people come to ignore these and other contemporary forms of racial resegregation. How is it that people believe that they live in a post-racial society when examples such as these suggest otherwise? If the work of Eduardo Bonilla-Silva and other social science researchers is to be believed, many white Americans genuinely believe that racism ended in 1965. How do they come to think this way?

Addressing these questions requires revisiting the notion of *hegemonic ideology*. In the previous section, I discussed the content of hegemonic ideology about African Americans that depicted Black people as gender outlaws and sexual deviants. This section focuses on the ways in which hegemonic ideology is manufactured and circulated—specifically, the racialized gender ideology of the previous section works well within a new racism that is founded on colorblindness. Stated differently, how does colorblind racism make use of racialized gender ideology to maintain social inequalities?

Colorblind racism takes its name from an ideology of racial colorblindness. By appropriating Martin Luther King, Jr.'s words that people should be judged by the content of their character, while well intentioned, this racism purports to do away with race altogether in order to facilitate fairness. "I don't see race," its proponents proclaim, "only talent." The rush to embrace the ideal of colorblindness fosters a shift away from the types of racially explicit language of anti-racist politics that facilitated political action. Racism didn't magically go away just because we refuse to talk about it. Rather, overt racial language is replaced by covert racial euphemisms that reference the same phenomena—talk of "niggers" and "ghettos" becomes replaced by phrases such as "urban," "welfare mothers," and "street crime." Everyone knows what these terms mean, and if they don't, they quickly figure it out. The reversal of language has been stunning. Late-twentieth-century affirmative action programs designed to remedy social inequalities of overt racial discrimination in jobs, schools, and housing became increasingly recast as reverse discrimination. Former racists can now claim to uphold the banner of racial neutrality by using the club of colorblindness to keep allegedly unqualified Black people out of desirable schools, neighborhoods, and jobs. If a colorblind system produces no African American hires or neighbors except a handpicked few, so be it. Ironically, the measure of fairness is the *absence* of Black people.

This ideology of colorblindness that reflects a new racial formation of imperfect desegregation draws on historic and new interpretations of racialized gender ideology. As mass media grows in importance, it creates, circulates, and reflects ideologies of gender, sexuality, and race that mask contemporary forms of race and class segregation. In particular, sexual stereotypes of African Americans projected in the mass media justify the persistent racial segregation and social inequality in our society. Images of Black people are everywhere—television, movies, sporting events, advertising, and news—a steady stream of images now circulate throughout the globe. Actual African Americans are far scarcer in mass media's corporate boardrooms, let alone the halls of the U.S. Senate. Overall, mass media repackages old ideas of Black people as gender outlaws and sexual deviants in new formats that help to uphold colorblind racism.

Because this theme of the repackaging and sale of images of Black people is so complex, here I focus on one question: "How do class-specific images of Black men and women uphold colorblind racism?" I suggest that contemporary controlling images of African Americans that draw up ideas of gender outlaws and sexual deviants are more class segmented. Just as the African American population has become more class heterogeneous in the post–Civil Rights era, so have the images applied to different segments of the Black population. In this context, the beast transforms into the contemporary thug, who symbolizes poor and working-class Black men, whereas the Uncle Tom becomes the modern Black sidekick, who symbolizes middle-class Black men. Moreover, in the context of a powerful mass media, depictions of the thug and the sidekick become justifications for inclusion and exclusion in jobs, schooling, and other economic opportunities as well as citizenship rights, such as voting requirements and eligibility for student financial aid. A similar logic applies to images of Black women—here the jezebel and mammy images reemerge as the "bitch" and the Black lady, also providing new social scripts for understanding how race, gender, and social class intersect in contemporary American society.

These images work in gender-specific ways, both with the social class system and with contemporary colorblind racism. Poor and working-class Black people encounter a set of depictions that both draw from historical images and uphold prevailing social class relations. Poor and working-class Black people are seen as being more "authentic" than their Black middle-class counterparts, primarily because they more closely fit the sexual stereotypes as gender outlaws and sexual deviants. They are heterosexual, are pro-Black, and typically live racially segregated lives in the 'hood. Because of racial segregation, very few white people and growing numbers of middle-class Black people encounter any of these seemingly authentic Black people in their everyday lives. Instead, spurred on by media images, we *imagine* that we know them. Listening to rap music and buying the latest hip hop, we can appropriate their style and somehow feel funkier, sexier, and closer to them because of it. That is the image of black authenticity: working-class, heterosexual, pro-Black safely ghettoized and consumed.

The images of poor and working-class Black people not only are retreads of old ideas but they are also gender specific. Bundling together ideas about gender outlaws and sexual deviants in new and entertaining mass media products, they construct a class-specific, racial authenticity using the stuff of gender and sexuality. For example, the glorification of the tough criminal through so-called thug life speaks to a certain kind of masculinity that may feel threatened by the gains of the women's movement of the past several decades. Representations of the thug serve a tangible political and economic purpose. An American society that cannot provide enough jobs for young African American men needs thugs, especially those engaged in the drug industry, to serve as commodities for a burgeoning prison industry. Their incarceration turns a profit for telephone companies, construction companies, food service vendors, and small towns where and McDonald's, Walmart, and the local prison are the major employers.

The image of the sexualized Black woman fulfills a similar function. It too seemingly emanates from "authentic" poor and working-class Black girls, and it now serves as a template for all women who can act the part. The representation of the hooker or the streetwalker drives styles in junior departments—short skirts, Daisy Dukes shorts, thigh-high boots, and lots of skin present an aura of sexualized women who are free to do what they want. This depiction undercuts the gains of the feminist movement concerning women's sexual freedom. These images mesh with new icons of black sexuality where actual Black people need not be present to invoke the meaning of black sexuality.

Middle-class Black people encounter a different set of depictions that also grow from historical images yet now serve to uphold prevailing social class relations. Here the notion is one of respectability, the absence of race, the successful excising of the allegedly authentic blackness so celebrated in mass media. Middle class, differently sexual, and white identified in some way, many African Americans question the blackness and therefore the imagined politics of this group far more than the actual behavior of African American lawbreakers.

Let me discuss one image, namely, the social script that constructs middle-class African American men as sidekicks of more powerful white men. Fictionalized versions of "sidekicks," or the "black best friend," are everywhere in film and television. The social scripts for middle-class Black women are equally narrow and complex. The comparable images bounce back and forth between the "Black ladies" and the "modern mammies." These women are aggressive, yet they also are ladylike. They work so hard that all they appear to do is work, for the company, for the corporation, for the university, for the government. They are completely devoted. In this era of including a few handpicked and loyal African Americans in the higher circles of corporations and government, as one of my colleagues puts it, the lone "top Blacks," it is important to remember that what I present here are social scripts telling aspiring Black people the behaviors they will need to succeed. This is not a commentary on these particular individuals. Instead, it is a commentary on the need for seemingly colorblind settings to include a few people of "color" so that the ideology of colorblindness is affirmed.

Combining these images of black masculinity and black femininity produces class-specific, gendered social scripts of black authenticity and black respectability that also rely on ideas about sexuality. Black authenticity is very often masculinized, hyper-heterosexual, and violent. This version of black authenticity privileges black masculinity and establishes a gender hierarchy among Black people as a defining feature of "real" blackness. Juxtaposed with this seemingly manly authenticity, black respectability becomes feminized, asexual, and assertive on behalf of white power, yet submissive to it. The subordinated sidekick and the Black lady are both feminized images.

These ideas are significant because they help to explain the placement of Black people in the new colorblind racism. In a context of colorblind racism, where only respectable Black people will be accepted, requiring respectability and then feminizing and devaluing it replicates existing class relations. Stated differently, poor and working-class Black people become safely contained, with new mass media technologies recording their every move and selling sounds and images of authentic blackness if they prove profitable. Conversely, if upward social class mobility becomes defined as a gender-specific process of selling out, decreasing numbers of poor and working-class Black youth will want to try to achieve it, and those who do are more likely to be girls.

Within this framework, the election of Barack Obama, who is married to an African American woman, was clearly a breakthrough moment, but not in the way that people think. Barack and Michelle Obama have had to tread carefully through the minefield created by this hegemonic ideology of gender, sexuality, and race. Despite the crack in the racial ceiling symbolized by the Obama family, the status of one family is far from being representative of the experiences of 42 million African Americans (13.6 percent of the total U.S. population of 308.7 million) identified by the 2010 U.S. Census.

The Need for a Progressive Black Sexual Politics

The conceptual framework that I develop in *Black Sexual Politics* concerning the relations of gender and sexuality within contemporary African American communities is designed to provide a set of conceptual tools that will help us not just analyze famous figures but also develop effective responses to the actual social issues and social problems that emerge in our current social context. Poverty, unemployment, rape, HIV/AIDS, incarceration, substance abuse, adolescent pregnancy, the treatment of children in foster care, intraracial violence (especially by young Black males as both victims and perpetrators), and similar issues have a disproportionate impact on African Americans. All of these social problems take gender-specific forms, and all require serious attention to the politics of gender and sexuality for solutions.

How will we solve gender-specific disparities in African American school performance without serious analyses of masculinity and femininity? African American girls are now outperforming boys in school, with differences becoming apparent as early as the fourth grade. One need only look at the demographics on any college campus to recognize that men are being left behind. Yet a gender-only analysis diverts attention away from how intersections of race and gender that shape black masculinity can make school a tough place for Black boys. Black LGBT youth also face major challenges in navigating the public schools, challenges that might fall more heavily on gay and bisexual Black boys. Gender and sexuality are operating in ways that remain largely unexamined.

Similarly, the complex forms of violence that diverse segments of the African American population face are unlikely to be addressed without multifaceted analyses that take sexism and heterosexism into account. African Americans are affected by violence in many ways, among them: (1) state violence against young African American men; (2) Black male violence against one another; (3) Black male violence against African American women (rape, incest, domestic violence); (4) African American adult violence toward children, in particular, childrearing practices with tactics of physical and emotional punishment that border on abuse; and (5) hate crimes against Black LGBT people. African Americans cannot generate an effective political response to violence by continuing to view these phenomena as competing. Rather, they are complementary forms of violence where one gains strength from the presence of the other. Developing a progressive Black sexual politics that takes gender and sexuality into account would enable African Americans to better address school performance, violence, vulnerability to HIV/AIDS, and similar social problems.

Although *Black Sexual Politics* is about African Americans, this specific project of developing a more progressive Black sexual politics resembles other social justice projects that grapple with similar issues. For example, women and men of African descent in South Africa, Brazil, Nigeria, and Great Britain face similar challenges in obtaining habitable housing, good nutrition, literacy, high-quality jobs, effective health care, and grappling with the effects of the spread of HIV/AIDS. In this sense, a more progressive Black sexual politics advanced by African Americans in the United States is one specific site of a broader global struggle for human rights. Because these important social issues transcend the particular forms they take among populations of African descent, they also constitute the foundation of social justice projects in a global context. Intersecting oppressions of race, class, gender, ethnicity, and sexuality touch everyone's lives, and social justice projects occur across societies and among very different types of people.

The ideologies and social practices discussed here clearly play a major part in upholding global social injustices by convincing us that social inequalities are natural, normal, and inevitable. If social hierarchies of race, class, or gender are beyond critique, why challenge the ideas that uphold them? Isn't it easier simply to go home, pop open a beer, and watch the latest YouTube video? Why try to change the actual practices that uphold social hierarchies, for example, high-stakes tests that tell us far more about a student's family income than about his or her potential for success in college? Human rights initiatives cannot advance without people who question what they hear and see, including this talk.

Existing social problems, whether school performance, poverty, HIV, voter apathy, the gendered contours of the new racism, or other issues that you care deeply about, are responsive to your thoughts and actions. Every single person has a choice. You do not have to leave the world as you found it. You need not move through the world thinking, "There's nothing I can do. I've been socialized this way." Because if you think of yourself that way, you uphold social injustice. It is your choice. I encourage you to choose the difficult path of social justice, to imagine new possibilities, and to act.

ADDITIONAL RESOURCES

Bonilla-Silva, Eduardo. 2003. *Racism without Racists: Color-blind Racism and the Persistence of Racial Inequality in the United States.* Lanham, Md.: Rowman & Littlefield.

Byrd, Rudolph P. and Beverly Guy-Sheftall, eds. 2001. *Traps: African American Men on Gender and Sexuality.* Bloomington: Indiana University Press.

Carbado, Devon W., ed. 1999. *Black Men on Race, Gender, and Sexuality.* New York: New York University Press.

Cohen, Cathy J. 1999. *The Boundaries of Blackness: AIDS and the Breakdown of Black Politics.* Chicago: University of Chicago Press.

Cole, Johnnetta B. and Beverly Guy-Sheftall. 2003. *Gender Talk: The Struggle for Women's Equality in African American Communities.* New York: Ballantine.

4

Resisting Racism,
Writing *Black Sexual Politics*

REFLEXIVE ESSAY: *In* Black Sexual Politics, *my thesis was that African American anti-racist projects would remain limited until sexism and heterosexism were made central to Black intellectual analysis. The difficulty I faced in writing the book was that African Americans were firmly wedded to race-only analyses, primarily because intersectional analyses of Black experiences were scarce. I realized that I could not concentrate solely on the ideas of my argument but also had to attend to the process I used in writing it. Because I envisioned* Black Sexual Politics *as scholarship that was placed in service to social justice, I faced decisions about not only the purpose of the book but also its intended audiences, content, and form (prose). Working with, for, and/or on behalf of oppressed groups raises a distinctive set of concerns that shape the choice of topics, research methods, and intended audiences. In this essay, I examine how these broader concerns affected the approaches I decided to take in* Black Sexual Politics.

BLACK SEXUAL POLITICS: *African Americans, Gender, and the New Racism* illustrates one site of my intellectual activism, where I place my scholarship in service to social justice. In this volume, I use the experiences of African Americans to examine the contradictions and tensions that surround anti-racist politics. I argue that African Americans must make gender and sexuality more central features of anti-racist political agendas. In essence, African

---

An earlier version of this essay was delivered at New York University in 2004 as part of a graduate student conference.

Americans need an adequate analysis of the new racism as well as new political strategies to deal with it.

In the book, I present the following set of ideas: (1) Black sexual politics consists of a set of ideas and social practices shaped by gender, race, and sexuality that frame Black men's and women's treatment of one another, as well as how African Americans are perceived and treated by others; (2) Black sexual politics lies at the heart of beliefs about black masculinity and black femininity, gender-specific experiences of African Americans, and the new racism in the post–Civil Rights era; (3) to confront social inequality, African Americans need an analysis of black masculinity and black femininity that questions the links between prevailing Black sexual politics, the connection to black gender ideology, and struggles for African American empowerment in response to the new racism; (4) taking into account the new challenges of the post–Civil Rights era, such an analysis would strive to point the way toward a more progressive Black sexual politics within African American communities; and (5) this politics in turn might both catalyze a more effective anti-racist politics and contribute to a broader social justice agenda. Collectively, this analytical framework shapes the core arguments advanced in the book.

Readers often think that ideas such as these fall from the sky and that the craft of writing a book matters little in relation to the final product. Yet when it comes to scholarship in service to social justice, the processes of intellectual production can be just as important as the ideas that find their way into print. For *Black Sexual Politics,* I was trying to engage in anti-racist intellectual activism during a period when the contours of racism itself were undergoing considerable change. It is difficult to analyze change, write about change, and try to effect change when you are living with the contradictions of change itself.

The challenges that I encountered in writing *Black Sexual Politics* illustrate broader issues associated with scholarship in service to social justice. The overarching goal of scholarship in service to social justice is not to explain social inequality or social injustice, but to foster social justice, to bring about some sort of change. Social injustice and social inequality are not necessarily the same thing. Situations of social inequality may or may not be unjust. Social inequalities exist that may be justified (e.g., power over young children to protect them from harm). In contrast, social justice traditions challenge *unfair, unjust,* or *unethical* social inequalities. For example, the abuse of children hiding behind ideologies that defend abuse with claims that it's natural to discipline them *does* qualify as a situation of social injustice. I use the term "oppression" to refer to the unjust structures, practices, and ideas that catalyze social inequality. Via its questions, methods, findings, and/or intended audiences, scholarship in service to social justice is against oppression.

We should ask how scholarship in service to social justice differs from traditional mainstream scholarship. Traditional mainstream scholarship is based on the quest for truth—the phrase "knowledge for knowledge's sake" captures this sensibility. Traditional scholarship has been extremely helpful to social justice projects, yet, because such scholarship sees knowledge as an end in and of itself, it need not be placed in service to social justice agendas. Much traditional scholarship, in fact, has been far more complicit with social injustice than is typically acknowledged. In part, traditional scholarship must play by a set of rules where neither ethics nor politics is deemed suitable for scholarship endeavors—these are seen as introducing bias into the scholarly process. In contrast, scholarship in service to social justice places ideas and the "truths" that emerge from mainstream scholarship in dialogue with broader ethical and/or political concerns. Such scholarship constitutes a tradition of engaged research designed to help people envision and build more equitable and fair societies, not to help them better fit into things the way they are. In essence, scholarship in service to social justice constitutes harnessing the power of ideas in service to social justice.

In this sense, there is an important distinction between scholarship *in support of* social justice and scholarship *in service to* social justice. Scholarship *in support of* social justice implies a lack of accountability on the part of the scholar—others are engaged in social justice projects and the thinker in question aims to make a contribution but is not held accountable for how his or her contribution works out. In contrast, scholarship *in service to* social justice invokes the responsibilities that are associated with the idea of service itself, namely, that service should be unpaid, freely chosen, altruistic, and may involve sacrifice. Positioning one's scholarship within a service framework by doing scholarship in service to social justice may mean being underpaid or even not getting paid at all, making choices that put one at odds with prevailing academic norms, having one's altruism mistaken for a passion for service, and/or assuming the risks of censure, failure, persecution, and other negative outcomes.

The specific decision points I encountered while writing *Black Sexual Politics* shed light on the challenges of engaged scholarship generally, and scholarship in service to social justice, in particular. Two overarching questions guided this project. First, what is the purpose of this book? Second, who make up its intended audience? These dimensions of purpose and audience are simultaneously intellectual and political. Together they define the context for the work. Let me address each in turn.

Purpose: Engaged Anti-Racist Scholarship

I had three main reasons for writing *Black Sexual Politics*. My first and most fundamental reason was to resist racism by writing a book about racism. I actually began working on *Black Sexual Politics* as a continuation of the analysis I advanced in *Black Feminist Thought* (1990). Then as now, I saw the need for a Black feminist analysis of the gender politics within African American communities that addressed the ways in which the politics helped or hindered anti-racist projects. My sense was that African American conceptions of both black masculinity and sexuality as ideological constructions weakened Black politics. In the 1990s, the scholarship that I needed to write *Black Sexual Politics* was in its infancy. Considerable scholarship existed on African American men, yet much of it was neither analytical nor considered masculinity as a gendered structure. Similarly, work on sexuality did challenge homophobia, yet racial analyses were scarce in the literature. Analytical arguments of black masculinity and/or sexuality that reflected robust intersectional frameworks were not fully developed.

The broader scholarly context of the 1990s also influenced my sense that my vision for *Black Sexual Politics,* namely, resisting racism by writing a book about racism, would be an uphill battle. I increasingly encountered scholars who were safely housed in elite academic institutions and simply had little interest in actual politics. From my perspective, many of these people engaged in "race" talk (always in quotations to suggest that they knew that race wasn't real), yet refused to walk the race walk at their own institutions. During this decade, historical and empirical research on racism that had inspired me morphed into decontextualized, abstract discussions that endlessly pointed out how race was an invalid construct. For some of my colleagues, talking about race meant constructing it, and for still others, such talk meant that one was "racist." I almost gave up on academia because it seemed to be moving away from my interest in engaged scholarship. The version of Black feminism that I espoused was under attack. Despite my anger at the growing disregard for the ideas of Black women (but not actual individual Black women who, ironically, were much in demand as visible entities within a new multicultural, colorblind racism), I could not write *Black Sexual Politics* in that intellectual and political environment. I would have to wait. In the meantime, I took on other projects that enabled me to track and learn the literatures of black masculinity and sexuality.

My second reason for writing *Black Sexual Politics* is related to the first. I aimed to develop an intersectional analysis of racism that did not rely on a race-only lens, but instead showed how it only made sense via intersectional analyses. Despite an outpouring of scholarship in the 1980s and 1990s that argued that race, class, and gender as intersecting systems of power shaped everyone's lives, the predilection to see certain topics (and groups of people) through race-only, or gender-only, or class-only lenses, for example, persisted. When I set out to explore how racism was alive and well, I joined a legion of scholars who were writing about the new colorblind racism. My contribution was to provide a theoretical argument about how the gendered and sexual dimensions of racism had also been reconfigured in the post–Civil Rights era. *Black Sexual Politics* provides an intersectional analysis of how race, gender, and sexuality as systems of power mutually construct one another. These systems take center stage in the book. Yet *Black Sexual Politics* also incorporates an intersectional analysis of class and nationality (explored via globalization) categories as well. Thus, the book focuses on racism, yet via its intersectional lens, it challenges mono-categorical analyses.

A third reason why I decided to write *Black Sexual Politics* was to develop arguments that might be useful to people working in political projects for racial justice. Academics routinely produce reams of articles, books, and conference presentations for one another that address pre-existing questions in scholarly literature. Yet we often seem far less interested in investigating the concerns of everyday people who are involved in social justice projects in their families, neighborhoods, schools, and places of employment. We study them for our own reasons, but we express less interest in studying what they want to know.

In *Black Sexual Politics,* by examining how African Americans confronted new forms of social injustice, I wanted to encourage readers to imagine new possibilities in their everyday lives. *Black Sexual Politics* is not a handbook about how to engage in political action. Rather it is a diagnostic tool that suggests that, when we think about the world differently, we often see different ways of being in it. One of the difficulties of writing "solutions" is that people want easy answers to hard questions when there are none.

In my own work, I have found that one important component of intellectual activism lies in learning how to ask good questions and drawing on the best ideas from many points of view in answering them. In *Black Sexual Politics,* I continued to engage a core existential question that guides my work: "What will it take for Black people to be free?" This question defies easy answers and formulaic thinking. For this particular project, this question pointed me toward gender and sexuality, and the kinds of political action that would be needed to move toward freedom in an era of colorblind racism. I needed to refine my question. A shift as simple as asking, "What will it take for African American men to be free?" or "What will it take for African American women to be free?" yields more nuanced answers to the question of freedom. This simple shift lies at the heart of *Black Sexual Politics,* and it is a shift that should catalyze new angles of vision on African American realities.

When it comes to the theme of scholarship in service to social justice, is this focus on the specificity of African Americans and freedom, even when refracted through intersectional arguments, enough? Many people think that engaging in social justice scholarship requires a direct connection with existing social movements and political activism. Yet scholarship in service to social justice suggests a bottom-up stance, one that respects the specificity of group experience while trying to see commonalities across differences. Many groups have had experiences that resemble those of African Americans, yet no group has had exactly the same experiences. Continuing to ask the same question with different groups at the center—"What will it take for Latinas to be free?" or "What will it take for youth in South Africa to be free?"—keeps the broader question in play, yet produces ideas that might be useful to the specific populations at hand. When placed in dialogue, the ideas developed from these multiple standpoints, each examining freedom from its own point of view, produce a whole that is greater than the sum of its parts. Social justice need not be an explicit theme. But it does need to be incorporated into the process of deciding what will count.

Black Sexual Politics is situated at this juncture between the specificity of one group's experiences and the universal themes that resonate throughout those experiences. I tell a story that is *both* specific *and* universal, working contrapuntally between the specific and the universal, trying to remain in an in-between space that allows me an angle of vision in both directions. Staying in this in-between space and using it creatively meant looking in both directions, namely, *both* to the specificity of African American experience *and* to the contributions of contemporary social theory. Moreover, each of these spaces has a variety of audiences attached to it, each of whom can have varying standards for what they deem to be important. Many authors resolve this difficulty by choosing one audience and writing to it, for example, writing a scholarly paper for publication in a refereed journal with the intention of writing a companion piece for the general public, or by writing directly for the public with the intention of figuring out how to make the ideas travel to the academic elite. *Black Sexual Politics* is written in both registers—two subtexts, one for the everyday people (in this case, African Americans and college undergraduates) and the other for scholarly elites. Rather than resolving the seeming contradictions between these two audiences, I choose to see how placing them in dialogue might shape the book. In practicality, maintaining this in-between space meant that I had to consider navigating multiple audiences.

Navigating Heterogeneous Audiences

The question of intended audience was crucial to *Black Sexual Politics,* framing virtually every decision I made in the research, writing, publication, and marketing of the volume. My target audiences consisted of scholars and academics, African Americans, both everyday and politically engaged, and a general public with an interest the themes of the book. Having multiple audiences that were very different meant that answers to my guiding questions shifted, depending on the actual topic, available material, and resources. I asked: "What are the concerns and issues of the intended audiences for *Black Sexual Politics?* What do they consider to be credible evidence and convincing arguments? What knowledge do they bring to this project? What is the best way to organize the content in regard to the concerns, issues, and worldviews of the intended audiences?"

Typically, these questions are recast as technical issues of writing style and reading level, yet, when it comes to the theme of intellectual activism, they are simultaneously intellectual questions and questions with profound political implications. Most scholars rarely stop and consider these questions, mainly because they need not do so. Most of us who produce engaged scholarship must confront these questions, primarily because we often have to work to create the conditions that make our own work possible. Scholarship that strives to step outside the seemingly objective standards of Western science must meet a higher standard of excellence, often by critiquing those standards and advocating new ones.

As writers and scholars, we can identify the integrity of the project and the challenges that might face us in writing for multiple audiences, but how do we frame what we really want to say? For this project, one danger lay in selecting examples that were too far removed not only from the everyday experiences of African Americans but also from their interpretation of those experiences. A related danger lay in making the arguments too "academic," typically received by people outside the academy as dense and boring. How sad it would be to bore people with a book about their own experiences! I was confident about my ability to write to the narrow specialty audiences of academia—but writing for a broad, heterogeneous public without unduly weakening one's argument is a challenge.

Let me share an example of what it actually meant to write for heterogeneous audiences and the public conversations that accompany this process. Recall the points of the working definition of Black sexual politics introduced early in this essay. This working definition works well with academic readers, but some of the main ideas prove to be far more relevant than others for different audiences. This became especially clear to me the first time I went on Black talk radio to "discuss" my book. One of the first questions stopped me in my tracks—"Do you think that Black men should date white women?" the caller asked, with a note of disapproval clearly expressed in the tone of her voice. The calls came hot and heavy afterward, with a heated debate about the merits of interracial dating. I never got a chance to make *any* of the "main points" of my book. Rather than blaming the callers, after that endlessly long hour was over (it was an early hour—morning Black talk radio!)—I reviewed my careful definition of Black sexual politics and realized that I needed to find different ways to discuss the material with different audiences or I had written the book for a select few who already lived in my academic world. *"Black Sexual Politics* 101" (Chapter 3) presents the polished version of the themes that were left standing as I returned repeatedly to *Black Sexual Politics,* mining the volume for themes that resonated with diverse audiences.

Yet another danger of writing for multiple audiences consists of pivots on rejecting epistemological frameworks of dominant groups. If Black intellectual production does not make sense to them or challenges dominant points of view too aggressively, that scholarship can be devalued and even suppressed. For example, within the framework of U.S. race relations, African Americans are typically studied in relation to whites, as a "minority" group or as a marginalized population, and not as a population with a set of interests, issues, and concerns that may be separate from those of whites. This has at least three common outcomes. First, it casts African American experience as a list of social problems (e.g., the issues that most concern whites are at the center of how African Americans are studied, such as unwed mothers, teen criminals, welfare cheats, racial gaps in test scores). Second, it assumes that African American experience can only provide evidence for some larger theory or perspective (white women have it bad as unwed mothers, but African American women have it really bad). Third, it assumes that African American experience is so exotic that it belongs in another category of analysis altogether (cultural deviance: "sexual practices of black folk" or the "natural predilection for violence").

Refracting African American experience through these lenses encourages African American thinkers either to do more "objective" work within a race relations framework or to move to the seemingly universal place of topics that are unrelated to people of African descent and/or that address issues that concern the general public. Currently, this first set of pressures suggests doing away with a black/white paradigm of race relations in favor of a more "modern" and seemingly theoretically complex analysis of difference. But what are the concerns of the general public? Who is this imagined general public? Within both of these strategies, African American concerns become subordinate to putatively more important issues.

The politics of knowledge that creates practices such as pushing the U.S. race relations' paradigm informs the specific decisions that I made in *Black Sexual Politics* concerning the overall purpose of the book, my imagined audiences of academics, African Americans and an interested general public, as well as the specific choice of topics. I explicitly centered on the experiences of African Americans, especially by identifying selected social issues that are important to Black people, and examined how they cannot be adequate addressed without attending to issues of gender and sexuality. Casting my argument in this fashion was designed to show how African Americans were negatively situated at the intersections of racism, sexism, and heterosexism as intersecting systems of power. Thus, when it comes to the question, "What will it take for Black people to be free?" answers that do not take all three systems of power and their intersections into account will be limited. How effectively I achieved my purpose of resisting racism by speaking to heterogeneous audiences through *Black Sexual Politics* remains to be seen.

ADDITIONAL RESOURCES

Angelou, Maya. 2009. *I Know Why the Caged Bird Sings*. New York: Ballantine.
Bell, Brenda, John Gaventa, and John Peters, eds. 1990. *We Make the Road by Walking: Conversations on Education and Social Change*, by Myles Horton and Paulo Freire. Philadelphia: Temple University Press.

5

Still Brave? Black Feminism
as a Social Justice Project

REFLEXIVE ESSAY: *In spring 2010, I attended a conference that focused on examining the thirty-year history of Black women's studies' in the academy. Many attendees were familiar with the 1982 publication of the groundbreaking anthology,* But Some of Us Are Brave: All the Women Are White, All the Blacks Are Men: Black Women's Studies. *For many of us, that book was a bible that helped shape our entry into Black women's studies. We gathered to mark the publication of a follow-up volume titled* Still Brave: The Evolution of Black Women's Studies. *I appreciated the commemoration, yet, for me, something was missing. I was far more interested in developing action strategies for the next thirty years than in celebrating the past ones. My efforts to rethink the issue of whether Black feminist thought within academic settings is "still brave" catalyzed this essay. I consider the core question that anchors the essay—What will it take for Black women to be free?—as fundamental to scholarship in service to social justice. This essay highlights the significance of audience— Who is our work for?*

The ideas in this essay developed over several events, including a 2000 American Sociological Association (ASA) plenary session at ASA's annual meeting; during my 2005 visit as a Visiting Professor at the University of Michigan–Flint; in a one-day celebration of the work of Senegalese sociologist Fatou Sow in 2008 at the University of Paris–Diderot; and at Mississippi State University in 2012. The focus on Black women's political activism explored here is treated extensively in *From Black Power to Hip Hop: Racism, Nationalism and Feminism*.

W HAT WILL IT TAKE for Black women to be free? This core question lies at the heart of Black feminism, shaping its themes, theories, and politics. Just has times have changed, so too have the conceptions of freedom pursued by women of African descent. For Black women, the forms that oppression takes vary tremendously from one society to the next and from one historical period to the next. The specificities of identities or experiences may differ, yet the overarching experience of oppression is essential. This fundamental theme of Black women's oppression simultaneously results in economic and social disadvantages and drives the need for and the contours of Black feminist theory and politics. Yet basic questions concerning freedom define Black women as a transnational Black population and forms of political action that Black women embrace and/or reject.

Oppression constitutes an unjust situation where over time one group systematically denies another group access to the resources of society. An individual can experience the effects of oppression, but oppression itself is an institutional phenomenon that characterizes a given social system. Social justice projects routinely aim to address social inequalities among groups that result from oppression. In the United States, for example, an individual can experience the *effects* of intersecting oppressions of race, class, and gender, and sexuality, primarily because those systems are important in the U.S. context. Similarly, while social justice projects require individual initiative, they are best viewed as heterogeneous, group-based responses to the myriad forms that oppression can take historically, cross-culturally, and/or within one social location.

Black feminism is a social justice project advanced by African American women and their allies in defense of the interests of African American women. Black women as individuals need not claim an identity as an "oppressed" person, yet each Black woman grapples with varying aspects of domestic and global social structures that routinely place Black women as a collectivity at the bottom of the social hierarchy. In this context, African American women have characteristic experiences that catalyze recurring political responses to their oppression in the U.S. context that may resemble and differ from those of Afro-British women, African women in Nigeria, or women of African descent in Venezuela. Although Black women's political responses carry different names, in the United States, Black feminism constitutes one generally accepted term that emerged in the late twentieth century to describe these oppositional political and intellectual responses. This grounding of U.S. Black feminism in African American women's quest for freedom positions Black feminism as a social justice project within a broader array of similar intellectual and political projects. Quite simply, if African American women were "free," there would be no need for Black feminism.

This quest toward freedom in contexts of oppression is what Black feminism has been in the past. But what forms might Black feminism as a social justice project take today? What challenges face contemporary U.S. Black feminism in moving Black women closer to social justice? What might it take to meet these challenges?

Challenges Facing U.S. Black Feminism
as a Social Justice Project

U.S. Black feminism rests on a synergistic relationship among three distinguishing features, namely: (1) Black women's everyday, lived experiences; (2) Black women's analyses of the meaning and significance of those experiences; and (3) Black women's actions that stem from and shape both experiences and analyses. Each of the three distinguishing features makes important contributions to the effectiveness of Black feminism writ large. Each feature stands on its own as a vital part of feminism, with patterns of relationship among these three concepts of experience, thought, and action varying from one historical era to the next, as well as across social settings.

First, African American women's experiences with oppression have been central to Black feminism. These experiences have been shaped by U.S. Black women's position within race, class, gender, and sexuality as systems of power.

The self-defined knowledge that African American women have produced to conceptualize their experiences, or Black feminist thought, constitutes a second distinguishing feature of U.S. Black feminism. Analyzing Black women's experiences with oppression has been vital to Black women's empowerment as well as to the stimulation of new knowledge about oppression itself. Knowing that Black women's freedom struggle necessarily proceeds on several fronts, against racism, sexism, class exploitation, and heterosexism in particular, has been central to this knowledge. The idea that Black women can never be free without addressing race, class, gender, and sexuality as systems of oppression that mutually construct one another has been a key tenet of Black feminist analysis. The framework of race/class/gender studies and its accompanying paradigm of intersectionality also emerge within this quest for freedom, because it was clear that gaining one kind of "freedom" (race or gender or class) would not free Black women.

A third distinguishing feature of U.S. Black feminism concerns African American women's politics or political action in response to oppression. Black women have approached their specific experiences with oppression not only by analyzing it but also by taking action. An everyday feminism, although it was rarely called such, characterized African American women's everyday struggles for survival, a long-term, albeit often unnamed, Black feminist politics. Ideas about Black women as the backbone of black communities and views of women as strong, self-reliant, and able to take care of themselves are part of this everyday politics about what it means to be a strong woman.

This everyday Black feminist politics also shaped patterns of African American women's political behavior across several social movements. In the 1950s to 1970s, for example, African American women were active participants within multiple social movements (Civil Rights; Black Power; women's movement; anti-war movement; gay/lesbian liberation movement), and modern U.S. Black feminism was shaped by these social movements. Not only did these movements affect one another but individual African American women also moved among them, often participating in more than one. These patterns of engagement framed initial expressions of modern Black feminism.

African American women who were intellectual leaders for modern Black feminism of the 1950s, 1960s, and 1970s typically participated in this synergistic and dynamic relationship among Black women's experiences, self-defined knowledge regarding those experiences, and a Black feminist politics. It's hard to categorize them as being either scholars or activists because they often were both. Toni Cade Bambara, Shirley Chisholm, Pauli Murray, Audre Lorde, June Jordan, Alice Walker, and many others drew on their own personal lived experiences as African American women. Yet Black feminist intellectual leaders also participated in organized political activities that enabled them to see beyond their own personal points of view. Building on their individual and collective experiences in Black women's politics, they used experiences to develop theoretical analyses of the intersectional nature of Black women's oppression. Moreover, they engaged in a Black feminist politics that was simultaneously free-standing (organizations for Black women) and that permeated other organizations (working with feminist organizations or Black nationalist organizations, for example) that incorporated these ideas.

From the social location of this synergistic relationship among experiences, analyses, and actions, these Black women intellectuals were able to look beyond the specificity of time and space to build on the ideas and actions of African American women from the past as well as Black women in transnational contexts. When it comes to questions of sexual violence, one can see links between the earlier work of researcher, journalist, and activist Ida Wells-Barnett and the later work of late-twentieth-century African American feminists. Angela Davis's groundbreaking work on sexual violence under slavery builds on Wells-Barnett's analyses of unmasking the violence visited on Black men as a site of racial and gender oppression that upheld class inequalities. Davis shifts the lens from Black men to Black women, pointing out how Black women have been raped by both white and black men, and that the control of Black women's bodies has been a terrain of struggle for masculinity. She also examines institutionalized rape as a tool of public policy, for example, the refusal of local municipalities to prosecute the rapes of Black women. When it comes to self-defined knowledge, modern Black feminists identify silences within African American communities as well as within dominant discourse as significant in minimizing sexual violence targeted toward African American women. More recently, sexual violence against Black women as a form of entertainment, the burgeoning pornography sites, is a new area of investigation. Modern Black feminists did not originate this type of analysis, nor will it stop with them. Because they crafted political responses to sexual violence as shaped within these power relations, this issue will persist as long as this expression of oppression continues to affect women of African descent.

Contemporary U.S. Black feminism faces many challenges that, if neglected, promise to leave this rich period of Black feminist intellectual production and politics marooned without ties to past movements or comparable cross-cultural initiatives. Staying the course of celebrating Black feminist accomplishments of the past few decades fosters a blindness to challenges. Many of the challenges faced by contemporary U.S. Black feminism require taking a hard look at shifts in U.S. society, the content and practices of Black academic feminism, and complacency within the U.S. context toward the issues that African American women continue to face. In essence, U.S. Black feminism is not a finished social justice project. Instead, it is one in the making, whose challenges reflect a weakening of the ties among experiences, analysis, and action.

One challenge concerns the need to refocus U.S. Black feminism on the everyday realities of Black women's lives. African American women who are working in community organizing roles are well aware of the list of social issues that face African American women and girls. At the same time, if the American media is to be believed, one could easily conclude that African American women are a privileged group that no longer needs Black feminism. Certainly, media figures such as Oprah Winfrey and political figures such as and Michelle Obama suggest that U.S. Black feminism has experienced some success in that some African American women are doing far better than the majority of U.S. citizens of all races.

Academia constitutes another important environment where Black feminism seems to be celebrated in order to be dismissed. This treatment of Black feminist thought within academia reflects pressures on scholars to sever our intellectual work from the group-based, social justice projects that initially stimulated them. We are encouraged to replace robust, empowering forms of knowledge that were developed within social movement contexts with narrow, individualistic, market-based solutions to social problems. This is the first historical juncture in U.S. politics where it is possible to have Black feminist analyses with neither substantive connections to Black women's lived experiences nor expectations that one would engage in Black feminist politics.

The visibility of prominent African American women within higher education, mass media, and electoral politics can be held up as an example of Black feminist accomplishments. Yet how deeply has the incorporation of Black feminist ideas actually penetrated in shaping the content of curriculum offerings, news and entertainment media content and public policy? The large numbers of Black women and girls who continue to face a litany of social problems suggest that considerable distance remains to be traveled.

In this context, a second challenge facing Black feminism concerns paying careful attention to how the language of Black feminism is being used, often in ways that are antithetical to Black feminist politics. Take, for example, the differences between the Combahee River Collective's statement on identity politics in the context of Black feminist politics of the 1980s and its redefined meanings within contemporary academic settings. The Combahee River Collective's approach to *identity politics* drew on the concept of the personal as political in ways that linked individual identity to collective political social location. Experiences were honed in this space, linking the individual and the collective, or the personal and the political. This concept was highly empowering for African American women, who often lacked a language that explained social inequality in ways that generated avenues for action. The major insight of the Collective also lay in identifying how African American women were positioned within multiple systems of power—their politics necessarily involved grappling with race, class, gender, and sexuality as intersecting systems of power that shaped individual identity and personal experience. The Collective advanced a powerful theory of action, one grounded in analysis and experience, with "identity politics" as the phrase that captures these complex relationships. In contrast, contemporary approaches to identity politics rely on an individualist notion of identity: identity as freedom from social constructions, no matter the power relations.

A third challenge concerns developing new standards for evaluating the effectiveness of Black feminism as a social justice project within a greatly changed political environment. What would an effective Black feminist politics look like now? Many people see the visibility of highly competent African American women as evidence of the effectiveness of Black feminism. Whereas the accomplishments of successful Black women should be applauded, seeing a Black female face in a highly ranked position as a proxy for African American women's economic, social, and political progress may be misguided.

Gaining visibility is not the same thing as exercising power. Many Black women who occupy positions of power and authority and who are trying to advance a social justice agenda continually find their way blocked. Take, for example, the impressive career of Congresswoman Eleanor Holmes Norton, an eleven-term representative of the District of Columbia in the U.S. House of Representatives. Despite being a nonvoting member of Congress, Norton has been a tireless advocate for the rights of children, women, Blacks, poor people, and the disenfranchised, all target populations of her congressional district. Her career illustrates the challenges that face even the most gifted and accomplished Black women who work on behalf of social justice. Moreover, the absence of accountability standards for Black women who claim to be leaders speaks to the disconnect between African American women as a group and the array of Black women who claim to speak for them.

African American women and their allies might benefit from a clear social issues agenda that is easy to understand, reflects issues that are important to African American women as a group, and can be used to shape Black feminist politics. This kind of clarity would make it far easier to evaluate whether a media figure or a newly hired Black woman professor is contributing to Black feminism as historically understood or is using it for her own career or personal gain. Such an agenda would also enable Black women and our allies to recognize and support the exemplary leadership of Eleanor Holmes Norton and numerous women whose Black feminism is not confined to the academy.

Confronting the Challenges: Revitalizing Black Feminism as a Social Justice Project

The continued relevance of Black feminism as a social justice project lies in its ability to reconnect with its traditional core, namely, the synergistic and dynamic relationship among Black women's experiences, self-defined knowledge regarding those experiences, and a Black feminist politics. Because many action strategies can address these challenges, here I sketch out three actions that I see as being especially pressing. They are: (1) setting a new social justice agenda that links African American women's social issues in the U.S. context with the concerns of global social justice initiatives; (2) reaching neglected constituencies by making African American girls and working-class women central as audiences for contemporary Black feminism; and (3) building coalitions *among* African American women who share a commitment to a social issues agenda yet are differentially positioned in relation to it.

Setting a New Social Justice Agenda

Highlighting a global social justice agenda identifies a list of social issues that concern social justice projects in general. They are: (1) struggles for political rights, especially citizenship; (2) struggles for economic rights, such as housing, food, and health; (3) struggles for economic rights issues of employment, poverty, and education; and (4) issues of bodily integrity, such as reproductive rights and elimination of violence. Whereas all social justice projects have a stake in this broad-based agenda, the work of U.S. Black feminism might lie in highlighting African American women's specific connections to this agenda. This would create space to see areas of consensus and conflict with other social justice projects and could form the foundation for new dialogues.

Here global feminism, especially a transnational Black feminism that embraces an intersectional framework, has much to offer African American women. Social issues that disproportionately affect African American women and girls in the United States—female-headed families, poverty, inadequate health care, and HIV/AIDS—also disproportionately affect women and girls of African descent in a global context. Black women in a global context do not reject issues of women's empowerment as women ("feminism," as a shorthand term). While they too often reject the term "feminism," they do see the need for female solidarity. African American women have greater difficulty achieving this solidarity because pushing for women's rights (especially if claimed under the banner of feminism) is seen as "white" and is often dismissed. Rather than confining U.S. Black feminism primarily to the terrain of race relations, the proverbial question, "Black and white women—can we get along?"—developing links between African American women and women of African descent in a transnational context creates space for new issues and points of view.

For example, reproductive rights—retaining one's own bodily integrity—are a fundamental premise of women's rights in a global context. Yet this social issue takes varying forms for women who have different social locations within racism, sexism, heterosexism, class exploitation, age, and religious fundamentalism. Fighting for the rights of Black women is central to much broader debates concerning reproductive rights. In this regard, given Mississippi's history as a staunch opponent of the rights of African Americans, Mississippi voters' rejection of the personhood amendment is extremely noteworthy. The amendment had implications beyond banning all abortions—if implemented, it had the potential to ban many forms of birth control and fertility treatments. How were Black women positioned in relation to this decision?

There would be no need for a transnational Black feminism if women of African descent as a collectivity were well housed, healthy, educated, well fed, employed, and safe from violence, and had loving relationships with their partners, family members, and friends. The core of a transnational Black feminism must begin not with discussions of who can participate in such a movement but rather by acknowledging that a disproportionate percentage of people who are poor, homeless, and hungry are women, are black, and are young. The convergence of systems of racism, sexism, class exploitation, age discrimination, citizenship, and heterosexism converge most intensely to create a global population of people called "Black women." Most certainly, there is significant social and cultural variation in how groups of Black women experience these social issues. But it also is important to remember that there would be no need to discuss Black feminisms of any kind in the absence of these kinds of social issues.

Here, the challenge is to take the main ideas of U.S. Black feminist thought, many of which are now theoretical frameworks and cultural analyses that are developed within academic settings, and use this framework to rethink the social issues that are of most concern to African American women. These issues include violence, education, health care, jobs, housing, family, body politics/sexuality, and a whole host of other social issues that threaten the vitality of Black communities. A Black feminist social issues agenda will recognize that some of these issues take gender-specific forms. For example, a responsive Black feminist agenda would critique violence against African American men at the hands of the police state, while recognizing that much of the violence experienced by African American women (and all women?) is at the hands of men. Thus, a crucial component of this social issues agenda lies in bringing U.S. Black feminism more in line with these social justice initiatives as they are articulated within the global women's movement. At the same time, a parallel component is to make sure that the global women's movement is attentive to the specifics of African American women's experiences. Women may share a common global position, yet building a global women's movement against women's poverty and powerlessness cannot come at the cost of ignoring how racism and heterosexism also affect women.

Women who are concerned with the need to create a common social issues agenda responsive to the heterogeneous social context in which Black women live form the backbone of transnational Black feminism. Transnational black feminism can share how other ways of living provide a different interpretive context for the same social issues experienced by African American women. Extracting the social issues of Black women from the race relations paradigm of the U.S. context and positioning such issues instead in a context of transnational Black feminism would be an important first step in addressing the challenges that currently face U.S. Black feminism.

Reaching Neglected Constituencies: Working-Class Black Girls as a Target Audience for Black Feminism

Black feminism currently reaches a far broader constituency than African American women. At the same time, the patterns of access to a discourse whose very reason for being is to advance social justice and whose specific form resists racism, sexism, class exploitation, and heterosexism are shaped by these very same systems of power. Within this broader constituency, are African American women still target audiences for Black feminism?

If Black feminism were reaching a broad constituency of African American women, one would assume that African American girls, the next generation of Black feminist intellectual leaders, would know about it and value its contributions to bettering their lives. Yet African American women and girls, the population on whose behalf Black feminism emerged and whose lives were supposed to be changed by this work, typically remain remarkably unaware of Black feminism. Moreover, if they have even heard of Black feminism, they reject it. In this context, I have become increasingly concerned about who exactly gets to develop Black feminist ideas as well as who has access to those ideas. Black feminism cannot be effective if those who are aware of this history hold distorted understandings of it. Black feminism has a limited future if it is invisible to Black girls and to the working-class African American women they are likely to grow up to be.

Currently, Black feminism is carefully rationed, with women and girls from already privileged groups gaining access to its ideas, primarily through college and university classrooms. Yet Black feminism in the academy decreasingly reaches college-age African American women, in part, because they form a shrinking percentage of students on elite college campuses. Black women must continue to do high-quality scholarship across many academic disciplines. However, we must ask ourselves, does our scholarship speak to the concerns of African American women, or are we increasingly addressing issues that reflect academic agendas? Should our intellectual talents be devoted to yet another dissertation, journal article, or book on well-trod academic topics, for example, the maternal politics of Toni Morrison's *Beloved*? Surely Morrison's work is of tremendous value for understanding motherhood, captivity and resistance. Yet who are the intended audiences for our dissertations, journal articles, and books on Morrison and for the current preoccupation of academic Black feminism?

If Black women intellectuals both inside and outside the academy considered ways of reaching Black girls and working-class Black women as neglected target audiences for our work, we might develop organizational capacity for reaching African American boys and Black men. Black feminism argues that gender matters in shaping the experiences of African American women. This does not mean that gender means girls. It does mean that Black feminism would think about Black women and men as target audiences for our work. This is an issue of need.

How would we go about building organizational capacity? Most likely, we would pay more attention to schools and similar social institutions that facilitate Black feminism or serve as gatekeepers. Black girls, especially poor and working class African American girls, need a critical education, which public schools are unlikely to provide. One important challenge that confronts Black feminism still aiming to be brave as a social justice project lies in educating Black youth not to fit into existing social hierarchies, but rather to challenge them. Education has long been the central theme of African American politics, and Black feminism that ignores this fact does so at its own peril.

Schooling is the social justice battleground for Black girls. Black feminism has made some progress into classrooms of higher education, but even there Black feminism remains contained within Women's Studies, Cultural Studies, and to a lesser extent, Black Studies programs. The works of individual African American intellectuals may be incorporated into the mainstream curriculum, yet a robust treatment of Black feminism remains rare. K–12 education shows even less interest in Black feminism, beyond teaching material on Black women worthies like Sojourner Truth. However, incorporating the ideas of Black women is no substitute for recruiting, educating, and graduating Black girls, especially girls from poor and working-class backgrounds, from colleges and universities.

The handwriting has been on the wall for some time concerning the steady pressure to exclude African American students from elite colleges and universities. The next Black feminist frontier must be K–12 education, not simply a watered down "shero" curriculum modeled on the "hero" curriculum for boys. Talk of "sheroes" and heroes assume that Black girls and boys are unaware of the accomplishments of African Americans and that they need accomplished role models to encourage them not to be like the people in their families and communities. Role model approaches assume that Black youths lack an analysis of their own situation, have low self-esteem, and can be motivated by exposure to images of African Americans who have "made it." Just because Black boys know about Tiger Woods doesn't mean that they are going to take up golf.

There is nothing wrong with exposing Black girls to images (if not actual) Black women who have achieved. Yet a Black feminist "shero" curriculum that urges modeling one's life after Black women worthies without also helping girls further develop their own analyses of their lives remains incomplete. Black girls will be encouraged to better themselves one at a time, often by leaving their families and communities behind. Instead of this curriculum, I'd suggest using the broader social justice agenda discussed earlier to strategize how Black girls fit into it. A critical education would expose them to a kind of Black feminism that fuses experiences, thought, and action. If we asked Black girls to engage in projects where they examined their own lives (and not primarily in relation to the "sheros" of Black women worthies), what experiences would they share, what analyses might they offer, and what would they plan on doing with their knowledge? Stated differently, Black girls would not be consumers of Black feminism—instead they would create it.

How can we put poor and working-class Black girls at the center of Black feminism? Their lives are not marginal to intersecting power relations of race, class, gender, sexuality, and age. Rather, they are central to the future of Black feminism. Keep in mind that Black girls are over-represented among the poor. They disproportionately attend inferior public schools, have children young, and do not finish high school. They are more likely to end up as single mothers. They are more likely to grow up to be working class, if not poor. Their gendered lives occur primarily through their relationships with African American men as fathers, friends, brothers, sexual partners, husbands, sons, and grandsons. Any Black feminism worth its salt would not squander its resources on the children of elites. Instead, it would recognize that poor and working-class Black girls who are situated in families and communities are its special ground zero in the early twenty-first century.

Organizing Differently: Strengthening Coalitions among African American Women

Three important groups of contemporary U.S. Black women are positioned to make important contributions in meeting the challenge of developing a new social justice agenda and reaching out to working-class Black girls. Each group is differently situated within the U.S. context and brings a different skill set and experiential base to Black feminism. All three groups understand the existential question, "What will it take for Black women to be free?" but they interpret the question itself and its possible responses differently.

Black women community leaders constitute the first and, in many ways, the most foundational group. This is the group with skills of grassroots community organizing and a deep-seated commitment to developing African American communities. They are the ones dealing with recalcitrant schools, intrusive social service bureaucracies, and overzealous police. This is the group whose gender analyses include men, mainly because they see first-hand how the combination of race and gender places young Black men at risk. This is also the group that is least likely to claim Black feminism, even though their work embodies Black feminism's social justice agenda.

The second group consists of young women who personally identify with Black feminism. Most are introduced to Black feminism through Women's Studies classrooms and have had access to the rich idea base of an increasingly global feminism. Black feminism in the academy is often situated within Women's Studies, a field that has made tremendous strides in diversifying its study and staff. Within this area, young feminists of color discover each other as African American, Latina, and Asian American women and see the connections between what may have been understood in their home communities as separate struggles. They access a different, coalitional social justice ethos within the academic field of Women's Studies. Feminism advances an individual rights discourse, one that resonates well with the generational logic of young Black feminists.

Self-defined "hip hop feminists" may constitute a third group for a coalition among African American women. This group provides another forum of Black feminist politics with the potential to bridge feminist and nationalist strategies while encouraging African American women to develop, expand, and/or create new social institutions that house Black feminist praxis.

Building coalitional politics among these three groups of African American women would go far toward revitalizing Black feminism as a social justice project. Each has a distinctive angle of vision on Black feminism's traditional core, namely, the synergistic and dynamic relationship among Black women's experiences, self-defined knowledge regarding those experiences, and a Black feminist politics that reflects a broader social justice ethos. Yet this coalitional politics cannot happen without building organizational capacity that fosters such coalitions. To this end, Black women's organizations and organizations that have identifiable, internal Black women's caucuses might develop structural initiatives that are designed to bring together key agents from these three groups. It's not that one group contributes unexamined experiences and the other offers up theoretical knowledge that explains those experiences. Rather, all three have distinctive perspectives on the intersecting power relations that shape Black women's experiences. They also may propose different strategies for Black women's empowerment that stem from their placement in lived social relations. Moving the ideas and actions of U.S. Black feminism closer together might revitalize African American women's politics.

Still Brave?

Looking ahead, what direction and shape should Black feminism take? The answer brings the discussion back to the core question framing this essay: What will it take for Black women to be free? This question is straightforward, yet infinitely complex, and this essay has explored some of that complexity. I want to finish this presentation by revisiting this question in light of the previous discussion.

The meaning of "to be free" is important because freedom and social justice are deeply intertwined. *Freedom from* the social injustices that are structured by intersecting systems of oppression? This sense of the idea of freedom references issues of citizenship and emancipation, a widespread belief up until now that political freedom would yield tangible social benefits. With the growing disenchantment with representative democracy, it seems clear that political remedies, while crucial, are not enough. Freedom now must be recast through ideas about the economy. *Freedom to* live our lives as we want, with imagination and personal choice, to think what we want, go where we want, love whom we want, and dream big dreams that have some possibility of coming to fruition?

The heart of the issue concerns *what will it take*? Identifying examples from Black feminism that required women to be brave, to tackle thorny social problems that weighed more heavily on Black women than on other groups, reveals the multiple strategies that have been deployed to try to bring about this freedom. The need to ask the question at all suggests that this project is unfinished. This is a core existential question for Black women. I have also stressed African American women in my presentation, using Black women's experiences as a touchstone for broader social issues.

I remind you that the framework of intersectionality encourages an opening up of this question beyond the specific case of African American women. We need multiple cases, grounded within intersectional analyses that examine how this same question affects individuals and groups in a global context. For example, as refracted through the category of nation-states, one might ask, "What will it take for all young women citizens of South Africa to be free?" For stateless peoples, the question becomes, "What will it take for Palestinians to be free?" For subjugated ethnic groups, "What will it take for the Dhalit to be free?" For subordinated segments of national populations, the question might be, "What will it take for *beur* youth in Parisian suburbs to be free?"

Collectively, these questions remind us that "What will it take for us all to be free?" may be the existential question of human experience. Despite our disparate starting points, in moving along a path toward freedom, we might all tell ourselves from time to time, "Be brave," if only in a whisper. Yet we might be better served by remembering Fannie Lou Hamer's unshakable commitment to social justice. She found a way to "be brave."

ADDITIONAL RESOURCES

Combahee River Collective. 1995. "A Black Feminist Statement." In *Words of Fire: An Anthology of African American Feminist Thought*, pp. 232–240, ed. Beverly Guy-Sheftall. New York: New Press.

Davis, Angela Y. 1981. *Women, Race, and Class*. New York: Random House.

Hernandez, Daisy, and Bushra Rehman, eds. 2002. *Colonize This! Young Women of Color on Today's Feminism*. New York: Seal Press.

Hull, Gloria T., Patricia Bell Scott, and Barbara Smith, eds. 1982. *But Some of Us Are Brave: All the Women Are White, All the Blacks Are Men: Black Women's Studies.* New York: The Feminist Press.

James, Stanlie, Frances Smith Foster, and Beverly Guy-Sheftall, eds. 2009. *Still Brave: The Evolution of Black Women's Studies.* New York: The Feminist Press.

Norton, Congresswoman Eleanor Holmes. http://www.norton.house.gov/index.php? option=com_content&view=frontpage&Itemid=121. Accessed: June 24, 2012.

Pough, Gwendolyn D. 2004. *Check It While I Wreck It: Black Womanhood, Hip-Hop Culture, and the Public Sphere.* Boston: Northeastern University Press.

Ransby, Barbara. 2003. *Ella Baker & the Black Freedom Movement: A Radical Democratic Vision.* Chapel Hill: University of North Carolina Press.

II

Sociology of Knowledge

Learning from the
Outsider Within Revisited

REFLEXIVE ESSAY: *Much of my scholarship draws upon my expertise in the sociology of knowledge, a subfield within sociology that examines the links between knowledge and power relations. My 1986 essay "Learning from the Outsider Within: The Sociological Significance of Black Feminist Thought" provides an early example of my work in this field. In that essay, I introduced the* outsider-within *construct that I develop further in* Black Feminist Thought *and* Fighting Words. *Here I revisit this construct from standpoint epistemology, examining how the emancipatory potential of the* outsider-within *construct has increasingly been recast as a personal identity category of alienation from the mainstream that fits well with contemporary understandings of difference. This essay also introduces a foundational idea of sociology of knowledge that power relations and what counts as truth influence one another.*

ALTHOUGH I PUBLISHED "Learning from the Outsider Within: The Sociological Significance of Black Feminist Thought" more than twenty years ago, its ideas still speak to contemporary realities. I wrote this article because I wanted to understand my alienation in school and workplace settings where I was the "first" or the "only" individual in one category or another. Nothing in the literature that I consulted in the 1980s adequately described my

---

This essay was initially developed as the keynote address for a wonderful graduate student conference, "Liminality in the Humanities: An Interdisciplinary Exchange," that was held in 2004 at the University of Utah Humanities Graduate Conference in Salt Lake City.

state of belonging, yet not belonging. Sociological discussions of insiders, outsiders, and marginal men came close, but something was missing. Eventually, I chose the term *outsider within* to describe individuals like myself who occupied the edges between groups of unequal power.

As I initially envisioned it, the outsider-within construct spoke to the ambiguities of belonging, yet not fully belonging. In my case, my gender gave me insider status in my all-girls, public high school, yet my race rendered me an outsider in that same setting. In my African American neighborhood, I was an insider, yet as a girl, I was expected to take a back seat to Black men. In college, I competed with my classmates, yet recognized the many ways in which their middle-class backgrounds differed from my own. Whether the differences in power stemmed from hierarchies of gender, race, class, or in my case, the interaction of all three, the social location of being on the edge mattered.

In "Learning from the Outsider Within," I suggested that we might learn from people who lived in these border spaces, perhaps because they had an advantage in seeing the world differently than those in the center. Over time, what began as my search to come to understand my own *individual* experiences led me to propose that African American women as a group occupied a comparable *collective* social location. I argued that the space of being disempowered within intersecting systems of race, gender, and social class catalyzed a distinctive group standpoint on the world among African American women. I labeled this standpoint "Black feminist thought."

In hindsight, I see how unsettling it must have been for my more powerful colleagues to hear such patently outrageous claims from a junior scholar. In a society that to this day believes that only hand-picked Black women with JDs and PhDs can think, claiming that African American women as a group had something to say; that their collective social thought reflected their outsider status within social location in U.S. power relations; that they invoked a distinctive Black feminist epistemology in advancing their knowledge claims; and that this social thought constituted critical social theory that should be not at the margins but rather at the forefront of American social thought, was progressive, if not radical. I was so young then.

Much has happened since I drafted my initial arguments. I have been astounded by how the outsider-within construct has traveled beyond the experiences of African American women. We now know that few people can achieve the mythical norm of being wealthy, white, male, heterosexual, American, able-bodied, and Christian that Western social institutions tout as being natural, normal, and ideal. Instead, many people find themselves on the wrong side of the categories that matter most in their respective societies. In the United States, for example, people become outsiders because they are Muslims in a fundamentally Judeo-Christian country; or because they are Sansei, Korean American, Chicano, Chinese American, or Puerto Rican citizens confronting notions of American nationality that insist on viewing them as foreigners; or because they are physically challenged and face curbs that are too high and restroom stalls that are too small; or because they are working-class white women whose subjective experiences with upward social class mobility have been all but erased from social science research; or because they are lesbian, gay, bisexual, or transgendered (LGBT) individuals struggling to get insurance coverage for their partners; or because they are affluent, anti-racist, feminist, straight white men whose families cannot understand why they turned out that way— and the list goes on.

Globally, the transnational upheavals that have shrunk social welfare states in favor of market-based solutions to social problems have generated new outsiders within social locations and the experiences they engender for all sorts of people. Whether middle-class Hindu immigrants to Great Britain, or migrants to burgeoning world cities in Latin America and Africa, the ebbs and flows of diverse population streams challenge historically stable notions of belonging. Hindu immigrants who lived stable, even prosperous, lives in India, when compared with the poverty of farmers displaced by mega-dams, on arrival in Great Britain, may find themselves lumped together with black Jamaicans into a new ethnic identity, namely, "black British." These new "outsiders within" may see ideas about race and nation quite differently than their white British counterparts who never left home. The people who live on garbage dumps outside São Paulo, Brazil, as part of a global landless people's movement certainly have a different view of agribusiness and urbanization than the wealthy in the city's posh neighborhoods. The residents of Soweto outside Johannesburg, South Africa, may celebrate their freedom from apartheid in 1992, yet wonder when post-apartheid South Africa will make their neighborhood safe from crime. For the new urban migrants to Mumbai, Kingston, São Paulo, and Soweto alike, housing, clean water, electricity, and schooling for their children are not afterthoughts of national security—they are the essence of it.

Contemporary writers in varying race, gender, sexual, national, and class social locations use many terms to describe these changes wrought by racial desegregation in the United States and similar white settler societies, the multicultural challenges that face European nation-states, and the continuing struggles of decolonization. "Migration," "displacement," "liminality," "border crossing," "curdling," "marginality," "Diaspora," and "difference" reference varying dimensions of these new social relations. These terms suggest that the world looks very different from the edges of power than from its centers.

People who do intellectual work from outsider-within social locations can draw on a creative tension of being on the margins within intersecting systems of race, class, gender, sexual, and national oppression. They develop a critical consciousness of the need to remain attentive to the connections linking their scholarship and their in-between status of belonging, yet not belonging. This, to me, is what distinguishes oppositional knowledge developed in outsider-within locations *both* from elite knowledge (social theories developed from within centers of power, such as whiteness, maleness, heterosexism, class privilege, or citizenship) *and* from knowledge developed by oppressed groups whose energies are consumed by one especially salient form of oppression (e.g., patriarchal Black cultural nationalism, a racist feminism, or a raceless, genderless class analysis). In other words, intellectual production done from outsider-within social locations can produce distinctive oppositional knowledge. This knowledge can incorporate multiple points of view from many interpretive communities, yet remain cognizant of the power plays that created them.

As border crossers and boundary markers, people in outsider-within spaces contest the meanings of the categories themselves. The engaged scholarship they produce points out that freedom is meaningless without slavery, masculinity makes no sense without femininity, national citizenship rings hollow if it's given away freely to everyone, and who's really "black" or "white"? The view from the edge can be empowering. Replacing prevailing interpretations of how we are supposed to view ourselves with perspectives that reclaim outsider-within locations as places of intellectual, political, and ethical strength feels like a breath of fresh air.

That's the good news. Despite the actual and potential contributions of the outsider-within construct and its significance in empowering oppressed groups, I remain disappointed by how these ideas have been appropriated by and used within academia. For scholars whose intellectual activism is linked to outsider-within spaces, working creatively in such spaces has become more difficult. When scholars from privileged positions seem to celebrate, understand, and/or mimic the very differences that keep us down, it becomes hard to tell the difference between allies and enemies.

The changing meanings attached to the concept of the outsider within illustrate these trends. Removing the concept from its specific historical context of group-based oppressions and reinserting it within the new social realities of individual identities has changed its meaning. Current uses increasingly reduce the richness of outsider-within intellectual production to personal identity categories that far too often ignore racism, sexism, class exploitation, and heterosexism that house all individual identities. Social structures of intersecting systems of power disappear, to be replaced by an endlessly changing flow of individuals, each trying to understand him- or herself. In a U.S. context that often views choice and consumerism as synonymous, shopping for personal identities in the store of race, class, gender, and sexuality can devolve into meaningless narcissism. In this context, it has become difficult to retain focus on the big picture, the kinds of social phenomena that produce social inequalities and social injustices.

Let me give an example. Over the years, many people have approached me after my public lectures to share their own personal pain as self-defined outsiders within. Despite my discomfort with hearing so many sad stories of alienation, my initial receptivity gave way to my dismay as I saw a disturbing pattern emerge. As the term *outsider within* traveled, its meaning changed. For example, in one especially memorable exchange, a white woman shared a confessional monologue of how her Jewish identity had caused her pain as an outsider within. Yet the way she approached me, as if I were a mammy confessor figure from a long line of such figures, left me wondering about the depth of her racial analysis. She made no mention of Black/Jewish relations or of ways in which anti-Semitism and white supremacy draw meaning from one another. Both have been crucial in shaping Western racism, and both have generated distinctive outsider-within niches for African Americans and Jewish Americans, respectively. Instead, she wanted me to absorb her individual pain, yet rejected my efforts to refocus her attention to racism and sexism as systems of power. She wanted to bond with me in a social space where the marginalized were defined by and connected to one another via personal pain. She appropriated the outsider-within construct as a wedge issue to gain sympathy for her personal discomfort.

I do not fault her for failing to see how the growing emphasis on personal identity within American society in the 1990s has depoliticized the very language of dissent. In a climate where personal confessionals parade across American television screens via an endless stream of crying women on talk shows, and where social media such as Facebook and Twitter encourage people to share all every detail of their personal lives, ignoring structural power relationships of all sorts runs rampant. Reducing the complexities of outsider-within social locations to questions of individual identity resonates with distinctly American beliefs that all social problems can be solved by working on oneself. Removing the term "outsider" from its initial interpretive context means that *everyone* can now be an outsider within. Given the right setting, African Americans and whites, women and men, poor and rich—we can all be outsiders within and share one another's pain.

Currently, the concept of the outsider within falls victim to the same problems of redefinition that plague a host of terms. In a world where missiles are "peacekeepers," where "urban contemporary" means "ghetto," and where "welfare mother" invokes images of African American women who procreate to live off the dole, we may continue to use language, even though its meaning becomes changed. In essence, the interconnections between outsider-within social locations, outsider-within intellectual production, and any distinctive standpoints that may be produced have been stripped of their radical potential and have been replaced by an inordinate attention to the concept of difference.

A Telling Difference

There is much talk about difference in the academy today. Such talk sounds sympathetic to social justice projects, yet typically promises little to Black women and other historically oppressed groups and delivers even less. Because working-class African Americans and Latinos as well as poor and working-class whites find higher education less affordable, the campuses they can no longer attend change dramatically. Imagine this—a classroom filled with smart, middle-class young women, reading and discussing the ideas in Toni Morrison's prizewinning novel *Beloved*, with one lone African American woman in the class. The students struggle to make sense of a novel whose essence speaks to questions of slavery, freedom, and love that stem from the experiences of people in America. Ironies abound—"We're all the same under the skin," or "I'm glad that I didn't live during the racism of the past," the students say, confident that they are not upholding racism because they loved the book. Should the lone Black girl raise her hand and yet again become the spokesperson for her race? Or should she remain silent and implicitly condone yet another conversation that seems strangely removed from Morrison's intentions? Better yet, does she wonder why she is the *only* Black student?

Quite frankly, the academy has been quick to embrace the *idea* of outsiders within and the creative potential that their standpoints on the world might engender, yet has been far less willing to welcome the actual people who first advanced these ideas. From the perspective of African Americans, indigenous peoples, Chicanos, Puerto Ricans, and other historically oppressed groups in the United States, the emphasis on understanding differences rings hollow when Black and Latino kids are pushed into underfunded, failing inner-city schools that continue to prepare many of them far more effectively for prison than for college. One school district in the greater metropolitan Washington, D.C., area illustrates this cleavage between academic ideas and actual racial practices—instead of studying for the SAT, the district's African American high school student population received a visit from the local police department and students role-played how to get arrested. Ironically, this event was co-sponsored by the local NAACP chapter. What a Faustian bargain—because they are stopped so often, keeping Black kids safe requires training them in the skills of "assuming the position."

They are not alone. In the aftermath of 9/11, the general public also has to "assume the position," a practice that is painfully evident in airport security lines, where we remove our shoes and undergo full-body scans. As is true for the residents of many gated suburban communities, our fear stimulates us to incarcerate ourselves to protect our freedom. Abstract academic ideas of difference seem impotent in the face of practices such as these. We too are on lockdown in academic gated communities, encouraged to substitute "difference talk" for hard-hitting analyses of persisting social inequalities. It's a sobering thought—a world full of social problems that academic difference talk cannot help heal.

This late-twentieth-century and early-twenty-first-century academic preoccupation with difference could not have arrived at a better time for promoters and/or unconscious supporters of racism, sexism, heterosexism, class exploitation, and similar systems of social injustice. The shifting political climate in the United States has paralleled the growth of the corporate university, with its business-oriented ethos of serving individual students as consumers or clients. This shift from seeing structural issues and their impact on social groups to elevating the individual as central to all concerns has affected a range of constructs. Take social justice, for example, where conceptions of reparative social justice advocated by the social movements of the 1950s and 1960s have gradually been replaced with notions of an individualized distributive justice. Within conservative frameworks, social rights accrue to individuals, not groups, and should be adjudicated on a case-by-case basis. More expansive notions of difference first proposed during social movements by Blacks, Latinos, women, and poor people fell victim to conservative redefinitions of identity and difference as attributes and rights of individuals.

Ironically, difference talk may have flattened the richness of the outsider-within construct, yet the radical potential of construct of difference itself may also have fallen victim to these trends. In her classic essay, "Age, Race, Class, and Sex: Women Redefining Difference," published more than thirty years ago, Black feminist theorist Audre Lorde contended that much of Western European history has conditioned us to see human differences in simplistic opposition to each other. "We have *all* been programmed to respond to the human differences between us with fear and loathing," Lorde argued, "and to handle that difference in one of three ways: ignore it, and if that is not possible, copy it if we think it is dominant, or destroy it if we think it is subordinate." Lorde pointed out that difference itself is benign. Rather, the way that American society distorts differences and the meanings attached to them under systems of race, class, gender, sexuality, ethnicity, age, and citizenship status becomes the issue.

Not only is the meaning of difference shifting, when deployed uncritically, but the construct of difference also proves useful within contemporary power relations. For example, difference can be commodified and become a measure of worth that is counted and evaluated within the corporate university. Colleges and universities want people who are different in attendance, yet they are far less sanguine in accepting dissenting ideas that these different people might express. Conservative thinkers see the academy as overrun by tenured radicals who fail to appreciate the best of Western culture. Ironically, such thinkers misread the significance of difference talk within the corporate academy. Much difference talk is just talk—it poses minimal threat to business as usual.

Dealing with Difference through Domains of Power

In my work, I have been trying to think my way through these shifts in language and politics as illustrated by the changing meanings of the outsider-within and difference constructs. While critique of how the outsider-within construct has changed is important, engaged scholarship must go beyond "deconstructing" what is in ways that leave it to students to figure out appropriate action strategies on their own. Critique only pays the bills of people who have cushy academic jobs. Doing engaged scholarship from within outsider-within spaces means considering not only the content of our ideas but also how they might affect existing power relations.

My approach has been to develop a new vocabulary for analyzing power relations. Power may be everywhere, as French philosopher Michel Foucault points out, but what exactly does this mean? If power is manifested and organized everywhere, how might we develop a language of power that is useful? Understanding and responding to the shifts in meaning of terms such as "outsider" and "within" and "difference" requires attending to the power relationships that engendered these changes.

My response has been to draw from the widespread social theories of power and encapsulate them into a schema that might be useful not only for analyzing systems of power, such as racism or sexism, but also for crafting effective political responses to them. I settled on a *domains of power framework* as a useful way of thinking about power that seems to be everywhere and nowhere at the same time. The domains of power framework can be used to analyze social phenomena as historically specific as Black women's experiences, the approach I used in *Black Feminist Thought,* or as expansive as early-twentieth-century colorblind racism, my expanded treatment in *Another Kind of Public Education.* The framework identifies four interrelated domains where power is organized: (1) a structural domain, where social institutions of a society, such as banks, hospitals, schools, corporations, retail establishments, government agencies, and health care, routinely discriminate in favor of whites and against everyone else; (2) a disciplinary domain, where modern bureaucracies regulate race relations through their rules and practices, primarily surveillance; (3) a cultural domain, where ideologies, such as white supremacy, patriarchy, and heterosexism, are constructed and shared; and (4) an interpersonal domain that shapes social relations between individuals in everyday life.

The treatment of African American youth illustrates how structural, disciplinary, cultural, and interpersonal domains of power intersect. Structural power is expressed through the resegregation of housing and schools, with the most visible structural change being the hypersegregation of poor and working-class African Americans within cities. No matter how motivated a young Black man or woman may be, the experience of growing up in inferior housing, attending second-rate schools, and seeing no jobs in his or her neighborhood speaks to the structural constraints on a large segment of the African American population. Disciplinary power operates through unwritten rules that treat Blacks and whites differently (racial profiling of young Black men by the police comes to mind); through racial rules that few question but most people follow ("marry someone of the same race, different gender"); through policies that on the surface are racially neutral but that have racially disparate effects (relying on high-stakes testing for college admissions and job selection when the tests have not been shown to predict future success for anyone). School systems, the social welfare system, and prisons use more sophisticated mechanisms of social control, helped along by new technologies of surveillance. The cultural domain of power manufactures the new ideology of colorblindness, primarily through courts that view any differential racial treatment as being racist and through a powerful mass media that presents America as being more racially integrated than it really is. In the interpersonal domain, strategies of everyday racism become more important in the desegregated school and work environments associated with the legal structure of equal opportunity and a rhetoric of tolerance where to see race is to be racist. Although these everyday dominance strategies often constitute the most visible forms of racism or lack of it for ordinary citizens, they represent one dimension of this larger system of race.

The domains of power framework also sheds light on the ways that ideas about difference can uphold social inequalities within and across all four domains of power. For example, within the structural domain, new commodity relations have found the focus on difference profitable. In the search for ever-expanding consumer markets, understanding differences of race, gender, class, and sexuality helps in identifying segmented consumer markets. "Racial" profiling and market research are two sides of the same coin. Beyond this boon to business, the very idea of difference can be marketed as well. Take the housewares department in T.J. Maxx, or the success of stores such as Cost Plus, World Market, or Pier One. These retailers realize that American consumers like to collect and decorate their home with artifacts from different racial/ethnic cultures imported from around the world, resembling the colonialists who returned from distant journeys toting souvenirs from faraway places.

Because the disciplinary domain stresses the rules of replicating hierarchy within social institutions, it also draws on ideas about difference. Social inequalities operate via rules and regulations that keep the majority on the bottom. In a contemporary culture that places so much credence on the visual, showcasing the few disciplines the many. Disciplinary power is attached to bureaucracies, and such sites can no longer be organized as clear racial hierarchies where all the managers are white men and all the members of the cleaning staff are Black and/or Latino. If these historical patterns of exclusion did exist, they would be questioned as somehow violating current sensibilities concerning fairness and inclusivity. For the organization to run smoothly, everyone must buy into a new racial hierarchy that includes a few handpicked people of color or white women at the top to mask the many who hold service jobs at the bottom. Stated differently, new power relations predicated on token inclusion need an array of visible difference at the top to legitimate the continuation of business as usual at the bottom.

Within this context, people who claim outsider-within identities can become hot commodities in social institutions that want the illusion of difference without the effort needed to change actual power relations. Tackling the power relations that generate perpetual winners and losers within organizations always involves conflict. Bringing about more just school and work environments requires sustained commitment from the top that convinces people that conflict is a midpoint and not the endpoint of change. Unfortunately, far too many organizations lack this visionary leadership. Instead, they opt for cosmetic change, where retrofitting and marketing handpicked individuals as authentic outsiders serve as substitutes for substantive, organizational change. In these settings, it does not matter which outsider within or person of color you get. What matters is that someone convincingly plays the part.

The cultural domain also benefits from a focus on difference. The shifting contours of racism provide a useful case. Under color-conscious racial segregation, a language of exclusion held sway. Keep the others out; ensure that the home, neighborhood, profession, health club, swimming pool, locker room, golf course, or cemetery only contains those who belong. Colorblind racism relies on different strategies. The universalistic language of inclusion invoked by ideas about dreams, character, and colorblindness upholds the illusion of racial integration, yet masks the reality of persisting racial segregation for large segments of the American population. Hegemonic ideology that conflates the ideal of a colorblind society with its realization is vital in maintaining racial hierarchy. Yet fifty years after the momentous 1954 *Brown v. Board of Education* decision, poor and working-class African American and Latino children see how that universalistic language of inclusion does not appear to apply to them. The dream of Martin Luther King, Jr., that people be judged by the content of their character and not by the color of their skin is mouthed by many, yet actions speak louder than empty words.

Ideas about difference also organize the interpersonal domain of power. Currently, we each face pressure to create new personal identities that are grounded in apolitical notions of difference. Within this logic, race is no longer tightly bundled with racism, nor gender with sexism. Rather, my "race" and my "gender" become dimensions of my individual uniqueness, personal identity categories whose value lies in distinguishing me from everyone else. Each individual becomes a unique constellation of differences that makes him or her special.

While I am tempted to embrace the individual freedom that this approach to interpersonal relations promises, my work on intersecting power relations and the significance of seeing outsider-within social locations as embedded in power relations suggests otherwise. I see individual freedom as still substantially curtailed by limited opportunity structures. People who live in segregated neighborhoods and attend segregated schools are unlikely to meet and fall in love with anyone outside that neighborhood or school. Rich, white suburban kids simply live in different social worlds than poor, Latino, urban ones. After years of interacting within unequal categories as bosses and workers, social workers and clients, and police and neighborhood residents, by the time people reach adulthood to see one another as people is tough. Despite the structural barriers, many individuals manage to form friendships and love relationships that defy prevailing norms. Yet focusing on individuals who break barriers in order to ignore persisting, contemporary structural inequalities cannot erase the effects of deep-seated, historical systems of power.

A new multicultural, colorblind America no longer needs strict borders and theories of racial purity. Instead, it now welcomes mixed race and/or racially ambiguous people, because they serve as a sign of the demise of a white supremacist ideology that argued for racial purity. In this context, controlling the radical space of the margins becomes even more important because the ambiguity of *mestizo,* mulatto, biracial, and racially ambiguous individuals highlights the clarity of white and black as a fundamental and visible binary. This border zone is a buffer whose visibility shields the society against claims of racism (understood in binary terms) while fixing the two ends of the racial binary by focusing on the space in the middle. In this context, outsider-within spaces are required, not only to contain earlier radical critiques of the structures of power that produced them (the case of Black feminist thought as a collective outsider-within space) but also as places to encourage individual to perform new decentralized identities that are functional for new structures of power. These practices hollow out the radical potential of outsider-within social locations, refilling them with apolitical understandings of "difference" that gives the illusion of inclusion, yet allows old-fashioned power plays to reorganize.

The Outsider Within Revisited: A Coda

It has been an amazing thing to observe—the very category that I created to name, highlight, and thereby empower African American women can now, by recasting it as an individualized category of personal difference within commodity relations that package and sell difference, be used to *erase* African American women's experiences in outsider-within social locations. Mesmerized by the multiple identities of each individual Black woman that celebrates her unique differences, we fail to see how racism, sexism, class exploitation, and heterosexism shape her experiences as well as her analyses of her lived reality. Instead, current power relations ask that African American women stay in their devalued social location while more powerful others use greatly changed constructs, such as the outsider within, to write books and get tenure by explaining Black women's continued marginality. The acclaim granted Toni Morrison's *Beloved* as an important text on Black women's experiences illustrates this phenomenon. White girls get to read *Beloved* in their fancy colleges, most in classrooms with few African American women as students. Those who come to love Morrison's work get jobs as college professors, with some becoming specialists in African American women's literature. The Black girls whose experiences the book examines remain shut out of higher education, do not land the cushy jobs teaching African American women's literature, and watch from the sidelines as their experiences are repackaged and sold within commodity relations of difference. The white girls use ideas about difference and outsider-within theorizing to publish journal articles, using Morrison's *Beloved* as evidence for their arguments. The Black girls get to dust their computers and empty their trash.

Academic theories that hitch their wagon to the star of difference may soothe our fears that the shrinking numbers of African American and/or working-class faculty and students in elite institutions of higher education have nothing to do with us. We're not the ones who make policy. Instead, we are the ones who uphold the banner of social justice, in word if not always in deed. We are the ones who are morally and ethically innocent because we value difference and diversity and want each individual to be free to express his or her differences. We believe in individual freedom, spending time helping our biracial or LGBT students with their personal struggles.

Our desire to live in a socially just world that we have not yet created is completely understandable and commendable. Yet, when we expect students and faculty of color and similarly situated groups to bear full responsibility for social justice initiatives, we inadvertently strip oppositional language of meaning, burn out talent, and weaken the tools of resistance of historically oppressed groups. In the context of the growing corporatization of the academy, of the shrinking public commitment to humanities and liberal arts, of the closing of doors of opportunity to working-class and poor students from all backgrounds, we too need ideologies that convince us that all is right in Oz.

When it comes to the relationship between scholarship and social justice initiatives, we stand at a crossroads. In one direction, our scholarship does reveal how ideas about difference and its related constructs matter in both upholding and challenging racism, sexism, class exploitation, and heterosexism as systems of power. By sharpening our focus on power and developing tools that enable us to see how its domains are organized and can be changed, our engaged scholarship creates space for change. In the other direction, our scholarship about difference that is peppered with meaningless talk about race, gender, and class makes little difference in challenging the actual differences associated with social injustice. The words we use in describing both paths may be the same, yet the meaning of the paths varies greatly. Pick the path you will follow. I hope you choose wisely.

ADDITIONAL RESOURCES

Anzaldua, Gloria. 1987. *Borderlands/La Frontera*. San Francisco: Spinsters/Aunt Lute Press.
Chow, Rey. 1993. *Writing Diaspora: Tactics of Intervention in Contemporary Cultural Studies*. Bloomington: Indiana University Press.
Collins, Patricia Hill. 1986. "Learning from the Outsider Within: The Sociological Significance of Black Feminist Thought." *Social Problems* 33(6):14–32.
Lorde, Audre. 1984. *Sister Outsider: Essays and Speeches*. Freedom, Calif.: Crossing Press.
Said, Edward W. 1978. *Orientalism*. New York: Vintage.

Going Public

Doing the Sociology That Had No Name

REFLEXIVE ESSAY: *When I served on the program committee for the 2005 annual meeting of the American Sociological Association (ASA), I became especially intrigued by our program theme, "Public Sociologies." Participating in the process of planning ASA's annual meeting around this specific theme helped me articulate my ideas about the relationship of sociology to intellectual activism. Within the sociology of knowledge, the lion's share of attention had been focused on dominant knowledge, for example the idea structures of sexism or racism, with the corresponding idea that such knowledge was virtually hegemonic. Many scholars approached dominant discourses as if they could not be questioned. In contrast, this focus on public sociology created space for oppositional knowledge, ideas developed by people who were engaged in challenging social hierarchies and the ideologies that justified them. This essay contains my reflections on public sociology that came from this introduction to the name "public sociology" and my subsequent positioning of my own intellectual work within this framework.*

FOR YEARS, I have been doing a kind of sociology that had no name. In hindsight, the path that I have been on seems clear and consistent. In the early 1970s, as a teacher and community organizer within the community schools movement, I did some of my best sociology, all without publishing

This article was originally published as "Going Public: Doing the Sociology That Had No Name." In *Public Sociology: Fifteen Eminent Sociologists Debate Politics and the Professions in the Twenty-first Century*, pp. 101–113, ed. Dan Clawson, Robert Zussman, Joya Misra, and Naomi Gerstel. Berkeley: University of California Press, 2007.

one word. For six years, I honed the craft of translating the powerful ideas of my college education so that I might share them with my elementary school students, their families, my fellow teachers, and community members. My sociological career also illustrates how the tensions of moving through sociology as a discipline as well as engaging numerous constituencies outside of sociology shaped my scholarship. This impetus to think both inside and outside the American sociological box enabled me to survive within the discipline. Early on, I recognized that I needed to create space to breathe within prevailing sociological norms and practices. I wrote "Learning from the Outsider Within: The Sociological Significance of Black Feminist Thought," to create space for myself as an individual, yet that article simultaneously generated dialogues with a broad range of nonsociologists. Similarly, writing *Black Feminist Thought* for social theorists, sociologists, feminists, and ordinary people, in particular—African American women whose lives I hoped to influence—was an exercise in the energy that it takes to engage multiple audiences within one text. When colleagues tell me how much the ideas in that one book have traveled, I realize the importance of connecting scholarship to broader audiences. In hindsight, I see how important my years spent working in the community schools movement have been to my subsequent sociological career.

Over the years, my personal engagement in speaking with multiracial, multiethnic audiences from many social class backgrounds, citizenship categories, genders, sexualities, and ages has taught me much. As a professor, discussing my ideas with diverse groups at colleges, universities, community centers, academic conferences, and social activist arenas has improved my scholarship. Take, for example, how different audiences engaged the ideas in *Black Sexual Politics*. Writing a book is one thing—talking with different groups of people about what I had written was an entirely different experience. The generic lecture title "Introduction to *Black Sexual Politics*" fails to capture the wide range of talks that I actually delivered. The African American community residents in Tulsa, Oklahoma, who came out to their local public library to hear the version of the talk that I prepared for them had different reactions than the college students and faculty on the beautiful campus of the University of California, Santa Barbara, who encountered the same ideas, yet in a vastly different format. At times, I had to fall back on pedagogical skills honed during my days teaching seventh- and eighth-grade students, as when I addressed a lively group of Black and Latino high school students in Louisville, Kentucky. How different their reactions were to the ideas in *Black Sexual Politics* than those of the audience at the feminist bookstore in Cambridge, Massachusetts. The list goes on. I realize how diverse American society is, let alone the rich tapestry of global cultures and experiences that lie outside U.S. borders. Writing for and speaking with multiple publics has been challenging, but also worth it.

Despite this history, I initially found Michael Burawoy's ideas about public sociology unnerving. I certainly like Burawoy's model and think that it interjects a much-needed breath of fresh air into some increasingly stale sociological debates. At the same time, I'm not completely comfortable with it. Apparently, I had been *doing* public sociology without even knowing it. Moreover, I was not alone. Despite my inability to classify them as public sociologists, many other sociologists had also made the decision to "go public."

On one hand, I should be happy that the type of sociological practice that has so long preoccupied me is now gaining recognition. What has long been "out" now has a rare invitation to attend the party within American sociology that has not been particularly accommodating to changing its ways. Most certainly, individual sociologists have been at the forefront of many progressive issues, yet they do not constitute the center of the discipline of American sociology. On the other hand, I question whether this new visibility for public sociology is inherently good for practitioners of public sociology as well as for public sociology itself. What are the potential challenges that accompany Burawoy's gutsy move?

What's in a Name?

One challenge facing public sociology concerns the way in which naming it will help or hurt its practitioners. Is naming public sociology inherently a good thing? Most people assume that institutionalizing public sociology will be a good thing. Naming public sociology should help legitimate it within the discipline. Perhaps. Yet, as mental patients, runaway slaves, runaway brides, and prisoners remind us, institutionalization need not be good for everyone. It all depends on where you stand. Once a set of practices is named and thereby placed in a classificatory cell within an institution, these practices can become even more difficult to do. In this spirit, I wonder how discussions about public sociology will assist sociologists who currently practice public sociology? We assume that naming will elevate the status of current practitioners, but it may instead install a permanent and recognizable underclass that now carries the stigmatized name of "public sociology." Stated differently, will doing public sociology emerge as a new form of tracking within the discipline?

As an ideal type, public sociology seems glamorous. Yet, who actually does this kind of sociology? Current practitioners of public sociology are typically not housed in premier institutions, nor do many of them come from privileged groups. I suggest that individuals who are most likely to commit to public sociology have had experiences that provide them with a distinctive view of social inequality. African Americans; Latinos; new immigrant groups; women; working-class and poor people; gay, lesbian, bisexual, and transgendered (LGBT) people; and others who remain penalized within American society and their allies may gravitate toward a sociology that promises to address social issues that affect the public. If not predisposed before entering sociology, individuals from these groups and their allies may develop a public sociology perspective as a result of their sociological graduate training.

Many graduate students choose sociology because they are attracted to the vision of an until-now-unnamed public sociology that they encounter in their undergraduate classrooms. Most do not enter graduate programs to become professional or policy sociologists. For many, graduate training resembles a shell game—they look under one shell for the public sociology prize that they anticipated; yet when they pick up the shell, nothing is there. The real prizes, they are told, lie under the remaining three shells of professional, policy, and to a lesser extent, critical sociology. They are pressured to choose among types of sociology and to leave behind the idealism of public sociology and/or the "you'll never get a job if you keep that up" stance of critical sociology. Fortunately, my graduate training differed. I was encouraged to be an independent thinker, and I took my professors at their word. My own path within sociology certainly reflects this predisposition to focus on the recursive relationship between doing and naming.

I often wonder how I managed to carve a path for myself by doing a sociology that had no name. For me, this is not a new question, but rather one that has shaped my entire career. For me, being an African American woman in overwhelmingly white and male settings, as well as being raised in a working-class environment in situations that routinely privilege the cultural (and actual) capital of middle-class families, has been frustrating, yet immensely helpful. I am used to not belonging, to being stared at as the one who must introduce myself to yet another sociological clique at the ASA in order to put my colleagues at ease. Because I belong to groups that garner less value within American society, I hold ideas about democracy, social justice, colorblindness, feminism, and a long list of ideas and social practices that differ from those of the mainstream. I stand in a different relationship to power relations, and as a result, I hold a distinctive standpoint on those relations. Being committed to principles that are larger than myself has not been easy. I am the one who has been denied jobs for which I am qualified because I do not do the kind of sociology that is valued. Doing public sociology can make you strong, or it can kill you. Would naming the kind of sociology that I have been doing have made these struggles any easier?

Perhaps. Yet, at the same time, being classified under the banner of public sociology may foster a kind of sociological ghettoization, primarily because those who gravitate toward public sociology may already hold subordinate status within the discipline itself. Public sociology can thus become a convenient tool for getting African Americans, Latinos, women, community college teachers, and the like to do the service work of the profession, this time not just spreading sociology's mission to students or serving on endless committees because their "perspective" should be represented, but also by explaining sociology to multiple publics. In this endeavor, would time remain to "do" public sociology in its most robust form? Or would a legitimated public sociology be reduced to a service arm of the discipline, with the "real" sociology of professional sociology still holding sway? Is public sociology a "sociology of and for the Others," namely, all those people who cannot make it within other, ideal types of sociology? If so, then the irony of having those who have struggled so mightily to become sociologists serve as the public face of sociology, with the sociological center remaining intact, becomes especially poignant.

Beyond this issue of how legitimating public sociology via naming it might not necessarily help its current practitioners, the act of naming might also shift the very mission of this kind of sociology. I envision the spirit of public sociology as resembling historian Robin D. G. Kelley's notion of a "radical imagination;" the tenets of "magical realism" invoked by Lani Guinier and Gerald Torres as part of their project to transcend the limits of current thinking about race and democracy; or even sociology's own C. Wright Mills' clarion call for a new "sociological imagination." In my own work, I draw on these ideas via the concept of visionary pragmatism within Black women's oppositional knowledge, a creative tension that links visions for a better society and pragmatic strategies for how to bring it about.

Public sociology resembles these activities. It is a constellation of oppositional knowledge and practices. If American society were just and fair, if the American public were fed, clothed, housed, educated, employed, and healthy, there would be no need for public sociology. Its very existence speaks to the need to *oppose* social injustice, yet also to be proactive in creating a democratic and just public sphere. Naming public sociology strives to enhance the stature of these oppositional knowledge and practices by carving out spaces within the boundaries of an established discipline in ways that legitimate the public sociology that already exists and perhaps catalyze more. Naming aspires to redefine public sociology as no longer being a subordinated, submerged way of doing sociology, but rather seeks to elevate its stature.

Yet, in the American context, making the shift from outsider to insider knowledge may change the ethos of public sociology. Ironically, despite good intentions, naming public sociology may step on existing landmines of defining the purpose and practices of oppositional knowledge as well as the social location of insiders and outsiders who produce such knowledge. Naming public sociology and thereby opening the doors to the valid question of defining its distinguishing features can catalyze endless debates about boundary making. A subtle shift can easily be made from the doing of an unnamed, messy, and thus incorrigible public sociology to talking about public sociology in ways that shrink its possibilities. Public sociology can easily become yet another fad, a nugget of commodified knowledge that privileged sociologists can play at, just as a cat toys with a mouse. What comforting procrastination—one remains ethically honorable by paying lip service to public sociology while never having to take a stand by actually doing it. I can see it now—legions of dissertations analyzing the contributions and failures of public sociology versus dissertations that *do* public sociology. Better yet, what would the "Introduction to Public Sociology" course look like? Which sociological worthies would make the cut to become the required reading list, and which would be left outside to stare at a closed door?

What's in *This* Name?

Another challenge confronting public sociology concerns its chosen name. Is this a good time for the discipline of sociology to claim the term "public"? Is this the best name for this work, even as we persist in doing it? After more than two decades of sustained assault on public institutions in the United States, throwing in one's lot with the sinking ship of anything "public" may seem suicidal. Let's just paint a big target on sociology, some professional and policy sociologists could argue; sociology will become viewed as a field for losers.

In the United States, the privatization of public power seems ubiquitous. In the 1980s and 1990s, social policies dramatically reconfigured the meaning of "public" generally and defined the social welfare state as the quintessential public institution. Current efforts to privatize hospitals, sanitation services, schools, and other public services, and attempts to develop a more private-sector, entrepreneurial spirit in others by underfunding them—public radio, public television, subcontracting specific services via competitive bidding—illustrate this abandonment and derogation of anything public. Deteriorating schools, health care services, roads, bridges, and public transportation, resulting from public failure to fund public institutions, speaks to the erosion and accompanying devaluation of anything deemed "public." In this context, public becomes reconfigured as anything of poor quality, marked by a lack of control and privacy—all characteristics associated with poverty. This slippage between lack of privacy, poor quality, and poverty all affect the changing meaning of "public."

Much of this push toward privatization in the United States has covert yet powerful racial undertones. When African Americans and Latinos, among others, gained expanded rights, individuals and groups with power increasingly abandoned public institutions. Take, for example, the legacy of the 1954 *Brown* decision that outlawed racial segregation in public education. Thurgood Marshall, Derrick Bell, and other Civil Rights activists had no way to anticipate how a new colorblind racism would effectively stonewall school integration initiatives. The early trickle away from public schools by middle-class white parents, who founded private white academies so that their children need not attend racially integrated public schools, opened the floodgates of white flight from public institutions of all sorts. Public schools, public health, public transportation, and public libraries are all now devalued in the face of market-based policies that say, "Privatization will shield you from rubbing elbows with the public." These new social relations signal a distinct reversal—the public sphere becomes a curiously confined, yet visible location that increases the value of private services and privacy itself. Public places become devalued spaces containing Latinos, poor people, African Americans, the homeless, and anyone else who cannot afford to escape. In this context, privacy signals safety; control over one's home, family, and community space; and racial homogeneity—all qualities that can be purchased if one can afford it. This version of privatization dovetails with Guinier and Torres' notion of the privatization of power. If private spaces are better, then shouldn't private entities run the public itself?

In this political context, naming this sociology "public" sociology inherits this history and these social issues. What does it mean for sociology to claim to be for and about the public at this historic moment? Will this be perceived as sociology for the dispossessed, the displaced, and the disadvantaged? Despite Burawoy's efforts to generate much-needed dialogue that is designed to reinvigorate sociology, I suspect that those currently privileged within professional, critical, and/or policy sociology will express far less enthusiasm for an increased emphasis on public sociology than the internal integrity of doing public sociology might suggest. Following public sociology into the realm of the public raises too many uncomfortable questions about the discipline of sociology's merit, value, and purpose within contemporary American society. Currently, the term "public" invokes neither populist nor democratic sensibilities. Rather, it means "popular" (as in popular versus high culture), and more ominously, "inferior." Let the diverse public in and your discipline suffers. Let public sociology in and your scholarship deteriorates. Is sociology ready for that?

I certainly hope so. The social justice sensibilities of public sociology constitute one of its defining features. Caring about the public, seeing all of the others not as devalued entities that one must "mentor" or "help," but rather as potential partners for the betterment of society itself provides a core vision or ethos for this kind of work. People want ideas that matter both to them and within society itself. Public sociology suggests a recursive relationship between those inside the profession and people who are engaged in efforts to understand and challenge prevailing social inequalities that now characterize an increasingly devalued public. In this regard, if public sociology is unprepared to jump into the controversies that surround the term "public," then this may not be the best name for it.

Can We All Get Along?

A third distinctive challenge confronts public sociology in the United States. Now that public sociology has a name, when it comes to its relationship with professional, critical, and policy sociology, I wonder, can we all get along? American sociologists familiar with the circumstances that catalyzed the 1992 riots in Los Angeles might remember these words from motorist Rodney King, whose videotaped beating by members of the Los Angeles police department was shown around the world. It also catalyzed several days of rioting, during which Angelenos burned down entire city blocks because they couldn't envision living in Los Angeles the way that it was. The media loved to broadcast King's query, "Can we all get along?" His plea reified American assumptions that talking things through will yield a fair solution for everyone, that better evidence yields stronger public policy, and that if we just put our heads together and let rational minds prevail, we should be able to solve this mess.

However, can it ever be this simple? I have great difficulty imagining a mahogany conference table with representatives of the Los Angeles police force; African American, Latino, and Korean grassroots community groups; mayoral staff; the Los Angeles chamber of commerce; church folks; representatives of the Justice for Janitors and Bus Riders unions; and other members of the Los Angeles community putting aside their differences with an "oops, let's try this again" mentality. Most of us would recognize that the historical power relations in Los Angeles that created many of these groups in the first place make such a scenario unbelievable. The groups themselves are involved in a continually shifting mosaic of hierarchical relationships with one another—sometimes they operate as friends, other times as enemies, and they often have little knowledge of what the others are actually doing. Despite my incredulity about such a meeting, if it did occur, at least the people present would recognize that the knowledge that they brought to the table grew directly from the power relations that got them there. They would know that they could not achieve a new vision for Los Angeles without taking power differentials among them into account, let alone power differentials affecting those segments of the public that did not get invited to the meeting.

I wonder whether sociologists would have the same sensibility, if they even saw the need for such a meeting in the first place. Burawoy's four-cell typology gives the impression of parallelism among professional, policy, critical, and public sociology, yet it is important to reiterate that Burawoy proposes a Weberian *ideal type* framework. These four types have never been nor are they expected to be equal to one another. Therein lies the problem. Unless sociology itself expands (the old Reagan policy of creating a bigger pie so that newcomers like public sociology can cut a piece), creating space for public sociology means taking away from the space of the other three types. Will they move over to make room at the mahogany table? Or do professional, policy, and critical sociology see public sociology as the interloper in a game of musical chairs—because they occupied the three subdisciplinary seats when the music stopped, poor public sociology is left permanently standing.

This is the rub—in the U.S. context in the post–World War II period, professional and policy sociology have exercised imperial authority within American sociology in ways that obscure public sociology. One would think that critical sociology resists these impulses, but when it comes to the privatization of power, practitioners of critical sociology promise more than they deliver. Critical sociology often talks a good game, yet when it comes to the types of institutional change required to let in sufficient numbers of the unruly public, the intellectual blinders of many progressive sociologists keep them from delivering the goods. For example, the ideas of colorblindness and gender neutrality that underpin conservative agendas of the Right seem eerily similar to arguments on the Left. Longing for a progressive, class-based political agenda that supposedly addresses racism and sexism, some Leftist thinkers view race- and gender-based identity politics as undermining the integrity of class analyses. This failure to engage race and gender as deeply intertwined with social class limits critical sociology's contributions as a vibrant force within American society.

As the sociological pie shrinks, in large part because the demonization of the public outside sociology occurs via race- and gender-based bashing of large segments of the American population, fighting over crumbs within the discipline mimics behaviors that are as American as apple pie. Professional and policy sociology have well-established constituencies and do make important contributions. Critical sociology may have long contested the ideas of professional and policy sociology, yet it too has its well-established constituencies that can be just as resistant to a fully actualized public sociology as its well-heeled counterparts. Why should any of these three ideal sociological types cede territory to the upstart of public sociology, especially one that may contain disproportionate numbers of less desirable people? Given the derogation of anything public in the American setting, public sociology faces an uphill battle in finding its place at the sociological table.

Why Do Public Sociology?

Given these challenges, why would anyone willingly choose public sociology? When I share Michael Burawoy's typology of professional, policy, critical, and public sociology as four ideal types of sociology with some of my students, or even simply summarized its ideas, their eyes light up. There's the "aha" factor at work—"Public sociology is the kind of sociology we want to do," they proclaim. They resonate with the name "public sociology." Wishing to belong to something bigger than themselves, they know implicitly that doing public sociology constitutes intellectual labor placed in service to broader, ethical principles. They are drawn to the concept of a reenergized public where every individual truly does count. By positioning itself in solidarity with ethical principles of democracy, fairness, and social justice, public sociology seemingly offers a path away from provincial careerism and back toward the sociological imaginations that many students felt that they needed to check at the graduate school door.

Yet the inevitable questions that come next speak to their practical concerns. "Where do I go to study it? Do the top sociology programs offer a degree in it? Can I get a job doing it?" they query. Moving quickly through the preliminaries and honing in on the promises of mentoring and role modeling, they shift to the next set of questions. "How did you come to do public sociology?" they ask. "You appear to be successful. Can you teach me how to become a public sociologist?"

I don't fault the students. Their questions stem from the disjuncture between one set of promises within American sociology to place the tools of sociology in service to solving social problems and actual sociological practices that must pay attention to the challenges of paying bills. Unlike students of the past, contemporary students are much more cognizant of the fact that the bill will come due one day. So they feel pressured to choose wisely. Professional and policy sociology may position them to better pay off their student loans—what can critical sociology deliver, or worse yet, public sociology? They confront the contradiction of wishing to garner the moral capital of supporting social justice initiatives without taking personal risks such as having articles rejected from top journals or being denied their dream job. Can one truly work for social justice from the comfort of a cushy job and a tenured future? Derrick Bell labels this impetus "ethical ambition" and offers reassurances to his readers that it is possible to be ethical and successful at the same time. I sincerely hope that he is right, but I also know that the vast majority of people who actually do public sociology receive few perks and even less praise.

I suspect that people work at public sociology for very much the same reasons that some individuals become dancers, actresses, singers, painters, or poets—training for their craft may be part of their passion, but they would find a way to dance, act, sing, paint, or write even if no one paid them. The ardor of artists provides a template for the passion for social justice that many sociologists bring to their intellectual work. American pragmatism and its grand entrepreneurial spirit strive to stamp out this passion for justice, raising the question of whether there is even any room for public sociology sensibilities within American sociology. Yet, visitors from other national sociological traditions at the 2004 ASA meeting on Public Sociology remind us that public sociology not only exists but also holds a much larger place in their sociological vision than in the United States. It may be more difficult to see public sociology here, in the center of a major world power, but the stakes are too high not to.

When I look back and try to map my involvement in public sociology, I realize that, like love, I found it in unlikely places. For example, I love social theory—no secret there. But in hindsight, I recognize that the reason why I so appreciated early sociological theorists is because they all seemed to be doing public sociology, or at least, that is the way I was introduced to their work. Despite our current efforts to objectify, deify, freeze, and squeeze Marx, Weber, Simmel, Durkheim, Du Bois, and other classical social theorists into ossified boxes of their "most important contributions that you will need to know in order to get a job," I read the works of these theorists as public sociology. I remain inspired by their commitment to bringing the tools of sociology to bear on the important issues of their time. The public need not have been their direct audience—given literacy rates of the late nineteenth and early twentieth centuries, few could read their work—yet so much of what they did was on behalf of bettering the public. They talked to one another because they wanted to understand and better society.

Contemporary American sociology has moved away from this kind of energy and excitement. Yet, because public sociology demands that we consider the major issues of the day and that we bring tools of sociological analysis and empirical research to bear on them, it promises to breathe new life into sociological theory as well as the discipline overall. Despite the challenges facing public sociology as well as the difficulties that I have encountered in my career doing it, I would choose it all over again. At this point in my career, what we call it matters less to me than knowing that I am not alone in choosing this path.

ADDITIONAL RESOURCES

Bell, Derrick. 2002. *Ethical Ambition: Living a Life of Meaning and Worth.* New York: Bloomsbury.

Guinier, Lani, and Gerald Torres. 2002. *The Miner's Canary: Enlisting Race, Resisting Power, Transforming Democracy.* Cambridge, Mass.: Harvard University Press.

Kelley, Robin D. G. 2002. *Freedom Dreams: The Black Radical Imagination.* Boston: Beacon.

Mills, C. Wright. 1959. *The Sociological Imagination.* New York: Oxford University Press.

8

Changing Times

Sociological Complexities

REFLEXIVE ESSAY: *From 2005 to 2010, I developed and taught a graduate seminar on "Sociology of Knowledge" at the University of Maryland–
College Park. Each time that I taught my course, I learned something
new from my students about the importance of knowledge to contemporary power relations. Our topics ranged from classical work in the field,
to the expansive coverage of science as a form of knowledge, to the theme
of decolonizing knowledge as part of postcolonialism, to the emergence
of the Internet as a form of knowledge. In selecting essays for On Intellectual Activism, I rediscovered this earlier essay, where I examined the
social construction of knowledge within sociology.*

A FEW YEARS BACK, a colleague and I struck up a conversation at the
book exhibit at an American Sociological Association annual meeting.
Looking guiltily at the vast numbers of new books, we confessed our
respective alarm at the exponentially growing list of sociology books. My colleague was especially concerned with the increasing number of books on social
theory. "How can I possibly read it all?" he bemoaned. "When I started teaching social theory in the early 1960s, we read Parsons and not much else. I could
cover it all in a semester. But now . . ." As his voice trailed off, I realized that we
were unlikely ever to read all the books in our specializations, let alone sociology as a discipline. There were just too many.

That book exhibit was a bittersweet experience—both unsettling and won-
drous. Our conversation in the middle of tangible evidence of U.S. sociology's
knowledge explosion spoke to the erosion of old centers of all sorts. Formerly,
everything of importance was classified, categorized, and assigned its own place

in space and time. Just as books in the library have only one place, libraries as repositories of Western knowledge assigned one number to each book. Books positioned near one another shared the same disciplinary neighborhood, with thematic differences distinguishing one book family from the next. Within this logic, sociology functioned as one section of an enormous library of categorized, symbolic space. Membership had its privileges. Access to the timeless traditions of sociology as a discipline distinguished those who belonged from everyone else. Things were peaceful then—or so goes conventional wisdom.

Lately, nostalgia for the golden years of U.S. sociology reappears in a surprising number of places. Senior sociologists in particular seem especially concerned that sociology as a discipline has lost its way. Because sociologists no longer have an agreed on set of books of required reading, some feel uprooted and anchorless. During the golden years of sociology, just as all books had their place, so did the sociologists who read them. Being familiar with a sociological canon, with its agreed on set of "classics," marked the boundaries of the field.

I wonder, however, exactly when these imagined golden years of U.S. sociology actually occurred. Certainly not during its early-twentieth-century founding decades, when sociology's future was far from settled. As a young, energetic, and often unruly field, sociology took on important questions and believed that it could make a difference in answering them. Articles published during the *American Journal of Sociology*'s early decades, for example, reveal a vibrancy that mystifies contemporary sociology's specialization and subfield sensibilities. There one finds articles written by social reformer Jane Addams, eugenicist Frances Galton, and others who not only disagreed with one another but who, by contemporary standards, also may not have been seen as sociologists at all. These fuzzy borders distinguishing sociological insiders and outsiders catalyzed similarly diverse subject matter. Industrialization, eugenics, imperialism, immigration, the so-called race problem, working women, urbanization, and the "savage mind" rubbed against one another. Authors took distinctive positions, yet, because they often knew one another, their proximity to one another generated debate. In this core journal of the emerging discipline, a diversity of questions, methods, and analyses was on public display.

The early twentieth century engaged its material of the social world. Its internal energy simultaneously reflected, manufactured, and challenged broader social concerns. The times themselves were in flux—a maturing imperialism that carved the world up into colonial empires ruled by a handful of nation-states provided a political organization that worked well with global capitalism. Structural changes of this magnitude created new questions, providing exciting material for a fledgling discipline.

I suspect that these early-twentieth-century decades are not the longed-for golden years. Because few people are now alive who lived through those founding years, we recreate those years as myth, not memory. Instead, the imagined golden years are those that can be remembered, often as myth. Reflecting the ascendency of Parsonian social theory and big science funding within U.S.

sociology, the post–World War II years of the 1940s through the early 1960s fit this profile. Sociology as a science came of age during these decades. Despite major social changes outside its borders, sociology's daily life moved toward science. Unlike the boisterous beginning of U.S. sociology, those years marked a mature, peaceful, seemingly homogeneous sociology. Sociologists were equally homogeneous. Because women, African Americans, Latinos, and sexual minorities were rare, the field could define itself as an imagined community unlike no other.

Those who are nostalgic for sociology's pastoral history may be mourning the passing of equally imagined familial relationships of normal sociology. Just as family members share some sort of unspoken affiliation with one another via blood ties, the sociological brotherhood (with selected wives and honorary sisters), for many, may have represented a comfortable, disciplinary "home." Within the boundaries of the discipline, sociologists typically accepted, without complaint, their assigned places in what appeared to be a naturalized sociological hierarchy. The senior socialized the junior; sociological fathers as male mothers mentored their sociological sons. Most members of the profession accepted these relationships because one day the junior would become senior. Membership had its privileges. C. Wright Mills may have railed against mainstream sociology's trajectory in works such as *The Sociological Imagination* and *The Power Elite*, and patterns of faculty promotion and publication in the so-called top journals reflected the wisdom of sociological insiders. Getting a job at an elite school, such as Mills' at Columbia, often rested on a handshake and who you knew.

Just as contemporary gangs wear colors as insignia that distinguish members from outsiders—red for Bloods and blue for Crips—disciplinary insignia that distinguished sociologists from anthropologists, and anthropologists from biologists, was less tangible but no less real. Similar to the 1885 gentlemen's agreement engaged in by European powers, who carved up the globe to avoid engaging in warfare against one another and to ensure a more efficient way of rule for all, academic disciplines had long ago colonized knowledge. In the United States, anthropology claimed foreign cultures and societies, political science planted its flag on government, economics hoarded business, psychology demanded the individual psyche, and sociology preoccupied itself with the functions of social structures. Just as each family is distinct among other families, sociology was distinct among disciplines. Sociology claimed areas of knowledge and research methodologies for itself. To belong to the sociological community, one had to learn that knowledge (typically, the canon of sociological theory) and master those methodologies (statistics as baptism by fire). Like nation-states that themselves set the stage for disciplines, sociology had self-contained borders and a constellation of citizens who imagined themselves as part of a community known as "sociology."

The borders were clearly demarcated among disciplines, and communities of practitioners within them were fairly clear-cut. Everyone and everything has an assigned place in geographic, political, economic, and symbolic space, yet border skirmishes did occur. Disciplinary borders were not as firm as everyone would have liked. Social psychologists, for example, never relinquished their position of straddling the borders of two disciplines, while a renegade sociologist occasionally wandered into the terrain of either political science or neoclassical economics with the taboo question, "Whatever happened to Marxism?" Despite these border skirmishes, the disciplines remained distinct from one another. Within this context, little need existed for defining identities of all sorts, including sociological ones. A smaller community of practitioners held smaller meetings and wrote fewer books. People were much more likely to know one another, and everyone knew what to read. There was no need to question sociological identity. As long as everyone left everyone else's intellectual, disciplinary, and professional turf alone—no matter how unequal or unjust the outcomes—peace ensued.

Peace without justice constitutes an illusion. No matter how we might feel about the passing of this vision of sociology, those days are over. The process of rebuilding Europe in the aftermath of World War II, global struggles for decolonization, and the rise of the Civil Rights and feminist movements within the United States disrupted the mistaking of quiescence for peace. Sociology's taken-for-granted assumptions of the parallels among conceptions of family and community, the organization of sociological knowledge and professional practices, and sociology's disciplinary identity crumbled. Sociology is no longer small, and it certainly is not homogeneous if, in fact, it ever was. Moreover, the logic that created the certainties of family, neighborhood, academic disciplines, and nations has eroded. As Zygmunt Bauman argued in his 1997 plenary address at the British Sociological Association's annual meeting, not only have self-contained borders collapsed but globalization has also wrought entirely new meanings of time and space. In the colonial era, physical and symbolic space (truth) were seen as finite and could be carved up, as I described earlier. Similarly, time was quantifiable, linear, and organized via the familiar trope of progress. Within the global politics of race, class, and gender, meanings of time and space have changed.

For the rich, time accelerates and the constraints of space disappear. Time is scarce, meted out, with increasingly blurry boundaries between work and leisure. Computers, telecommunications, and popular culture permit one simultaneously to work, play, and leave home without actually going anywhere. Advances in transportation allow those with resources to travel freely from place to place. Despite their longing for something new, these jet-setters want the familiar wherever they happen to be. The result—all Marriotts should resemble one another.

For the poor, suggests Bauman, time and space stand still. Unemployed and without a future, they mark time and kill time before it kills them. Contained in the crowded spaces of public housing, urban ghettos, and overcrowded schools, they exist in real places of resource scarcity, with nowhere to go. Some people migrate, trying to escape to places with more opportunity. But when they leave home in order to send money home, they realize that they can never go home again. They are changed by their journey and the homes they left have also been changed by time and circumstance. Literally and figuratively, home has disappeared.

For rich and poor alike, grappling with the shifting time and space relationships of globalization requires reorganizing boundaries, especially nation-state borders. Whereas global capital during sociology's founding decades required strong nation-states, ensuring the free movement of global capital and displaced populations needs weak nation-states.

These reconfigured social hierarchies within shifting time and space relationships present a real challenge for contemporary sociology. The disruption that changes of this magnitude create in people's everyday lives resembles those generated by the major global changes that were studied by a fledgling early-twentieth-century U.S. sociology. Is contemporary sociology equipped to confront these new challenges? In the context of a vastly different social, political, economic, and intellectual world that exists not just outside sociology, but within it, self-contained families, neighborhoods, races, even academic disciplines seem to be relics of the past. Wringing one's hands about how other disciplines are stealing sociology's thunder certainly represents one response to these changes. Many sociologists complain that gerontology, cultural studies, women's studies, media studies, business schools, colleges of education, and similar interdisciplinary and applied fields have poached sociological property. They've taken the best students, grant money, faculty lines, methodologies, and sociological subfields (survey research and organizational sociology come to mind) without giving sociology credit. Given the logic of sociological self-definitions, where people and ideas belong either to one discipline or to another, people either are sociologists or they are not, the both/and ethos of interdisciplinarity can feel chaotic. However, other alternatives exist.

For too long, sociology has defined itself either by what it's not—we're not like those "soft" humanities areas—or by what it would like to be—we're like physics and chemistry, and other "hard," or "real," sciences. This self-definition has always seemed odd to me because it enables sociology to avoid standing on its merits. I was initially drawn to sociology in part by its flexibility. I saw sociology as a field that maintained a creative tension among the diverse theoretical and empirical approaches within its borders, with an eye toward investigating important social questions. Then, as now, I liked the combination of the spirit of early sociology in going after difficult questions combined with the theoretical and methodological sophistication of sociology as a mature discipline. While specific content areas, theoretical perspectives, and methodological approaches certainly have experienced ebbs and flows, the strength of sociology lies in its resiliency.

In a sense, sociology constitutes a border discipline between the humanities and the social and physical sciences. Some purists may be horrified by my use of these terms, yet in hindsight, sociology to me resembles what is now valorized as hybrid, mulatto, *mestizo, métissage,* and in my own work, outsider-within theorizing. These terms describe this space of defining and then violating the borders between ostensibly pure spaces of all sorts. Theoretically, sociology's flexibility enables the field to accommodate a range of theoretical perspectives within its borders without losing its center. The fact that it now contains a larger and more heterogeneous constellation of practitioners and ideas than in the past is less a hindrance than a strength for its future.

Rather than rejecting sociology's position as a border discipline as a weakness—sociology is neither pure science nor pure humanities—the flexibility of sociology's structural and intellectual organization may better equip the field for the challenges of the twenty-first century. On one hand, sociology constitutes a science of the social that creates intriguing possibilities for rethinking the types of social issues raised by Bauman and others. I still see the need for analyses of social phenomena that transcend the offerings of the humanities, the traditional physical and natural sciences, and past definitions of the social sciences. Valorizing individual narrative and human subjectivity to the point of erasing social structure, a position exemplified by extreme postmodernism, seems awfully dangerous. How can we examine and solve social problems, such as poverty, hunger, homelessness, environmental degradation, and the spread of HIV/AIDS, without analyzing social structures? Paradigmatic approaches to social phenomena embraced by the physical and natural sciences seem strangely devoid of human agency. For example, neither the machine model of social organization from nineteenth-century physics nor the society as organism model of biological sciences that has inordinate influence on sociology's own structural/functionalism seems able to explain contemporary phenomena. Physics and biology have moved on, and so should sociology.

On the other hand, and more importantly, sociology's flexibility may help clarify new definitions of what counts as science. What does it mean to be a *social* scientist in ways that go beyond former paradigms advanced within the natural sciences? Sociology's unique social location as a contested space of knowledge construction allows it to think through new ways of doing science. Even those sociologists whose work is most influenced by postmodern social theory are, in some sense, social scientists. I cannot imagine why anyone would be a sociologist without appreciating the possibilities of the science of sociology in addressing important social issues. What first intrigued me was how, despite their varying approaches, all of the now classical sociologists grappled with important social issues of their time and thought that they could craft sociology as a science of society in doing so. Weber, Marx, Durkheim, Simmel, and Du Bois, among many, analyzed how sociology as a science could shed light on capitalism, industrialization, and imperialism as macro-sociological phenomena. The issues that concerned the sociological "founding fathers" varied, but the basic mission was the same. Social issues and science were inextricably linked because the tools of science fostered new understandings of the social. A science of society was not only possible but also necessary.

Given this history, why would sociology back off from its flexible organization, its heritage as a science, or its commitment to grappling with important social issues? Just as society has changed, so must sociology as a social science in exploring it. There is no lack of social issues—take your pick—the next millennium provides new variations on some very old problems. I think the real task lies in moving sociology closer to new areas of inquiry across the social, physical, and natural sciences. The science that everyone imagines science to be—the Newtonian physics from which early sociology gained inspiration—is useful for certain sorts of problems and not others. In other words, there is no one overarching scientific method reminiscent of what I learned in seventh-grade science class that stands in proxy for Western science writ large.

New directions in the sciences, broadly defined, demonstrate an increasing commitment to the concept of complexity that might prove extremely useful in crafting sociological self-definitions. This new science that explores complexity is much more humble than the science of conquest associated with linear time and colonial space. As a science of order, traditional science was especially well suited to the social goals of nineteenth-century imperialism, namely, prediction for purposes of control. It reduced complexities or differences by suppressing them or explaining them away. It was a sociology of studying centers and explaining away dissent as outliers. In contrast, a sociology as science developed within assumptions of complexity would resist reducing intricate social phenomena to their most basic and essential elements. Recognizing the complexity of the social as subject matter, such a science would aim to understand apparent disorder and chaos, not by reducing complexities, but by embracing them. Stated differently, trying to order the messiness of differences by assigning them neat, categorical boxes arrayed in proper order would be increasingly replaced by new conceptual and methodological tools dedicated to understanding complexities.

Some areas of sociology are already moving in this direction. Take, for example, the area of race, class, and gender studies and its emerging paradigm of intersectionality. In the 1990s, some theorists and practitioners within the subfields of race, class, and gender, respectively, came to recognize that the logic of segregated intellectual spaces that characterized their respective areas left them virtually oblivious to developments in other areas. Moreover, working exclusively within the confines of their subdisciplines left them increasingly unable to explain complex social phenomena. This growing recognition that the complex social issues that they wanted to study could not be accommodated within singular frameworks of either race *or* class *or* gender sparked interest in exploring the intersections among these areas. Examining how racial meaning is constructed in gendered terms and how gender shapes class formations allows a complex web of understandings and social relationships to emerge. Moreover, this emerging paradigm of intersectionality moves beyond race, class, and gender to encompass additional categories, such as nation, sexuality, ethnicity, age, and religion.

I see race, class, and gender studies as being much more closely aligned with emerging emphases on complexity in the physical sciences than its current classification within sociology as being on the margins of "real" science. Many scholars persist in seeing race, class, and gender primarily as identity categories, and the issues raised by scholars working in these areas as reflecting some particularistic and therefore unscientific (nonuniversal) agenda. However, this interpretation seriously misreads the theoretical and methodological potential of the richness of examining the relationships among these fields. The increasing interest in the complex relationships among race, class, and gender as intersectional categories of analysis represents a significant, albeit basic step toward developing a complex social science. Such a science requires that we learn to think across separate categories of all sorts, examining not how they differ from one another, but their connectedness and relationality.

I share my colleague's dismay at not being able to read all of sociology's new books, yet I reject his pessimism that this represents the downfall of sociology. Instead, I see sociology's disciplinary location as well as the intellectual diversity within sociology as holding the potential for a different type of excellence. Such excellence would emerge from the heterogeneity of sociological practitioners and ideas within a sociology that itself occupies a border space. Its goal would be to develop sociology as science adequate for dealing with complexities. Instead of defining "excellence" in the former terms of homogeneity and exclusivity, such excellence emerges from creating new ways to handle complexities both within and outside of sociological borders. Within this new way of thinking and being, it becomes neither possible nor desirable to believe that any one individual can read all of the books. Instead, each of us must continue to specialize, read what we can, but realize that, for each of us to do intellectual work, we must nurture relational structures for sharing ideas. Sociology cannot continue unless we all pull together differently. For now, I'll read my books, you read yours, and someday we really must talk.

ADDITIONAL RESOURCES

Bauman, Zygmunt. 1998. *Globalization: The Human Consequences*. New York: Columbia University Press.

Feagin, Joe R., and Hernan Vera. 2001. *Liberation Sociology*. Boulder, Colo.: Westview Press.

Lemert, Charles. 1995. *Sociology after the Crisis*. Boulder, Colo.: Westview Press.

Mulkay, Michael. 1991. *Sociology of Science: A Sociological Pilgrimage*. Bloomington: Indiana University Press.

Weber, Lynn. 1998. "A Conceptual Framework for Understanding Race, Class, Gender, and Sexuality." *Psychology of Women Quarterly* 22:13–32.

The Racial Threat

REFLEXIVE ESSAY: *I include this short piece that was published as part of a 2006* British Journal of Sociology *symposium devoted to Bryan Turner's article "British Sociology and Public Intellectuals: Consumer Society and Imperial Decline." Turner's article analyzed the effects of post-9/11 social phenomena on British sociology. Three points were especially salient: (1) British social science has depended heavily on the migration of intellectuals, especially Jewish intellectuals who were refugees from fascism; (2) intellectual innovation requires massive, disruptive, violent change; and (3) British sociology reflects a distinctive tradition advanced by public intellectuals whose social criticism examines the constraining and divisive impact of social class, race, and gender in the context of expanding social citizenship. Turner was optimistic that, stimulated by the new threats of the post-9/11 world, public intellectuals would produce innovative sociology. I examine here how a similar set of links between marginal intellectuals, critical thought, and public sociology might work within U.S. racial politics.*

TURNER OFFERS a provocative argument, namely, that times of massive, disruptive, and violent change have often catalyzed great sociology, in part because the issues raised are so compelling, and in part because intellectuals who are directly affected are more likely to address them. The stock story of the founding of sociology, when Marx, Weber, and Durkheim analyzed the many social issues associated with rapid industrialization, seem-

---

This piece was first published in 2006 in *The British Journal of Sociology* 57(2):169–188. Bryan Turner's article is in the same volume.

ingly follows this pattern. Building his compelling history of post–World War II British sociology on a similar conceptual scaffold, Turner suggests that during this period of massive change, many UK intellectuals found themselves with theories that did not fit the events around them (Zygmunt Bauman's work on the Holocaust), whereas others tried to make sense of the social relations they encountered as new migrants from Britain's former colonies (Stuart Hall's initiatives within British cultural studies). Turner speculates that a similar set of relationships associated with the uncertain post-9/11 present may shape British sociology's future, one where "sociology of security and terrorism will become the next growth area of sociological research and theory."

Maybe this is the case in Britain, yet I wonder how effectively this argument travels to the United States. I agree with Turner that these are indeed scary times, yet I remain less convinced that discrete, albeit tragic, social events, such as the attacks of 9/11, by themselves, will catalyze the type of intellectual virtuosity within American sociology that Turner envisions. Is post-9/11 America all that different than the period that preceded it? Moreover, I question whether American sociologists will generate the kind of innovative intellectual production as that created by the displaced, marginalized, and/or exiled European scholars of the post–World War II period.

First, the terminology of security and terrorism may be new within a British society still grappling with how its seemingly homogeneous national identity has been profoundly disrupted by postcolonial migrations, yet the notion of threats to so-called American security is far from a novel idea within domestic American politics. In particular, the concept of the racial threat, namely, ensuring security for white American citizens from racialized others, remains deeply rooted within American national identity. The United States has long grappled with how to manage its black, native, Asian, and Latino immigrant populations. In essence, powerful groups in the United States have often constructed groups who differ by race, ethnicity, and religion as potential threats to American security and to the profitability of American markets. Inassimilable groups within the borders of the American nation-state pose certain risks—the indigenous folk who refuse to give up their land and their traditional ways, the black people whose ghetto art catalyzed hip hop, and Latino immigrant populations who insist on speaking Spanish and sending money home to their relatives all constitute potential threats to the American way of life until they willingly assimilate. The tragic events of 9/11 expanded the nature of the perceived racial threat from the domestic "others" to a new foreign enemy. Thus, the very concept of threat remains racialized (e.g., the shift from the internal enemy of native peoples, black people, and Latino immigrants to the external threat of Muslim and/or Arab populations, a racialization that hides under the term "terrorist").

In essence, the language of security and threat may sound new, yet the idea of an American public scared out of its wits by stereotypes of difference is not. Keeping the American public ever fearful of the next amorphous threat has characterized domestic and foreign policy for at least the last fifty years. In his classic 1956 book *The Power Elite,* C. Wright Mills points with alarm to growing normalization within American society of a perpetual state of warfare, one that encourages the American public to remain ever-vigilant in response to a nebulous threat. In the 1950s, Mills wrote that the threat was communism, symbolized by the "enemy without" of the Soviet Union and the "enemy within" of stealth communists who could easily be one's next-door neighbor. Removing the rose-colored glasses of an American media that has depicted the 1950s as an extended episode of *Leave It to Beaver* and American sociology's embrace of Parsonian structural-functionalism as the penultimate theoretical framework of that era reveals the stultifying practices of McCarthyism, where Americans were pressured to rat out family members as potential communist sympathizers.

Communism is no longer the external and internal threat. Instead, terrorism is rapidly replacing it. Yet there's one important difference—whereas anyone could potentially be a communist (according to the same kind of generalized threat, anyone could be a Jew or a homosexual), the contemporary terrorist threat carries an anonymous brown or black face. Rather than melting into normal society as "one of us," the terrorist is imagined to be Arab, Muslim, immigrant, foreign, brown, and/or black, a social meaning that only makes sense in the context of American understandings of the racial threat. Thus, when it comes to the U.S. situation, the concepts of security and terrorism are inextricably bound to America's racial past, one that gives meaning to contemporary ideas of risk and security and that continue to drive American public policy. I question whether these really are times of massive and disruptive change in America. Current preoccupations with security may constitute social practices that shift their form, but not their essence.

This brings me to my second concern about the applicability of Turner's claim that the best sociological theory emerges during periods of crisis and that people who are displaced, exiled, and/or marginalized within a crisis are more likely to advance such theory than those who are not. For 100 years, American sociology has managed to coexist with these historical ideas about security that reside in the notion of the racial threat. If contemporary panic about security constitutes American business as usual, only now on an international rather than a domestic stage, then it stands to reason that American sociology can easily borrow from its existing tools of dealing with the racial threat to counter the seemingly new security risks of terrorism. Why would we expect that a new iteration of the racial threat in the form of Muslim terrorists would unsettle standard sociological understandings of racial deviance, criminology, primitivism, socialization, and the like?

I wonder whether there is room for the kind of public intellectual within an American society whose very understanding of security has been refracted through the lens of the racial threat, as well as within an American sociology that has so long been complicit with these ideas. Turner's rendition of the important historical contributions of Jewish immigrants to social theory in the United Kingdom suggests that similarly placed contemporary thinkers might invigorate American sociology. Like Michael Burawoy's call for a revitalized "public sociology," Turner wishes for a rejuvenated tradition of public intellectuals who remain dedicated to thinking through important social issues, engaging democratic publics of civil society, and whose own insecure placement serves as a catalyst for their innovative intellectual production. Following Turner's logic, one would think that black, native, Latino, Muslim, and similar racial/ethnic thinkers would be spearheading the kind of intellectual vanguardism of their Jewish predecessors.

For a variety of possible reasons, one would be hard pressed to find this kind of intellectual leadership within contemporary American sociology and within American society. For one, standard disciplinary practices within American sociology militate against intellectual innovation. Here the British case is illuminating. Turner argues that the "best" sociology (that known for intellectual innovation) is *not* done at major British universities; rather, the area of "cultural studies" has captured the imagination of British students. Turner's observation offers a provocative look at what happens when mature disciplines, like American society overall, require assimilation as the price of citizenship. Within American sociology, the impetus toward institutionalization and establishment of the discipline within the structuralist-functionalist, empiricist traditions of government-funded social science research has taken a toll on critical sociology. In essence, the kind of people who might engage in intellectual innovation may now be less likely to be in sociology at all, and if they are in the field, may not be employed at the "best" institutions. Without the imprimatur of being in a top-tier sociology program at a top-tier institution, their ideas never make it to the sociological forefront. Displaced, exiled, and/or marginalized intellectuals rarely get cushy jobs at big institutions.

In addition, intellectuals often occupy a distinctive niche within American mass media, namely, as media-selected expert spokespersons for a body of knowledge or group of people. Turner suggests that the United Kingdom does not have public intellectuals because "we do not have a social role for them." In the United States, there is a role for intellectuals, yet it is one that will not necessarily foster intellectual innovation. The case of black public intellectuals is suggestive here. In the 1990s, selected black intellectual celebrities commanded substantial media attention concerning issues of race (Cornel West and Henry Louis Gates come to mind), primarily because they helped assuage the American public's fears about African Americans as a racial threat. Whereas these and other black intellectual celebrities may have spoken eloquently on behalf of the displaced, exiled, and/or marginalized, they themselves were not displaced, exiled, and/or marginalized. I do not doubt either the sincerity or the intellectual prowess of these thinkers; rather, media practices that produce black intellectual celebrities militate against the kind of intellectual innovation among African Americans that Turner envisions. Ironically, after 9/11, the media moved on to new forms of racial threat, leaving many of these domestic black thinkers behind.

Turner's essay taught me much about British sociology, yet I remain unconvinced that its thesis of social crisis catalyzing the "best" sociology that is spearheaded by marginal intellectuals applies to contemporary American sociology. There, another story remains to be written, one that, unlike Turner's treatment of race as a peripheral identity category within the pantheon of race, class and gender, sees the concept of the racial threat as fundamental.

ADDITIONAL RESOURCES

Cruse, Harold. 1967. *The Crisis of the Negro Intellectual*. New York: William Morrow.
Gouldner, Alvin. 1970. *The Coming Crisis in Western Sociology*. New York: Avon.

Rethinking Knowledge, Community, and Empowerment

An Interview

REFLEXIVE ESSAY: *An earlier version of this interview was published in* The Griot, *the newsletter of the Association of Black Sociologists. The interview examines general ideas concerning intellectual activism as they apply to this specific organization as well as to Black scholars. I have left the questions intact but have edited many of my answers to clarify my arguments as well as coordinate them with other essays in this volume. I wanted to maintain the flow of the conversation, yet sharpen my presentation of ideas.*

The Griot: Do you think the ASA [American Sociological Association] has been successful in dismantling the barriers [for Black sociologists and other minority scholars] that led originally to the creation of the ABS [Association of Black Sociologists]?

Patricia Hill Collins: One way to approach this question is to recognize that we're in a new racial period of so-called "post-raciality." We need to figure out what post-raciality and colorblindness mean for organizations like ABS. ABS

This interview was conducted via telephone by Philip Kretsedemas, who patiently edited an unruly draft of the original transcript. It was originally published in the February 2010 and June 2010 issues of *The Griot*, http://www.associationofblacksociologists.org/Association_of_Black_Sociologists/Home.html.

was formed during a period of racial segregation that was organized by excluding Black people from the best jobs, schools, neighborhoods, and public space. Organizations that challenged racial segregation did so by developing strategies that demanded inclusion. Anti-racist projects could follow a simple formula that applied to racial, gender, class, and sexual segregation: There are barriers. Remove the barriers, recruit people, and let them in. This political philosophy has characterized anti-racist political activism for the past thirty years and certainly affected the founding ethos of ABS. So if you look at Black people, women, and similar groups that were historically excluded, the battle has been to get them included within schools, jobs, neighborhoods, and all institutions of American society.

In some areas these inclusionary strategies have been more successful than in others. My election as the 100th president of ASA speaks volumes about the changes that occurred throughout ASA over the past twenty years, in part, because ABS actively pursued a strategy of racial inclusion and diversity. Based on the trajectory of past presidents, I was a very unlikely presidential candidate. I didn't come straight through an elite school; I wasn't even working in a sociology department for quite some time, and the substance of my scholarship was not highly valued within elite segments of the profession. Yet my experiences and scholarship are more representative of the diversity of people and perspectives in U.S. sociology. Within the field, many professional associations have also made real strides in including formerly excluded people—SSSP [Society for the Study of Social Problems], the regional associations, ABS, Sociologists for Women in Society [SWS]—many of these organizations, if not all of them, are making concerted efforts to be inclusive and diverse. Sociology's accomplishments parallel those of other professional associations. In 2009, I attended a summit titled "Madam President: Summit on Women of Color, Leadership and the Learned Societies." Representing ASA, I was in good company—the American Studies Association, African Studies Association, American Political Science Association, Organization of American Historians, and the National Women's Studies Association, to name a few, had all elected women of color as presidents.

Programs to increase participation should continue, yet when it comes to professional associations, I don't see the exclusionary practices of ASA or other professional associations as the *primary* problem. Rather, we need to pay more attention to the terms of our participation within the colleges and universities that excluded our parents and grandparents. Inclusion works differently across different organizations. Impacting ASA has been far easier over the past thirty years than changing the policies and procedures of higher education. Feeder schools for college, from elementary schools through high schools, still show a high degree of segregation by race and class. Schooling still performs an important gate-keeping function that excludes talented students of color. If capable Black and Latino students do not attend college and continue disproportionately to drop out of high school, discussions concerning their participation in organizations like ABS are moot. Educational equity is an old issue that now plays out on the new battleground of the illusion of inclusion.

The Griot: I think you may have implicitly answered this question, but what role do you think the ABS could play in this broader process of opening up more space in the institutions themselves?

Patricia Hill Collins: I see it as a two-pronged process, one dealing with knowledge and the other with the power relations that produce knowledge. Organizations like ABS and the Black scholars supporting such organizations can do two things. The first is to work to change knowledge about race. The second is to try to change the patterns of participation in the institutions that produce racial knowledge.

Regarding knowledge, it is important to remember that ABS was not founded to get a few Black people jobs. Instead, it wanted to transform knowledge about race in America initially and about race globally, in ways that empower Black people. Because racial knowledge is very much created in the academy and also in the media, we have to look to other institutional locations if we want to produce the kinds of outcomes that I think ABS wanted initially.

I see the terms of our current inclusion in colleges, universities, and professional associations as being a much greater issue. We certainly should continue to do what we've been doing in our disciplinary associations in terms of the programs that are in place. The success of the ASA's Minority Fellowship Program (MFP) comes to mind. For me, receiving MFP support was vital to my professional success. At the same time, we have to develop new ways of opening doors for one another that guarantee continued participation. Because I have been an insider for some time, I see how my hard-earned insider knowledge shows me different opportunities and options than those who stand outside universities and professional organizations such as ASA. From my current vantage point, I am especially bothered by people who, once they become established, give scant attention to making sure that they provide a path for others to follow.

I think that there are many great up-and-coming young scholars who have new and innovative ideas about race. But they are less heard than people like me. For example, Black sociologists working in community colleges often have a heightened sense of contemporary racial politics. Their daily work with people who are trying to better themselves provides a distinctive angle of vision on how race, class, gender, citizenship status, and sexuality shape their students' prospects for social mobility. Despite this on-the-ground knowledge, it's often far more difficult for front-line workers to be heard. Instead, we return to African American professors at top institutions (regardless of field), who typically know far less about the everyday realities of race and social mobility than their community college counterparts. This example suggests that we need to look at the structures of higher education and realize that certain questions don't even *become* questions because of who is raising them and where they are located.

We need to create new spaces for doing intellectual work on race and racism so that we can get more innovative ideas on the table. If not, we'll continue to recycle old debates that may have outlived their usefulness. ABS could do a real service here by identifying talent in community colleges, state schools, and new media ventures, and making sure that a broad array of ideas can be heard from people who care about fighting racism in their everyday lives, and not just studying it in their scholarship. All around us, students and young professionals point out how they live in a different world than the world of the Civil Rights movement, than the world of the Black Power movement, than just living in the United States. *We* have to come up with another way of analyzing not only how race and racism are organized but also how they can be resisted in a seemingly post-racial society. I would like to see organizations like ABS be on the front end of that. ABS need not turn its back on its traditional advocacy function for its membership. Junior African American scholars will need support for all aspects of their career development. But we need intellectual leadership from the association concerning the big ideas about race and racism in American society. To make those ideas heard, we need to create spaces for our discussions.

The Griot: I would definitely second that. There are many ways you could go about it, but it seems to me that you're talking about something like creating more journals and other spaces for dialogue.

Patricia Hill Collins: Absolutely. But I would push even further. We need to think creatively about the spaces that we currently control and see them as beachheads that, with imagination and creativity, might be put to different use.

The Griot: Just as a side note, I find—I teach a lot of race and ethnicity courses— there are issues that I deal with in the context of the course that I realize are much harder to deal with in the real everyday workings of academia, but you can talk about them in class.

Patricia Hill Collins: But that's exactly what I mean. If you look at the founding moments of an organization like ABS, there were clear links between practice and knowledge, similar to those linking pedagogy (what you can accomplish in the classroom) and the curriculum (how teachers and students make new knowledge by how they engage the material). We always have to create the social conditions that make our intellectual work possible. That was the impetus for the creation of ABS as an organization—founding members saw the need for structural change and were able to develop a critical consciousness when they talked to each other in private, safe spaces. Having an organization that created that space so that you could talk about different things and so you could have an impact on institutional processes was crucial.

Repairing these fraying links between political practice and knowledge creation constitutes one of the greatest challenges for contemporary Black intellectual production. In today's seemingly post-racial society, if we're not careful, this robust understanding of praxis that was reflected in the founding moments of ABS can become reduced to toothless, symbolic discussions of race and racism carried out by people who are just trying to advance their own careers.

The Griot: What you've just said really sets the stage for the next question, which is what kinds of issues do you think Black sociologists or anyone interested in critical race theory should be addressing today?

Patricia Hill Collins: I would like to see more attention given to the interconnectedness or *intersections* of race and class. I think we definitely need to shift gears to questions of economic opportunity and economic justice. We can *both* focus on intersections of race and class *and* keep Black people central to economic analyses. I happen to believe that when things work for Black people they tend to work for everybody a lot better. Blacks are not a special case, an exception to the rule of normality for everyone else. Instead, Blacks are like the canary in the mine, as Guinier and Torres explain in *The Miner's Canary*. We're on the front line. Negative social phenomena tend to affect Black people earlier and often more harshly than the general population. Conversely, when poor Black people have opportunities, then society will be fundamentally changed in ways that are fairer.

Despite the significance of economic issues, how Black people go about addressing them in the current political climate requires rethinking longstanding strategies. The Civil Rights movement focused on marshaling state power to fight exclusionary, discriminatory policies of racial segregation in schools, jobs, and housing. The movement assumed that, if the state protected civil rights, Black people could compete equally. Gaining access to better economic opportunities would eventually reduce poverty among Blacks. To a certain extent, until the 2008 global capitalist crisis, this strategy appeared to be working. The creation of a Black middle class is one important outcome.

Now, however, we can see the limits of that particular strategy. In the United States, intellectuals have spent so much time fighting about whether race or class is more fundamental in explaining Black poverty that we fail to imagine developments that do not petition the state. I'm not arguing that holding the state's feet to the fire needs to go away, but I'd like to see greater emphasis placed on building African American economic capacity through other means. The government need not be the sole engine that builds economic capacity within African American communities. Despite the discouraging news about how the housing crisis and the shrinking of government jobs has shrunk Black middle-class wealth, African Americans still constitute a massive consumer class that could exert considerable clout if we spent and invested our money differently.

I would also like to see more attention paid to economic development from the bottom up. Here, we have much to learn from the global context. In countries with little or no credible welfare state sector, people have simply abandoned hope that larger state programs are going to deliver anything to them, whether it is socialism or the democratic social welfare state. We have much to learn from the economic strategies deployed by people in these settings. For example, I want to see more focus on questions that examine the kinds of things that are occurring globally around issues of micro-credit and sustainability. There are some very interesting and innovative solutions from people on the ground.

The Griot: Of course, Black feminist inquiry has made some important contributions to the analysis of race and class—in addition to the situation of women and sexual minorities. So are there any questions that are specific to Black feminist inquiry that you think should be explored?

Patricia Hill Collins: Directions in global feminism pointing us toward the gendered nature of building economic capacity are really very interesting in this regard. When you look at people who are in a difficult economic situation—I don't mean people who are entrenched in the consumerism that we're encouraged to follow in this country, but folks who are dealing with real bread-and-butter issues and trying figure out a way to move forward with their lives, whether it's globally or here—women have been quite central. When women gain money or find ways to earn it, they tend to spend it on families, health care, their children, and education. These are all activities that build economic capacity by caring for those who might generate income. In some ways, the global feminist agenda is already inherently an economic agenda. Societies where women are more empowered tend to do better overall economically. Women are quite central to economic development. When it comes to economic issues, Black women are especially well represented in the African Diaspora. Many African American women remain unaware of this aspect of global feminism and would certainly benefit from seeing other options than an American-centered, race relations framework. Then they could see that women, and especially Black women, are central to any agendas for enhancing economic capacity.

Black feminism, however, is not just the study of issues that affect Black women. The theoretical framework of Black feminism is also important, especially the need to develop intersectional analyses of important social issues. One important area of emphasis for critical race scholarship concerns developing better intersectional analyses of the status of Black youth, broadly defined, especially in a global context. We need to continue some of the excellent work done by Cathy Cohen in *Democracy Remixed* on how the future looks to African American youth who have come of age after the Civil Rights Movement. Cohen examines contemporary youth's perceptions of politics and how a very different set of conditions concerning race, class, gender, and sexuality shapes their political ideas and behavior. I think we need to develop new ways of thinking about the new racial realities that Black youth face and also strategies that will enable them to become effective political actors. That's a little different than looking for racial or gender discrimination under every rock. Do not hear me wrong—I know that discrimination remains an important frame for anti-racist scholarship. Rather, I think racial discrimination has already received considerable attention. I'd like to broaden our agenda to focus on the needs of Black youth and other populations who want to do something about contemporary forms social injustice.

The Griot: How would you apply those priorities to the field of sociology as a whole? One original question I had was "What sort of questions do you think the field of sociology should be addressing?" But I guess it could also be framed as "Do you think the field of sociology is doing a good job of addressing the sorts of questions you've just outlined?"

Patricia Hill Collins: Absolutely. I'm a huge fan of sociology, and I see a vital role for traditional, applied, critical, and public sociology. I think that the field brings structural analyses to the forefront, a vital contribution in the current U.S. political context, with its inordinate focus on individualism and personal responsibility as the causes of and cures for social problems. Sociology brings a much-needed structural analysis to issues of unemployment, job creation, homelessness, schooling, and other important social issues that are increasingly recast as economic concerns solely within the purview of economists. We have solid theoretical traditions, far too often under-recognized, that ask big, tough questions about society. Sociology as a discipline also has a wonderful toolkit of methodological approaches—whether we're talking about quantitative methodologies that generate statistical information that convince people that social problems exist or qualitative methodologies whose studies explain people's experiences with community and cultural practices as well as with broader social policies.

At the same time, I think that the field of sociology could do a better job of embracing its existing strengths. Sociology is a border discipline that touches political science, philosophy, some of the natural sciences (biology and genetics come to mind), anthropology, and literary criticism. Yet sociologists often do not see sociology's interdisciplinary inclinations as a strength. Ironically, as the world itself becomes more interdependent and interconnected, it needs interdisciplinary analyses that can make sense of these relationships. Sociologists are well positioned for interdisciplinary collaboration, both with the fields that border it and with one another within our own boundaries. Yet efforts to purify the discipline, in a misguided effort to elevate its status, belie sociology's actual strengths. Ironically, chasing the dream of redefining sociology as science impoverishes the field. Instead, strengthening sociological science and placing it in dialogue with sociology's other internal traditions, as well as with sciences from other fields, promises an exciting future.

I think the field needs to be bold and claim what it already is and does, which is to put many different things in play and have them work. I would like to see a more robust understanding of sociology, both in the United States and globally—which is now possible because of available technology—applied to some of the important issues that sociology has traditionally examined, such as economics and race, and more recently, questions of gender and sexuality. Because our subject matter is society, sociologists will never run out of interesting and important things to study and say.

The Griot: I wonder if I could take you on a little tangent—because I thought your description of sociology as a border discipline was really compelling. I think there's always been a kind of split identity in sociology. There's a lot of critical work—including your work—that is solid sociological work and has defined a good part of what sociology is, but sometimes that work gets portrayed as if it's marginal to the canon because it's critical. I imagine everyone is familiar with the conflicts that have occurred between qualitative people versus quantitative people or other conflicts over epistemology or theory. I think sometimes it leads sociologists who are trying to do original, critical work to wonder if what they're doing is really sociology or whether it will be taken seriously by other sociologists. That's why I'd be curious to learn more about how you see sociology as a border discipline.

Patricia Hill Collins: I began this interview talking about ABS's responses to U.S. racial segregation, but I see segregation as a metaphor for a broader set of social relations stemming from colonialism and nationalism. These political systems required drawing strict boundaries to determine citizenship, status, and the benefits and costs of belonging. Historically, sociology was uncomfortable with itself because it was a border discipline during a period of separation where, to know who you were, you had to pick a side. You were, for example, black or white, or you were a sociologist or you weren't one. You had to be whatever it was . . . not that "other" race, religious group, or discipline. Areas that had messy, porous borders, that seemed to be "not pure" in some way—a mulatto or *mestizo* racial identity or sociology as a border discipline—had trouble in terms of the way they situated themselves in relation to their neighbors. We don't live in that world anymore.

In our interdependent, interconnected world, people who are on the front end of creating knowledge—creating innovative programs or innovative research designs—recognize that they cannot answer questions by themselves, from one vantage point, and from within one particular category. Interdisciplinarity is certainly one way that this is expressed in the academy. The irony is that sociology has historically had the potential for tremendous heterogeneity *within* its borders and in other ways has served as a crossroads, an interchange of ideas from *outside* its borders. Yet, depending on which national setting you're looking at, national sociologies, American sociology included, have attempted to purify themselves by quieting selected segments within their borders.

Sociology is a field with tremendous potential. Fighting about what belongs within sociology and what stands outside can impoverish us. Efforts to purify the field are ineffective in these current intellectual and political conditions, because the world is not going in that direction—so I see that as a failed project. Programs or departments that continue to fight specious battles over whether qualitative or quantitative methodologies constitute the best forms of sociology, or that fail to appreciate how cultural sociology and media studies constitute an important part of the sociological future, or that reject the intersectional paradigms of class, race, and gender that I discussed earlier are really looking backward more than they are moving forward.

Moving forward involves analyzing the actual and potential relationships among ideas, social practices, and people that historically may not have been seen as connected. The focus on inclusivity and the terms of relationships is crucial for understanding contemporary patterns of race and racism. What does it mean if you *are* participating, if you *are* connected, if you *are* in a relationship? How do we think about inclusion differently so that we go beyond reacting to patterns of being excluded?

The Griot: I think it's important to hear someone like you, who's occupied a position at the top of the discipline, say that. I know there are several other sociologists who have said similar things.

Patricia Hill Collins: To build on these ideas, I see a substantial generational difference within the field in terms of receptivity to new ideas. The kinds of battles that you describe, in some ways, are really about my cohort, sociologists who are nearing retirement who have been in the field twenty-five years or more. Despite public rhetoric, many senior faculty implicitly aim to impose the worldview they gained during their graduate training, and this includes beliefs about the relative merits of quantitative versus qualitative methodologies, on graduate students and junior faculty. Yet these issues speak more to past debates than they do to contemporary sensibilities of junior scholars. Graduate students and junior faculty may specialize in certain methodologies, yet they seem far less concerned about maintaining strict borders. There's much more openness on their part to doing things differently. I am encouraged by these trends in that the field itself already has within it traditions of doing things differently that, if embraced by junior scholars, can be quite exciting. For example, in my Presidential 2009 ASA meeting in San Francisco, I was thrilled to see the high numbers of junior scholars who attended the meeting, many of them with children in tow. They brought wonderful energy to the meeting. I love my senior colleagues, especially those who have been tireless defenders of doing the right thing, but I was excited by the energy of our junior scholars. I just wanted to give a little shout out to the junior scholars.

The Griot: Great! I guess I could say "thanks" on behalf of a lot of them. What you just said actually relates to the next question. You've written about the challenges of balancing the professional demands of being a sociologist with your commitment to doing social justice work or producing work that's relevant to social justice issues. Maybe that divide is not as relevant now as it might have been some time ago, but I'd be curious to get your thoughts on how you've managed that tension or how you see it playing out today. Is it something you see in the lives of other sociologists? I'm thinking back to some of the things you wrote in *Black Feminist Thought*.

Patricia Hill Collins: I've always recognized that one can do intellectual production in many different locations. When it comes to my scholarship, I have survived by reminding myself that I always have a choice. I never mistake my job as being synonymous with intellectual activism or my own life's work. I also remind myself that, despite the fact that intellectual work remains devalued within U.S. society, I know that the power of ideas matters.

This view enabled me to see a bigger picture beyond simple career choices. When I started off in my twenties, I wasn't even heading for a career in the professoriate; that wasn't a career goal for me. Make no mistake—I have been quite strategic about my career. But for me, my life's work has always been bigger than the issue of individual career advancement. For years, I did not work in a sociology department, yet I thought of myself the entire time as a sociologist. I did not approach my work as trying to have a career as a sociologist. Rather, a career as a sociologist could facilitate my work, but I could do that work in other places as well. Given this philosophy, it is quite shocking to me that I have done as well as I have as an academic and that I have been embraced by the field of sociology.

If people want to do what I do, they have to look at what I had to do to get to this point. On one hand, the costs of trying to do scholarship on your own terms can be high. In my case, I didn't have the best jobs or work in the best institutions, and for a very long time I was underpaid. But on the other hand, I gained a degree of intellectual freedom that has sustained me over several decades. I was willing to pay for as much intellectual freedom as I could afford. I wonder about people who want scholarly "careers" in social justice. They want the benefits of taking the moral high road without the struggle. They want to do social justice work without pain. They fail to recognize the inordinate risk that accompanies social justice work and how committing to such work always requires a contingency plan.

Being a Black woman has given me advantages in social justice work, and not for the reasons that many people think. For Black people in this country, it really has been a history of knowing that there is no safe place for you, even when times are good. I have not gone through life assuming that because of my credentials and demonstrated experience I would receive fair and equitable treatment. Instead, I assumed that I had to be prepared to struggle to get everything—even the things to which I was entitled—and I had hoped that I would not need to do so. Having access to the collective standpoint of African Americans and the standpoint of Black women in particular showed me that I was not alone. The collective consciousness given to me as a gift by my family and people in my neighborhood institutions helped me develop an individual critical consciousness that provided me some protection within broader social institutions who aimed to keep me down.

Over the years, I have met many other people who have also struggled to maintain intellectual freedom, whether their social justice projects targeted racism, sexism, heterosexism, poverty, immigrant status, ability, or age, to name a few. What felt like a lonely struggle early on, the longer I stayed with it, became a journey of finding so many other people of like mind. There as so many different kinds of people from all walks of life who care deeply about building a better future. We need to develop better ways of recognizing and finding one another. Continuing to do social justice work, including intellectual activism within sociology, requires building communities of practice of people who value social justice work, especially if they look quite different than us.

The Griot: This raises questions that I've always had about how you create an intellectual community or whether it's important to have one. On one hand, I've found that intellectual work can be a very solitary experience, but I imagine that we're all inspired by some idea that what we're doing is informed by some collective obligation to solve these issues that are bigger than we are. But again, it can also be a solitary struggle. When I read your work, I get this sense that there's an intellectual community that you're referencing and trying to support. It's not necessarily just a professional, academic community—even though it involves academics—but it doesn't seem as if it's just that. So I was wondering how you went about creating community, or how important it was for you to have these support networks, or whether you really just had to be on your own a lot in order to produce the kind of work that you ended up writing.

Patricia Hill Collins: Because I selected "The New Politics of Community" as my 2009 ASA meeting program theme, I've thought deeply about what I mean by "community" in all of its manifestations. I see community as being a much more powerful and political construct than a social support network, with its associated bureaucratic language of role models and mentoring.

To me, the construct of community encompasses people who have a shared agenda, who may have a shared worldview, and who see their lives as interconnected. It may be people you grew up with—it may not. You may have nothing in common with the people you grew up with. So the whole notion of constructing a community that's political and that's bigger than each individual doesn't necessarily match up with understandings of social networks. Political communities require social networks, but social networks are not inherently political.

In far too many cases, this language of social networks, mentoring, and role modeling has been hijacked by bureaucracies that tell us we need to seek help that we may not necessarily need. Within the academy, this kind of thinking basically disempowers students and junior scholars by convincing us that we need institutionally supplied role models, mentors, and professional networks to be successful. I am not disputing the importance of mentoring in terms of certain information or networks of people who will put us in touch with resources. But do we really need bureaucratically sanctioned social networks that make us feel that we have to send a blast to the listserv or call up all these people and cry every time something negative happens to us in our sociology departments? Social media enable us to be embedded in ever-expanding social networks, but these networks are far from being communities.

The Griot: There are times when I've wanted something like that—a more developed social network—but I can also see that there's a certain freedom you have in being able to make decisions without having to vet everything little thing you're doing with this network of colleagues.

Patricia Hill Collins: Exactly. The power of a free mind consists of trusting your own mind to ask the questions that need to be asked and your own capacity to figure out the strategies you need to get those questions answered. Over time, this requires building communities that make this kind of intellectual and political work possible. My scholarship on *Black Feminist Thought* began as a solitary endeavor before I even realized that I was working on that project. No matter how hard it tried, my public school couldn't convince me that Black women had no serious ideas *(laughter)*. I attended the Philadelphia public schools for twelve years. That's a long time to spend in classrooms and never encounter the ideas of one African American woman or one woman of color anywhere. Even though I, as an individual Black girl, was included in the school, the exclusion of Black women from my public school's curriculum sent the message to me that Black women had no independent intellectual tradition worth knowing. No one ever stood up and directly said that, but over time, it became clearer to me that I had to research Black women's lives to convince myself that my public school education was wrong.

In the course of investigating the absence, I found a nurturing political community among people whom I could not meet face to face. Many of them were dead, were unknown to the rest of academia, or were not considered to be intellectuals or theorists. Yet, their ideas spoke so strongly to my experiences. My experiences reading the ideas of others convinced me that such communities can be built if we ask the right questions and believe in our own capacity to act. It can be with things or people that you don't necessarily think you have anything in common with. It can be with a body of literature of a group that's not even your own group. I believe in opening ourselves up to a range of things as opposed to just feeling like we're constantly under assault—because clearly, when it comes to Black people, there is a high degree of assault and discrimination. I'm not underestimating that at all—what I'm talking about are the survival strategies that are necessary to protect the imagination and protect one's own intellectual self in the context of a society that still doesn't value Black intellectual capacity all that much. Building our own communities can serve not only to protect those within them but also to expand outward and find connections with others.

The Griot: I have one more question, which is just a way of reflecting on a lot of things that you've just covered. What is your view of the changing relationship between black feminism and other related forms of critical inquiry and mainstream sociology and similar disciplines, say between the 1980s and now?

Patricia Hill Collins: I think there's been this dual response—one good, one bad. Most things are always a both/and situation. On one hand, I see a substantial amount of co-optation of what used to be progressive scholarship. What happens when dissident scholarship or critical black theory or black feminist thought or Women's Studies or Ethnic Studies or Gender Studies or whatever gains visibility begins to influence political practice? Mainstream disciplines realize the power of these ideas and, to protect their own privilege, often appropriate ideas and recast them for their own purposes. On the other hand, if practitioners in critical areas are sufficiently strategic and do not mistake praise for acceptance, or inclusion for transformation, then progressive scholarship can become even stronger. The essence of progressive scholarship becomes tested in the crucible of academic experience. If you cannot find a way to be progressive within academia, how powerful are your ideas?

The area of race/class/gender studies illustrates both of these tendencies. Originally, race/class/gender studies came out of clearly defined social movement agendas from the 1960s and 1970s for challenging social inequities and unjust social hierarchies. Black feminism was at the forefront of birthing, in the academy, Black feminist thought, race/class/gender studies, and most recently, intersectionality. Black women argued that the solution to our problems was impossible through frameworks that focused exclusively on race, gender, class, or sexuality. Instead, Black feminist intellectuals argued that new and more empowering realities for Black women could be created only by conceptualizing how race, class, gender, sexuality, and age, for example, all worked together. Because that was an innovative and powerful statement in the context of social movement politics of the 1960s and 1970s, it traveled widely among social movements and into the academy in the 1980s and 1990s. The issue lies not with the flow of ideas but rather with how ideas travel, how some are shut down in some settings, and how they are expanded and embraced in others. This is the story that we're still monitoring.

The ways in which these ideas have traveled is simultaneously disappointing and encouraging. On the one hand, the phrase "race/class/gender" is widely used within academia. But sometimes it's just a phrase that is used to strip off or strip mine the best ideas from that body of critical thought. For example, many academics found that, if they incorporated some variation of the phrase "race/

class/gender" in the title of their paper or presentation, they became more marketable—even though they really had very little understanding of race or gender, or were not particularly interested in the field itself. This usage of the term "race/class/gender" in this fashion as a mantra impoverishes the area.

On the other hand, I am greatly encouraged by the growing number of scholars and activists who continue to breathe life into the issues raised within race/class/gender studies. Across diverse fields, many people are grappling with some big questions about how to do relational scholarship and how such scholarship connects with social justice practice. I sense a genuine shift occurring around the questions of race/class/gender within intersectionality studies, much of it advanced not by me, but by junior scholars. The story of this particular "changing relationship" of race/class/gender studies is still unfolding, and I look forward to seeing what happens.

III

Critical Education

Critical Pedagogy and
Engaged Scholarship

Lessons from Africana Studies

REFLEXIVE ESSAY: *C. Wright Mills' rich concept of the sociological imagination places individual biography, history, and society in dialogue with an eye toward sparking creative analyses of important social issues. Here I use the construct of the sociological imagination as an organizing principle to revisit two different sites of Africana Studies that had an important influence on my intellectual activism. Both illustrate these relationships among my personal biography, the historical times in which I was doing intellectual work, and the specific social settings where I was located. In both social locations, I was neither blindly trying to change society nor dispassionately studying it. Rather, I was actively engaged in trying to foster social justice, using the power of ideas as my weapon of choice.*

MANY PEOPLE THINK of me primarily as a professor of sociology who teaches classes, writes books, and serves on endless faculty committees. Others view me as an accomplished scholar of Black feminism whose interdisciplinary work inspires their own. Still others have met me during my more than twenty years of service to the American Sociological Association. I suspect that many other points of view on who I am exist—a role

I presented a working outline for the ideas for this essay during a symposium on my work at the 2011 Annual Meeting of the Eastern Sociological Society. A version of that conference presentation was published in 2012 as "Looking Back, Moving Ahead: Scholarship in Service to Social Justice." *Gender and Society* 26(1) February: 14–22.

model to junior colleagues whose work has followed in the footsteps of my work on Black feminism and intersectionality; a puzzle to my progressive white colleagues who wonder why I'm not as outspoken as they are; a straw woman to my African American colleagues who question my blackness; an African American woman whose intellect scares some people if I say what's really on my mind; or an anonymous, ordinary Black woman who can't get a good table in an upscale restaurant if she has left her business suit, attaché case, or expensive jewelry at home.

I am all of these things some of the time, but none of these things all of the time. The fluid nature of how others view me as well as how I see them has shaped the content and process of my intellectual production. My work reflects distinctive, competing, and often contradictory angles of vision that shift not only with physical and intellectual social locations but also as times change around me. While it has been tempting to simplify my intellectual travels into a homogeneous narrative to make the world more comfortable for me, my challenge has been to sustain a commitment to dialogical knowledge production, especially in situations of conflict. Stated differently, I consistently seek out connections among entities that seem disparate, resisting the temptation to synthesize things into a tidy story prematurely, yet also recognizing that a story needs to be told.

We can throw up our hands at the magnitude of the task of negotiating the complexities of our individual experiences and the viewpoints they engender, or we can embrace forms of engaged scholarship and critical pedagogy that reflect a commitment to intellectual activism. In this essay, I examine the relationship between critical pedagogy and engaged scholarship in my own work by revisiting two different phases of my career. My six-year engagement with the community schools movement in Boston, Massachusetts, and my twenty-three-year career as a professor in the African American Studies Department at the University of Cincinnati (now renamed the Africana Studies Department) each provided distinctive angles of vision on the meaning of intellectual activism.

Laying the Foundation: St. Joseph's Community School

I arrived at St. Joseph's School in 1970 to work as a middle school teacher, curriculum developer, and community organizer. At that time, the school was undergoing a transformation from a traditional parochial school to a community school. Operating both as a K–8 community school and a demonstration project of the Harvard University Graduate School of Education (HGSE), St. Joseph's aimed to forge new relationships with the working-class and poor African American residents of its surrounding neighborhood. Our students were homogeneous, but our staff was not. The school community included a heterogeneous group of teachers, parents, nuns, lay teachers, neighborhood volunteers, and HGSE doctoral students and faculty. If you wanted diversity, we had it. We faced the challenge of building a community across differences of race, class, gender, age, region, education, religion, and ethnicity that would enable us to achieve excellence (sexuality was there, albeit still in the closet, but there nonetheless). Building a community across such differences was an uphill battle. We agreed on practically nothing except the need to do everything we could to teach, nurture, and empower the African American and/or poor children in our care.

We each brought our specific talents to the project of crafting a pedagogy that might provide the critical education that our students needed. I mined my education for both content that our students of African descent would find meaningful and skills of critical thinking that would enable them to put that content to good use. My goal was to encourage our students to think in far more expansive terms than memorizing factoids for standardized tests. The teachers, staff, and parents at St. Joseph's did not want to teach our students merely to fit into the system, although for reasons of survival, knowing how to fit in without selling out was essential. We knew that our students also needed to know how to analyze, critique, and change the systems of inequality that disempowered them. I saw my intellectual production as tethered to a broader commitment to intellectual activism whereby my engaged scholarship and critical pedagogy shaped one another.

I quickly realized that the critical thinking component of my formal education was first rate, whereas the content, especially concerning people of African descent, had tremendous holes. During my twelve years in the Philadelphia public schools, I had not taken one Black Studies course, mainly because such courses did not exist. Brandeis University did somewhat better. There I was able to enroll in all of the courses in the entire curriculum devoted to people of African descent. There were two courses, one on African Americans and one on Africa south of the Sahara (code for Black Africans, not the Arabs of Northern Africa). I enrolled in both. It became clear to me that I would have to take ownership of my own education if I wanted to learn about people of African descent. I majored in sociology because its emphasis on and progressive approach to race and racism came closest to my growing interest in studying Black people. By my junior year, I began writing papers that reflected my independent research on race, racism, and Black people. I am especially proud of a term paper that I wrote on Franz Fanon's *The Wretched of the Earth* that I recently discovered while going through some really old papers. I was also fortunate that the Rev. Dr. Pauli Murray agreed to supervise my senior honors thesis on "Community Control of Schools." My senior honors thesis provided a conceptual foundation for my subsequent work that took me through my efforts in the community schools movement in the 1970s to my program theme, "The New Politics of Community," more than 30 years later, when I was elected president of the American Sociological Association. It also left me with a love for engaged scholarship.

Given my path in coming to terms with my own engaged scholarship, bringing this sensibility to my first full-time job as a seventh- and eighth-grade classroom teacher felt right. I did not have the luxury of arriving with my fancy degree and untested ideas of how the world worked, expecting to share them with appreciative, complacent, docile students. My students were smart and feisty, with considerable street savvy that enabled them to overcome years of traditional parochial school training. They talked back, acted up, and acted out. They also had small biographical horizons—many had never been out of their Roxbury neighborhood to see downtown Boston or experience the wealth of cultural material in the greater metropolitan area. What we both needed was material that did not yet exist, questions that, to our knowledge, had not yet been asked.

To this day, I believe in testing ideas in the crucible of experience, and my classroom teaching at St. Joseph's Community School provided many such tests. In that setting, my engaged scholarship consisted of diligent research for my lesson plans. Responding to the historical and social context of the Black Power movement, I read everything I could on everything related to race and Black people, domestic and global. I was astounded at how much I found that, to this day, remains neglected within dominant curricular offerings. I had to teach myself before I could teach others, thus practicing the skill of creating new frameworks versus endlessly criticizing those advanced by others. Doing research with the understanding that I would have to talk to people about it almost immediately shaped how I viewed what I read and what I chose to make public. My adolescent students quickly told me when I missed the mark. Chaos in the classroom is no fun. But when I got it right, it was magical.

My engaged scholarship at St. Joseph's Community School focused on in-depth research in search of substantive ideas, whether they were written with my students in mind or not. While others in my cohort (who by then were in graduate school preparing to be professors) were reading *The Wretched of the Earth* in their graduate seminars and debating with each other, I was re-reading this book in the context of community politics, trying to figure out how to translate what was useful for my seventh- and eighth-grade students, their parents, and members of the St. Joseph's community. Because elite academics were not my intended audience, I neither published what I wrote nor saw my intellectual work as tethered to my own career trajectory. Unfettered by a scripted curriculum and undisciplined by an established field of study, I found that the intellectual freedom of this period enabled me to experience ideas and actions as iterative.

Although this was not the language that we used at the time, I can see how the ideal of social justice constituted a core principle at St. Joseph's Community School. This overarching idea enabled us to negotiate differences that ultimately enabled us to build an effective community. We did not approach our differences to erase them, because in the context of education as a site of political struggle, we knew that we needed everyone's contributions. Our view of excellence did not embrace an exclusionary politics of elitism, one where weak members are weeded out through competition, leaving the strong or excellent behind. Instead, over time, the St. Joseph's community came to embrace an inclusionary vision of excellence, one that tried to bring the best ideas to the table to solve the problems at hand.

From our separate paths to St. Joseph's, we brought several social justice traditions that made different contributions to the collective project of building a community school. Drawing on the ethical frameworks of Catholicism, the nuns shared how poor people throughout the globe used liberation theology to challenge their subordination. From them we learned how vitally important taking principled stances is in struggles for social justice. What keeps people going in political struggles is principled commitment, not simply information.

Influenced by traditions of participatory democracy inspired by the works of John Dewey, as well as works on adult literacy and empowerment by Myles Horton at the Highlander Center and Paulo Freire in Brazil, the Harvard contingent brought critical pedagogical perspectives on social justice. From them we learned about freedom schools and the centrality of critical education to social justice struggles. Our school was not alone. Many others saw the significance of literacy for political empowerment. Our efforts were part of this broader social justice initiative.

I brought my own personal social justice perspective to St. Joseph's, one developed as a Brandeis University undergraduate. My sociological training exposed me to the work of exiled Jewish intellectuals, whose commitment to ensuring that the atrocities of the Holocaust would never be repeated (encapsulated in the phrase "never again") influenced my understanding of social justice. Reflecting continental philosophy, especially critical theory as advanced by the Frankfurt School, and Marxist social thought, my sociological training taught me much about the significance of engaged scholarship for social justice.

The parents, neighborhood volunteers, and the kids themselves were especially critical to the social justice mission of St. Joseph's Community School. Social movements for Civil Rights and Black Power, collectively referred to as the "Black Freedom Movement," reflected and encouraged a social justice ethos among African Americans, and the parents, neighbors, and kids themselves engaged the ideas of these movements from varying vantage points. Influenced by the social justice visions of political leaders, such as Martin Luther King, Jr., and Malcolm X, Nina Simone's "Mississippi Goddam" served as a soundtrack for our especially political parents. The kids also drew ideas from popular culture. When I found a group of my eighth graders listening to the Last Poets' song "The Revolution Will Not Be Televised" during recess, I knew that we had to speak to their issues. Claims for social justice embedded in the language of freedom now and Black Power shaped our students' sense of the world and ourselves in it. They drew inspiration from the commitment of these figures to remedy longstanding injustices rendered by racism and class exploitation.

These foundational experiences at St. Joseph's Community School have shaped my scholarship and teaching ever since. I never intended to be a college professor, yet the high bar that I set for myself in preparing lesson plans for middle school students in a context where I had to engage multiple social justice traditions influenced my subsequent decision to become one as well as the kind of scholar and professor that I became. St. Joseph's enabled me to explore the connections between critical pedagogy and engaged scholarship, thus delaying for a decade the deadening "publish or perish" ethos of higher education. Instead, it put me on a different path of being a rigorous scholar and a public intellectual, with an eye toward social justice traditions. From the nuns who worked so tirelessly in community organizing, my elite colleagues from HGSE, my spirited middle school students, and a broader community of working-class, African American citizens thirsty for sophisticated yet accessible analyses of inequality, I learned that intellectual activism requires a synergy of thinking and doing, in this case, the dialogue between engaged scholarship and critical pedagogy.

Africana Studies and *Black Feminist Thought*

A few years back, a high school teacher in inner-city Baltimore sent me a link to a YouTube clip featuring one of his debate team participants. He thought that I would be interested in knowing how a young African American girl used my analysis of Black feminist epistemology to frame her arguments. After viewing her video, I was impressed. Seeing this young debater wield the ideas of Black feminism made my struggle to get *Black Feminist Thought* published worth it. Her intellectual activism helped validate my twenty-three years as a professor whose tenure line appointment was solely within the Africana Studies Department at the University of Cincinnati. Some people use their joint appointments to dabble in Black Studies, retreating to their home departments when the going gets rough. With my tenure line solely in Black Studies, I didn't have that option.

Intellectual freedom is a wonderful thing, but you have to fight for it. In the 1980s and 1990s, Africana Studies was a difficult space to be, primarily because universities devalued these units. Black Studies remained chronically underfunded and largely disrespected. Despite the challenges of being a professor *within* a Black Studies unit with no graduate program, I chose to stay because, in several ways, I understood my involvement in Africana Studies as an extension of the kind of engaged scholarship that I began at St. Joseph's Community School. I loved the students that I taught at the University of Cincinnati. I felt at home with them, not only because they reminded me so much of my St. Joseph's students but also because their issues closely resembled my own. They were trying to better their lives and saw school as an important part of their hoped-for upward social mobility. Many sacrificed to attend college, working jobs that supplemented their student loans and substituted for the scholarships they never received. The vast majority of my students, including my white students, were from working-class backgrounds, and many were the first in their family to attend college. Africana Studies courses also enrolled a high percentage of African American students, and the majority of those students were women, populations with whom I have a special affiliation.

I also valued the pedagogical freedom that I had in Africana Studies in developing my individual courses as well as the overall curriculum. Our ongoing struggles to ensure our right to exist at all repeatedly reminded us of how politics shape the social construction of knowledge. As a unit, we were not examining "race" and "racism" exclusively as abstractions. Instead, the Africana Studies curriculum had palpable ties to African American politics as well as scholarly knowledge of the academy. As at St. Joseph's, my time in Africana Studies provided a vehicle for what I now call a "contrapuntal reading" between everyday lived experiences and scholarship that seemingly explains those experiences. Despite the difficulties of remaining in a devalued academic unit, that same unit provided me with the freedom to fuse engaged scholarship with critical pedagogy. Stated differently, building the Africana Studies Department was a site of community organizing, a direct descendent of the hard work that we did at St. Joseph's Community School. Both sites were devoted to building vibrant intellectual communities that served their respective populations.

When it came to questions of gender and/or sexuality, there were some significant differences between St. Joseph's Community School and the Department of Africana Studies. In the 1980s and 1990s, Africana Studies was a friendlier place for Black women than the rest of the academy, but only if we accepted second-class citizenship within the department. At that time, paradigms of Afrocentrism held sway in ways that routinely relegated Black women to second-class citizenship. One way that Africana Studies fended off external assaults from the academy that questioned its very right to exist was to embrace patriarchal Afrocentric frameworks. These frameworks routinely elevated the needs of Black men over those of Black women. Because I came from traditions of strong Black female leadership, such as that at St. Joseph's School, I found the patriarchal norms of Africana Studies confining. At the same time, it was clear to me that even the most sexist Black man in Africana Studies cared far more about the welfare of Black people than did my academic colleagues outside the department. If I really cared about gender, I needed to stay in Africana Studies.

In hindsight, I now see how my years within Africana Studies at the University of Cincinnati constituted a rich, albeit often painful, influence on my intellectual activism. My undergraduate teaching not only provided intellectual freedom for me and my students but also helped shape the distinguishing themes and main arguments of *Black Feminist Thought*. For example, my course "Contemporary Black Women" served as a vehicle for a dialogical knowledge project on Black feminism. Each time I taught this course, I revised it and eventually used my syllabus as the table of contents for the first edition of *Black Feminist Thought*. When it came to selecting the book's title, my students taught me about the politics of naming. I knew that a book titled *Black Feminist Thought* would be more marketable than one titled *Contemporary Black Women* or *Black Womanism*. Yet, when it came to African American women and their perceptions of Black feminism, I faced an uphill battle. My students flatly rejected the term "feminism." In their minds, feminism was for white women, but not for them. I grappled with that issue throughout the course by teaching the main ideas of Black feminism, yet without the use of the term "feminism." Imagine my students' surprise at the end of the course when I told them that our course was an extended exploration of the main ideas of Black feminism. They loved the material when they didn't know it was called "Black feminism." I concluded the course with the question, "Who benefits from your rejection of the term 'feminism'? Who benefits when you claim Black feminism and its main ideas?"

Critical pedagogy within Africana Studies also enabled me to explore the significance of standpoint epistemology. For example, my students in the "Contemporary Black Women" course pushed me to see how my earlier understanding of situated standpoints as an *individual* concern was too narrow. Situated standpoints were also *collectively* constructed angles of vision on the world that often drew on alternative epistemological criteria (standards for assessing truth). The revelation came in class one day when, for unknown reasons, the white students skipped class, thereby creating a class composed entirely of Black women. The entire classroom atmosphere changed. Everyone seemed more relaxed, including me. We were scheduled to discuss an article by a prominent sociologist on African American love relationships. My students had no interest in delving into the reading—they wanted to know about the author. "Was he a Black man?" "Did he have a white girlfriend?" "Was he married?" Not only the atmosphere of the class, but also the very rules of class itself had changed. Initially, I was frustrated by my students' seeming lack of scholarly engagement with his arguments. But then I realized that these Black women were using an alternative epistemology, one grounded in knowing who produced knowledge and how that person's social location might shape his or her analyses. In that setting, they rejected dominant classroom norms of uncritically accepting ostensibly objective scholarship by academics whose God's eye on the world legitimate the truths they see. Instead, these Black women refused to read knowledge projects outside of power relations, reminding me of the iterative nature of knowledge and the power relations that produce it for people seeking social justice.

At the same time, I wondered how I could continue to challenge my students to move outside of their comfort zones without putting myself in a similar situation. If I planned on developing Black feminism as foundational to my intellectual work, I needed to engage Women's Studies and the feminist politics it advanced. In the 1980s, Women's Studies programs were overwhelmingly white and lacked today's diversity, primarily because racial segregation was prominent in U.S. society overall. As someone who believed passionately in Black feminism, I felt hemmed in by the kinds of questions that racially segregated

Women's Studies units pursued. I was tired of being asked, "How can black and white women get along?" This was an important question for white women, but it was not my top priority. Furthermore, I wondered, if I managed to develop Black feminist analyses within patriarchal Black Studies settings, without the help of white women, why were they seemingly so in need of my help in bringing a hard-hitting racial analysis to feminist theory and politics?

By the 1990s, things were changing, and for the better. Women's Studies students became increasingly diverse, a shift that facilitated my decision to teach graduate courses for the Women's Studies program at the University of Cincinnati. I'm glad that I did. Beyond giving me the opportunity to work with some terrific students, the Women's Studies program enabled me to develop further my foundational ideas about intersectionality. I developed three graduate courses: "Race, Gender and Class"; "Race, Gender and Nation"; and "Race, Gender and Sexuality." These courses were vital in giving me the intellectual space to develop an analysis of intersectionality that, while generated by my experiences in Africana Studies, catalyzed an important intellectual and political foundation for my subsequent scholarship.

These classroom and pedagogical experiences from both my Africana Studies and Women's Studies classes were vital to several of my books, from the content of each volume to the processes I used in writing them. For example, standpoint epistemology is an important theme in *Black Feminist Thought* (1990), one that I further develop in *Fighting Words* (1998). The intersectional analysis advanced in *From Black Power to Hip Hop: Racism, Nationalism and Feminism* (2006) stems directly from both my Women's Studies graduate seminars and my undergraduate teaching. Two sections of *From Black Power to Hip Hop* contain essays where I analyze the politics of race, class, gender, and sexuality that emerged from my position as an "outsider within" Africana Studies and Women's Studies at the University of Cincinnati. For *Black Sexual Politics* (2005), I placed the ideas from my graduate Women's Studies seminar on "Race, Gender and Sexuality" in dialogue with my undergraduate course "Introduction to Black Sexual Politics." *Black Sexual Politics* constitutes the culmination of strategies of dialogical knowledge production from the critical pedagogy that I pursued.

I am convinced that my subsequent work on intersectionality was enhanced by the challenges of making intersectional arguments about Black feminism intelligible within Black Studies settings as well as within Women's Studies. I see my focus on analyzing how race, class, gender, nation, age, ethnicity, and sexuality mutually construct one another as unjust systems of power, as well as my choices to analyze intersectionality as a knowledge project that is embedded in power relations, as reflections of my years at the University of Cincinnati. In sum, the social location of where we engage in our intellectual activism shapes the characteristic themes in our work, the perspectives we take, and what we believe counts as legitimate knowledge.

ADDITIONAL RESOURCES

Collins, Patricia Hill. 2006. "Black Nationalism and African American Ethnicity: Afro-
centrism as Civil Religion." In *From Black Power to Hip Hop: Racism, Nationalism and Feminism*, pp. 75–94, ed. Patricia Hill Collins. Philadelphia: Temple University Press.
———. 2006. "When Fighting Words Are Not Enough: The Gendered Content of Afro-
centrism." In *From Black Power to Hip Hop: Racism, Nationalism and Feminism*, pp. 95–122, ed. Patricia Hill Collins. Philadelphia: Temple University Press.
Marable, Manning, ed. 2000. *Dispatches from the Ebony Tower: Intellectuals Confront the African American Experience*. New York: Columbia University Press.
Perry, Theresa, Claude Steele, and Asa Hilliard III. 2003. *Young, Gifted, and Black: Promoting High Achievement among African-American Students*. Boston: Beacon Press.
Rojas, Fabio. 2007. *From Black Power to Black Studies: How a Radical Social Movement Became an Academic Discipline*. Baltimore, Md.: Johns Hopkins University Press.

Teaching for a Change

Critical Pedagogy and Classroom Communities

REFLEXIVE ESSAY: *When it comes to helping people who are on the bottom empower themselves, oral truth-telling, or telling the truth of their own experiences, constitutes an important part of intellectual activism. In* Fighting Words, *I wanted to unsettle assumptions that knowledge is a top-down creation. This essay explores ideas from a series of talks that I delivered in the mid-1990s, when I was working through these ideas. This essay illustrates how the critical pedagogy gained from my teaching, in this case, an experience with inner city second-grade students, can serve to guide more complex theoretical arguments. This essay also shows how critical pedagogy and scholarship in service to social justice are interconnected, both providing a foundation for intellectual activism.*

IN *FIGHTING WORDS,* I describe an experience that I had as a classroom teacher in the community schools movement. I include the following detailed passage taken from the "Introduction" because the experience it describes shaped my subsequent understandings of both critical pedagogy and the multi-layered significance of community.

In the early 1970s, I was assigned to teach a curriculum unit entitled "The Community" to a class of African American second graders. The community in my students' textbook consisted of single-family homes nestled in plush, green grass, populated by all sorts of friendly white people they had never met and probably would never meet. Sentences such as "Let's visit our men at the firehouse," "Cross only at the corner," and "The policeman is your friend" peppered the text, all designed to reassure my second graders that children are loved, cared for, and safe in their communities.

My students lived in quite a different community, however. Most resided in a nearby, racially segregated public housing project. Their neighborhood experienced all of the social problems that typically accompany poverty and political powerlessness. As I read to them from the pages of their text and saw their blank, bored, and occasionally angry expressions, I realized that I was lying to them. Worse yet, we all knew that the book and I were lying. So I asked them to tell me about their community as they experienced it. One little boy tentatively raised his hand. To my shock, he shared a story of how, because the housing commission had left the doors open, his best friend had fallen down an elevator chute the day before. His friend had been killed.

At that moment, I faced an important choice. I could teach the status quo, or I could teach for a change. I could not see how I could lie to my students, no matter how pure my intentions to "prepare them for the third-grade entrance test on community vocabulary." So we closed those texts full of smiling, affluent white people and began to talk.

At first, my class could not quite believe that I wanted to hear from them. Despite their young age, so many had been silenced by classroom practices that rewarded their obedience and punished their curiosity that they were justifiably afraid to question the public transcript known as their curriculum. They kept their own oppositional knowledge hidden, relegating it to discussions on the playgrounds, on the streets, and in the privacy of their apartments. But because they were still young, they were able to come to voice much easier than those of us who have endured years of such silencing. With minimal prompting, they shared their feelings about the horror of their friend's death, especially their sense of vulnerability that something similar might happen to them. In some cases, they exploded, sharing deep-seated anger.

Through dialogue, these children began to develop the voice so typical of any relatively powerless, outsider group that begins to frame its own self-defined standpoint in hierarchical power relations of race, class, gender, and in their case, age. Some blamed the victim, claiming "he had no business being near that elevator anyhow." Others condemned his mother for being at work while it happened. "Why couldn't she stay home like she was supposed to?" one little girl queried. Still others wanted to "tell somebody" that something was wrong with the way that people in their community were treated. One little girl summed it up, saying, "It's just not fair, Miss Hill. It's just not fair." (*Fighting Words*, ix–x)

For me, this incident marked the day when I realized how important teaching for a change can be. Educational reform often begins by revising existing bodies of knowledge within academic journals, scholarly books, textbooks, and teaching materials. Other reform efforts place faith in retraining teachers to do a better job of accomplishing the predetermined mission of schools by revising their existing syllabi or incorporating technology into the classroom. These efforts are certainly of value, yet they merely scratch the surface.

Teaching for a change involves more than this. If we centered classroom practices on empowering both students and teachers who are disempowered by systems of social inequality, how might classrooms be different? The list of people who occupy positions that simultaneously privilege and penalize them within race, class, gender, and sexuality as intersecting systems of oppression is much longer than we might think. African American women and men, Latinos, Asian Americans, Native Americans, white women, working-class and poor people, gays and lesbians, bisexuals, the very young and the very old, the physically challenged, and progressive and conservative white men all have some degree of privilege and penalty. What forms of critical pedagogy might work to address their needs?

I see two areas where we must teach for a change. The first involves developing a critical consciousness in our students and ourselves about these social conditions. The struggle for critical consciousness starts from the premise that to be other than what is defined as natural, normal, and ideal by dominant curriculum offerings and classroom practices is perfectly acceptable. Each individual struggles to create an honest self. Such identities can never be finished. Instead, as lifelong endeavors, they require skills of critical thinking, dialogical engagement, and empathy. For educators, doing this kind of work involves recognizing that not only our students but also we ourselves have been differentially privileged and penalized within intersecting systems of oppression. For teachers and students alike, the struggle for self-definition means developing a critical posture on what we have been taught about ourselves and others.

Although necessary, critical pedagogy aimed at critical consciousness is far from sufficient. Teaching for a change involves struggling for institutional transformation so that we leave the social institutions that educated us better than we found them. Thus, the struggle for self-definition must be joined to the struggle for institutional transformation of classroom communities. My second-grade students needed to develop a critical analysis of the failures within their own community that led to the death of their classmate. Yet they also needed the tools to envision a more socially just community as well as a skill set that might move the communities they build for their children closer to this valued social ideal.

Critical Consciousness and Classroom Communities

More than twenty years ago, I published an article titled "Learning to Think for Ourselves: Malcolm X's Black Nationalism Reconsidered." I opened that piece with the following excerpt taken from the transcript of a conversation that Malcolm X had with Black youth. His response gets at the heart of critical consciousness: "One of the first things I think young people, especially nowa-days, should learn is how to see for yourself and listen for yourself and think for yourself . . . this generation, especially of our people, has a burden, more so than any other time in history. The most important thing that we can learn to do today is think for ourselves" (59). On my first reading, I found his answer puzzling. Malcolm X was a brilliant Black intellectual, yet he refused to tell young people what they should think.

Learning to think for themselves is equally needed by the second graders I taught decades ago and the students enrolled in my graduate courses on social theory. Thinking for ourselves is virtually impossible if we do not understand how we are situated in the social world. Developing a critical consciousness involves coming to see how our individual biographies are shaped by and act on our specific historical and social contexts. These individual biographies in turn provide the foundation for understanding distinctive group histories that grow from power differences of privilege and penalty.

Members of oppressed groups have special need of critical conscious-ness, because social institutions have routinely worked against their develop-ing it. Developing habits of questioning social injustices maladapts people on the bottom to stay there. This issue framed the first class I ever taught on Af-rican American women, a class consisting of junior high school girls attend-ing an inner-city school in Boston, Massachusetts. In one class assignment, I asked my students to think about anything associated with the words "black" and "white." When we shared our lists, they began to see the magnitude of the negative associations with blackness and darkness that pervade Western cul-ture. Nothing on the list was new or unfamiliar. These students *knew* that black cats brought bad luck, villains in Westerns wore black hats, and black was the color of mourning at funerals. They *knew* that whiteness symbolized purity, goodness, light, and virginity. They *knew* that they were "black." Yet, despite this experiential knowledge, they had not yet learned to think for themselves about these widespread racial meanings. Their knowledge remained subju-gated, suppressed, and scattered. The classroom exercise was designed to make this knowledge explicit and self-defined.

In developing a critical consciousness, my middle school students resisted separating reason from emotion, thought from feeling, and feelings from ac-tions. Just as they examined their experiences in holistic ways, the process of developing a critical consciousness took a similarly holistic form. When they saw the negative patterns and associations with the term "black" and realized that they were Black, they began to talk from the heart. It was this talking from the heart—expressing the pain, the anger, the energy, the criticism of adults who had knowingly and/or inadvertently taught them to feel this way about themselves and each other—that was the first step along their path of iden-tity politics.

It is empowering to reject interpretations of one's own experiences that serve the interests of other groups and empowering to claim those that serve our own. Gaining this clarity fosters a confidence in Black women or any oppressed group about larger institutional contexts in which we reside. Without the foundation of a critical consciousness, subordinated groups continue to view their experiences through the framework of the dominant group. "The master's tools will never dismantle the master's house," contends Audre Lorde. "They may allow us temporarily to beat him at his own game, but they will never enable us to bring about genuine change."

Developing a critical consciousness can position individuals and groups to challenge social injustices. Learning to think for oneself often leads to action. In speaking out about the necessity of addressing social problems that face African American communities, Hadiyah Rashid, a student in my classes, succinctly put it, "We must be bold." Black feminist thought and similar forms of self-defined knowledge can empower members of subordinated groups to "be bold" enough to question social injustice and demand change. Such knowledge is central both in reforming dominant curriculum offerings and classroom practices and in developing alternatives to them.

Learning to think for oneself can foster a paradigm shift, an unsettling recognition that the world is not as one believed it to be. The facts no longer fit what one held to be true. This dynamic space of being unsettled creates space for seeing and creating alternative truths. Black feminist thought and similar knowledge created by people on the bottom often read like a breath of fresh air to people who are searching for new truths when the old certainties no longer deliver.

Classroom communities that aim to teach students *how* to think, not *what* to think, can be vitally important in this move toward critical consciousness. Just as Malcolm X refused to deliver a lecture on his principles of Black nationalism to Black youth, teaching for a change means teaching people to think for themselves. It is exciting to help students grow in their ability to craft their own self-defined standpoints on their worlds.

Such clarity often takes surprisingly little to accomplish. I once asked a sixth-grade class of African American students to listen carefully to a twenty-minute lecture on American history. I told them that I was going to tell them three "lies." Their task was to raise their hands when they thought they heard a lie. At first they protested, "Miss Hill, this is silly. We know you wouldn't lie to us!" Thinking of my second graders, I responded, "People lie all the time, even when they love you and have the best of intentions." So they listened and raised their hands, sometimes in unison, sometimes in small groups, and sometimes in solitary dissent. Whenever even one hand went up, I stopped the lecture and we discussed the patterns of hand-raising. Why did some people think the fact in question was a lie, while others trusted its credibility? This exercise made the process of knowledge legitimation visible. Someone had decided what counted as truth and what would be dismissed as a lie. This was a very different kind of classroom practice than the standard pedagogy of requiring students to listen passively and write down nuggets of truth we call "notes." My students were being encouraged to listen analytically and to use their own experiences as a starting point for critiquing classroom knowledge. Importantly, this exercise helped each individual and also showed the importance of collaboration in figuring out the lies.

Living one's life as a person on the bottom involves listening for lies all the time. The challenge lies in thinking critically about race, class, gender, and sexuality without driving yourself and your loved ones crazy. When oppressed groups embrace their own experiences to challenge dominant curricular offerings and classroom practices, they create space for their own self-defined view of the world.

Institutional Transformation and Classroom Communities

Whatever the group, whether my second graders' point of view on their community or Black feminist thought created by African American women, developing a critical consciousness inevitably confronts structural barriers that limit what is possible under existing power relations. Critical pedagogy can aim to stay at the level of curriculum reform, yet developing and fully engaging the self-defined standpoints of the less powerful involves institutional transformation. As James Baldwin points out, one of the problems of education is that "precisely at the point when you begin to develop a conscience, you must find yourself at war with your society. It is your responsibility to change society, if you think of yourself as an educated person."

Being at war with society means seeing the small and large ways that institutions foster social injustice, and working for transformation involves thinking through how institutional transformation might occur. When it comes to education, the lion's share of attention has gone to curriculum transformation projects. Yet, because transformation projects aim to change idea structures and not decision-making institutional structures, these efforts remain partial. At best, curriculum transformation projects believe that rewriting the curriculum will foster different behaviors in learners. At worst, such efforts believe that adding information without changing the paradigms themselves will be sufficient. Neither approach goes far enough. Institutions change when people change both knowledge and power structures from the actual social locations where they find themselves. Because classrooms are currently the bedrock of educational institutions, changing classroom practices becomes an essential part of institutional transformation. I see institutional transformation not solely as a top-down series of reforms initiated by elites but also as a bottom-up, grassroots community organizing endeavor, one classroom at a time.

Rather than bemoaning the fact that we do not teach in ideal multicultural, economically diverse classrooms where the students are well mannered, get along, and learned to read when they were three, we might imagine possibilities in the classrooms as they actually exist. Teachers matter. The materials and texts that we use are less important than how we use those materials. If it's not too dangerous, the school itself can become the material that we study. The possibilities for learning to think for ourselves are as infinite as the situations that we encounter in our daily lives. Yet we are simultaneously constrained in teaching for a change by the established organization of educational institutions. Race, class, and gender shape preschools and graduate programs alike. Schooling in the United States reflects the segregation of race and class in the United States, with layers of gender and sexual segregation encapsulated within.

Working in Segregated Classroom Communities

In an ideal world, we would all participate in heterogeneous, multiethnic communities where people could struggle directly with one another to develop a critical consciousness on their own experiences and those of others. Yet the structures of segregation that shape society overall also structure the kinds of classrooms in which we find ourselves. Homogeneous classrooms of wealthy white students in prestigious liberal arts colleges and working-class Black students in two-year community colleges reflect the institutional policies of race and class segregation. What are some of the constraints and possibilities for critical pedagogy within homogeneous classrooms?

Homogeneous classrooms predominantly, if not exclusively, composed of poor white students, or female students, or Chicano/Chicana students, or wealthy African American students can become effective sites for institutional transformation. Just as survivors of domestic violence benefit from support groups where they can talk with each other, so do groups of people experiencing any form of domination. Imagine how difficult it would be to develop a critical consciousness on your own victimization as a survivor of sexual assault if your support group contained individuals who, through no fault of their own, resembled your abusers, or worse yet, were themselves rapists. Despite their significance, homogeneous groups functioning to support their members were never meant to be a way of life. Their intent is to assist people in articulating a critical consciousness in spaces of safety. Groups that separate themselves to develop a critical consciousness on the world differ from those that separate to retreat from the world.

The patterns of student dialogue varied when I taught classes where African American students were the clear majority. Black students tend to raise issues in classes where they feel empowered that rarely surface in racially heterogeneous classrooms. African American students wanted to discuss how they could better their neighborhoods. For many of them, their daily lives were spent grappling with the myriad expressions of everyday racism—my African American male students were routinely stopped by the police for no apparent reason, my African American female students were routinely followed around stores as potential shoplifters, and because the large majority were from working-class backgrounds, they all struggled with chronic financial worries about how to pay for school. Given these everyday realities, African American students did not want to spend their time convincing white students that racism was real or helping white students better understand how it felt to be "black."

White students have a different challenge. Their experience is also one of racial segregation, typically with considerable class segregation as well. Yet they do not see spaces where they are in the clear majority as racialized spaces. For white students, such spaces are not racially marked until a student of color enters the space and "brings" race with him or her. Colleagues have asked me how they can teach about race when they only have one or two Black students in their classes. They assume that it is the responsibility of African American students to educate whites about racism or that Black people possess the "experiences" that will sensitize whites. My reply is that such educators begin to think creatively about how to use racially homogeneous spaces differently.

Like support groups, racially homogeneous spaces can become safe spaces for white students to get on with the task of developing a critical consciousness toward whiteness. Many white students feel that only people of color have "race," and that they themselves somehow stand outside of the racial order as "individuals" or just human beings. This is a perfectly reasonable thing to believe, given that white students have come of age in a context of colorblindness where many believed that to speak of race was to *be* racist. These students need a new model of how to talk about race that takes race into account and challenges racism.

Early-twenty-first-century scholarship on whiteness should be very helpful in developing critical pedagogy for overwhelmingly white classrooms. For example, Mark Warren's book *Fire in the Heart: How White Activists Embrace Racial Justice* is a must-read volume for white students who are grappling with contemporary racial politics. Classrooms can provide safe space for students to engage Warren's ideas. We may not like some of these ideas because they may make us feel uncomfortable or guilty. But since so many white students are already in racially segregated classrooms, we must make them aware of how they got to that classroom and how they might get to another type of classroom that contains people who don't all look like them.

Working in Diverse Classroom Communities

Because knowledge results from collaboration between teachers and students, classroom communities are dynamic political spaces where this knowledge production continually happens. Given the significance of classrooms, what actually happens when diverse classrooms become organized around critical pedagogies that encourage critical consciousness? Unlike homogeneous classrooms where teachers help students see existing diversity that may be hidden, diverse classrooms may be where people encounter diversity for the first time.

Teachers are not merely technicians who can be trained to implement someone else's ideas and theories. Classrooms organized around a critical pedagogy do not resemble the metaphor of the symphony, one where every instrument has a scripted part, where there is a clear hierarchy of first violin, second violin, and the like, and where a conductor is needed to "keep order." In this model, individual players are interchangeable in and out of predetermined social positions. While this model of classroom community can produce beautiful music by one set of aesthetic standards, it is predictable, leaving little room for human creativity and improvisation.

Ideally, teachers and students in classroom communities might all strive to become more like jazz combo facilitators. In such groups, the goal is to get all instruments to come to voice, to sing their own songs, but to do so in dialogue with each other. There are clear differences between the instruments—the drums could drown out the saxophone if the standard of who can talk the loudest were the standard of participation—but the goal of the facilitator is to ensure that balance is maintained, that ethical turn-taking occurs. The goal is not cacophony of sound or anarchy of political practice. Allowing for individual difference does not necessarily degenerate into blind relativity, meaninglessness, and loss of community. Instead, one hears a different kind of music (or knowledge), ever changing, full of surprises, and much more adept at responding to the everyday needs of the people playing the instruments.

What will be required for developing such classrooms? How do we develop classroom communities that are organized around democratic processes? Ideally, for the struggle for institutional transformation, we each need to see the partiality of our own individual and group experiences. No one group possesses an objective view of constructs, such as community, or paradigms for interpreting human experience, such as positivist science or postmodernism, or epistemologies for deciding what will count as knowledge. No matter how much sense they may make to us as individuals, the constructs, paradigms, and epistemologies we develop that emerge solely from our own experiences necessarily remain partial.

Because classroom communities put people in touch with one another in actual time and space, and through the materials that community members bring to the space from other times and places, classroom communities contain the potential to negotiate this partiality of experiences. For example, I love African American women's fiction for what it tells me about my own experiences. Yet I limit myself when I concentrate exclusively on my own group. Moreover, how I engage other groups is crucial—I do not aim to recast their experiences into a preconceived notion of the world that has been developed solely using my own experiences. This is how dominant knowledge works. Mimicking this process only replicates its worst features.

Reading fiction by women of color gives me a sense of the types of connections that exist between African American women and other historically marginalized groups. But it also gives me a sense of how Black feminist thought provides a partial perspective. For example, Amy Tan's path-breaking book on Chinese and Chinese American women, *The Joy Luck Club*, resonates with themes that pervade the work of Black women writers: mother/daughter relationships, domestic violence, racial/ethnic identity, generational differences, and the constraints and contributions of culture. But in reading Tan, I realize how she is differently positioned than I am in discussing these issues. I read her works because I want to hear her point of view, I want to develop empathy for Chinese and Chinese American experiences, I want to develop interpretive communities that can sustain multiple points of view. I read her novel neither to study uncritically at the feet of a putative expert on motherhood nor to prove her view of motherhood wrong and mine right. To me, we each have a partial point of view that stems from the specificity of our experiences. We need each other's partiality to make more sense of our own.

Empathy constitutes an important skill within critical pedagogy. We can't remake another group's experience by collapsing it into our own, but we can use our own experience to imagine what that group experiences, thinks, and feels. Developing a critical consciousness on one's own experiences is a vital first step, with this self-knowledge becoming the basis for imagining a comparable human experience for other groups. Empathy enables us to identify points of similarity and divergence between the aspirations of our own group and those of other groups, to engage in dialogues with other groups, and to enter into workable coalitions.

Grounding classroom communities in critical pedagogy potentially leads to alternative epistemologies, or ways of knowing, that legitimate what counts as knowledge. Those ideas that are validated as true by African American women, African American men, Latina lesbians, Asian American women, Puerto Rican men, and other groups with distinctive standpoints become the most "objective" truths. Each group speaks from its own standpoint and shares its own partial, situated knowledge. Yet, because each group perceives its own truth as partial, its knowledge is unfinished. Each group becomes better able to consider other groups' experiences without relinquishing the uniqueness of its own or suppressing other groups' partial perspectives. "What is always needed in the appreciation of art, or life," maintains Alice Walker, "is the larger perspective. Connections made, or at least attempted, where none existed before, the straining to encompass in one's glance at the varied world the common thread, the unifying theme through immense diversity." Partiality, not universality, is the condition of being heard.

Why Teach for a Change?

Classroom communities that are grounded in a critical pedagogy are vitally important for social justice projects. The knowledge that emerges from classroom communities may create more useful constructs, paradigms, and epistemologies than those offered in the dominant curriculum. Moreover, the processes used to arrive at that knowledge may be equally, if not more, important.

My second graders had an angle of vision concerning the meaning of *community* that grew from their lived experience. Many middle-class white children and increasingly children of color may also live in communities that resemble the version of community in my second graders' text; many do not. There are so many other variations on community in the United States that resemble neither my students' realities nor the lives of white middle-class children idealized in the texts. How do homeless children living in the parks of Berkeley, California, experience community? What's the meaning of the term to the children of undocumented Asian and Mexican immigrants? How do the Haitian children incarcerated in Florida camps awaiting a judgment on their bid for asylum feel about the term "community"? Poor white kids are conspicuously missing in debates about community services. How do middle-class white children really feel about growing up in these idealized communities? Is this how they see their world, or does this perspective represent the beliefs of the adult textbook writer? The community life of American children is deeply textured and different. Moreover, if these children do not readily encounter each other in their second-grade classrooms, they may later on in high school, college, or the workplace. Shouldn't these individuals collectively be allowed to redefine the meaning of the construct "community" so that it reflects the differences of their multiple realities?

Content matters, yet an even more significant benefit stemming from teaching for change is that everyone in the classroom actively creates knowledge rather than passively receives it. My second graders needed to know much more about their community than how the rules of the game worked. They needed skills that would equip them to change those rules. When we create vibrant classroom communities, we each know that we are not alone in this quest.

ADDITIONAL RESOURCES

Collins, Patricia Hill. 1992. "Learning to Think for Ourselves: Malcolm X's Black Nationalism Reconsidered." In *Malcolm X: In Our Own Image*, pp. 59–85, ed. Joe Wood. New York: St. Martin's Press.

———. 2009. *Another Kind of Public Education: Race, Schools, the Media, and Democratic Possibilities*. Boston: Beacon Press.

Lorde, Audre. 1984. *Sister Outsider: Essays and Speeches*. Freedom, Calif.: Crossing Press.

Mills, C. Wright. 2000. *The Sociological Imagination*. New York: Oxford University Press.

Warren, Mark R. 2010. *Fire in the Heart: How White Activists Embrace Racial Justice*. New York: Oxford University Press.

13

Another Kind of Public Education

REFLEXIVE ESSAY: *From its inception, I envisioned* On Intellectual Activism *and* Another Kind of Public Education *as complementary volumes of public sociology. Together, they are expressions of intellectual activism aiming to speak to a general public. I include the preface from* Another Kind of Public Education *because it provides a succinct statement of how my analysis of critical education in that book constitutes extensions of core themes of Black feminism that I present in Part I of* On Intellectual Activism. *The ideas in these companion books reappear across many of my publications.*

ON AUGUST 28, 1963, Martin Luther King, Jr., stood on the steps of the Lincoln Memorial in Washington, D.C., and delivered his famous "I Have a Dream" speech to an estimated 200,000 to 300,000 people who were gathered at the March on Washington for Jobs and Freedom. One line stands out: "I have a dream that my four little children will one day live in a nation where they will not be judged by the color of their skin but by the content of their character." Some would say that the outcome of the 2008 U.S. presidential election has been either the realization of King's dream or evidence of its failure. We can speculate endlessly about how and why Barack Obama won and John McCain lost, but this may not be the best use of our time. For the United States and the globe, too much is at stake to concentrate too closely on winners and losers.

Quite frankly, no one wins and everyone loses if the social issues that face growing numbers of the world's population are not given serious thought. We know the list—environmental degradation, illiteracy, poverty, HIV/AIDS, a global fiscal crisis, hopelessness, and violence in all its forms require critical analysis coupled with new action strategies. Everyone loses if we continue to think of the world's population itself as divided into winners and losers. Who wins, for example, if the children and youth of the world lose?

This framework of winners and losers is unlikely to shed light on the complex issues of our times. In this context, political parties or any other group that claims to have quick and easy solutions may itself be part of the problem. When times are tough, people look to leaders to give them hope and tell them what to do. It is seductive to see our most cherished leaders as responsible for solving problems—vesting them with authority enables us to praise or blame them for the answers they propose. Yet the more sobering realization is that they can only lead us where we are willing to go. We must learn to think for ourselves as individuals and also to act collectively. We are each unique, yet each of us is also part of something bigger.

I think that the United States is at a turning point in its history and that it should look to the lessons of world history for guidance. Blind faith in strong leaders has gotten many groups of people into trouble. In countries where a small group seizes power and imposes its will on an unwilling populace, we recognize that shift of power as an illegitimate coup. But we are less skilled at seeing how individuals and groups manipulate structures of power for their own ends, often within legitimate structures of government. For example, the National Socialist German Worker's Party was elected to office in Germany in 1933. There was no palace coup—the Nazis did not seize power. Instead, a legitimate democratic election bought them to power, and once in office, they so quickly changed the rules of the game that they eviscerated the meaning of democracy. There are numerous cautionary tales such as this, of how democratic power was wrested from an unwilling public, or worse yet, willingly relinquished by a public that confused its own interests with those of its elected officials. In democratic societies, people who passively follow the rules and uncritically obey their leaders open up their countries to undemocratic outcomes. Unquestioned obedience may be the best way to run an army, but it can be the death knell for democracy if a citizenry chooses this path.

The United States prides itself on being one of the greatest democracies of all time and calls on each individual citizen to defend democracy from its enemies. The enemy, however, is not the historically imagined enemy of brown or black youth, more often depicted as America's problem than as its promise. The enemy is not the nameless, faceless, yet ethnically imagined terrorist that we have been encouraged to fear in the post-9/11 environment. Rather, the greater enemy to American democracy is more likely to be an uninformed and uncritical American public that can be manipulated by soothing political slogans, feel-good photo ops, and an endless round of holiday sales.

What the United States needs is another kind of public education, one that encourages us to become an involved, informed public. What this country needs is a recommitment to schools and other social institutions whose mandate lies in delivering the kind of public education that will equip us for this task. We miseducate the public and students when we dumb down big ideas and shy away from politics. We do not need a public that stands on the sidelines, cheering on political candidates as if they were heavyweight contestants in boxing matches, or a public that passively listens to political commentary with an ear attuned to the latest put-down. Voting, for example, is more serious than calling in one's opinion to *American Idol*, or text messaging one's fan favorite to *America's Next Top Model*.

In *Another Kind of Public Education: Race, Schools, the Media and Democratic Possibilities*, I argue for another kind of education that better prepares the American public for democratic action in our contemporary social and political context. Two core questions shape this entire project: First, what kind of critical education might the American public need to envision new democratic possibilities? Second, what changes can we envision in schools and other important social institutions that might provide this critical education? Because these questions can never be answered in any one book, here, I focus my discussion on four important themes.

First, I emphasize the persisting effects of race in a seemingly colorblind society. Because of its history, race has been tightly bundled with the social issues of education and equity in the U.S. context. Moreover, in the current seemingly colorblind context, where the next generation of Americans is increasingly of color, the United States must find a way to build a democratic national community with an increasingly heterogeneous population. Rather than equating excellence with elitism—the posture that encourages keeping people out—we might define excellence as being compatible with diversity. Only with a range of points of view involved in the democratic process will the United States get the kind of innovation that it needs. I posit that grappling with this deeply entrenched challenge to U.S. democracy should yield provocative ideas and new directions for dismantling similar social inequalities.

Second, I focus on schools as one important site where these challenges are negotiated. Because public schools in America are vested with the responsibility of preparing each generation of new citizens, schools are inherently political. I also focus on pedagogy as a crucial component of democratic practice. Teachers have vitally important jobs, not simply delivering skills for jobs or acting as simple conduits for information. Rather, teachers are front-line actors in negotiating the social issues of our time. Teachers are the ones who black and brown youth turn to for guidance for upward social mobility. Teachers can be facilitators or gatekeepers of this fundamental democratic ideal.

Third, I focus on the media. If you define public education as what public institutions teach us about our place in the world, schools are by no means the only institutions educating young people and the broader public. In this book, I would like you to watch out for how kids get another kind of public education beyond school-based learning from the media. Whether we like it or not, for youth, the media provide an education that often contradicts and supplants school-based learning. New technologies are the currency of youth, and a critical education requires media literacy that prepares youth to be critical consumers of media as well as cultural creators.

Fourth, I speak to and about youth. When I think about the American public, I envision a heterogeneous population of youth characterized by vast differences in wealth, religion, appearance, sexual orientation, gender, linguistic competencies, immigrant status, ability level, ethnicity, and race. Some are in schools, some are not, and all are trying to figure out their place within American democratic institutions. I see the talent and potential of this heterogeneous population as crucial for American democracy. Yet I also see tremendous differences in opportunities that are offered to youth. In this context, just as school is inherently political, so is this youth population.

As young adults in early-twenty-first-century America, youth see the challenges that face them—a deep-seated worry about the uncertain future that awaits them in such volatile times; a growing disenchantment with the seeming inability of the United States to provide equal opportunities to a sizable proportion of its youth of color; their impatience with parents, teachers, clergy, and others who struggle with the rapid technological shifts that brought the wonders of the Internet and cell phones. But mostly, the politically savvy among them see the significance of themselves as the next generation of leaders.

Youth will not be following us. Rather, we will be following them. I want them to be prepared to lead me in directions that eschew complacency and put some genuinely new ideas on the table. I do not want to follow them down a path of hopelessness, but rather look to them to envision and take action toward new possibilities that I could not consider in my life. Therein lies the critical significance of delivering another kind of public education to youth. They will inherit not only social issues but also the responsibility for addressing them. To meet these challenges, youth will need another kind of public education that equips them with tools to take informed action.

As you read, I'd like you to keep in mind several factors that shaped this book. First, *Another Kind of Public Education* grew out of my activities as a public intellectual and sociologist of race. The issues that I investigate come not only from academic settings but also from the ordinary conversations of everyday life. I talk with different kinds of people on a regular basis about a wide range of topics. I don't seek out issues—rather, they come to me through my talks on college and university campuses, conversations with friends and neighbors, chats with people while standing in line in supermarkets and airports, or commiseration with people after my exercise classes. Because I have been working on the ideas in this volume for some time, the arguments presented here have been honed through dialogue with a variety of people.

My career as an educator constitutes a second factor that influenced this book. I have spent more than twenty-six years teaching in public systems of higher education. Before that, I spent four years as a university administrator and six years teaching elementary and middle school in the community schools movement of Boston, Massachusetts. As a lifelong educator, I understand how important teachers are at all levels of education. I also see how education is vitally important to solving the major social issues that confront democratic societies such as ours. Thus, I write not only as a scholar of education but also as a practitioner. In this book, I draw on many examples from my own teaching, not as examples of best practices to emulate, but rather as examples to carry the main ideas of my argument.

Third, this book had a specific catalyst, a factor that influenced how I wrote it. *Another Kind of Public Education* was developed from a series of lectures that were originally given in spring 2008. When I received the invitation to speak to the public as part of the *Race, Education and Democracy* lecture series at Simmons College, I had been thinking about these ideas for some time and had this title in mind for the actual book. The invitation to participate in the lecture series could not have come at a better time. The chapters presented here reflect a choice of language and tone commensurate with the lectures. Unlike much of my other writing, I occasionally use a more personal, informal style. Whenever possible, I have also incorporated some of the many rich ideas that characterized each lecture's question-and-answer period. The fact that these were lectures helps explain my ambition for the book—to bring to a general audience a line of thinking and ideas that are usually talked about in scholarly conversations. I remind readers that public dialogue and debate is the cornerstone of democracy, and I was fortunate enough to develop this book in that context.

Fourth, I should point out that this approach to using conversations with a wide range of people and, in this case, the more focused dialogues of the *Race, Education and Democracy* series constitutes a contemporary expression of a longstanding thread within American democratic social thought. In writing this book, I consulted not just current debates about education but also a broader conception of public education that draws inspiration from traditions of American pragmatism. John Dewey's work on democracy and education, as well as that of William E. B. Du Bois, Jane Addams, and Alain Locke, among others, has a special place here. In the early twentieth century, thinkers such as these emphasized the significance of educating the American public for democracy in a rapidly changing society. We face similar challenges today. I draw inspiration from and amplify their historic calls for linking democracy and education. I place myself (modestly, but ambitiously) in a tradition of public intellectuals speaking to these issues.

Finally, the intertwining themes of race, schools, the media, and youth are woven throughout the entire book. The volume focuses on racism and its effects on American youth, yet I suggest that if we can diagnose racism, we can envision new democratic possibilities. In what ways do schools perpetuate racism and other forms of social inequality, and what can parents, schools, teachers, and students do about it? How might youth in a consumer society speak the truth to a powerful force of media that now holds sway? What will it take to prepare youth from heterogeneous backgrounds for the challenges they will face in sustaining democratic institutions?

Writing this book without knowing the outcome of the November 2008 elections was a real nail-biter for me. In hindsight, I am glad that I did not know. Not knowing required me to think more broadly about the core ideas of my argument, the ideas that are larger than any political party, any media figure, and the specific expression of broader issues concerning democracy as they are expressed at this historic moment. Today we confront our particular variation of the struggle to craft an American democracy that is adequate to the challenges of our times. We can learn from the achievements and unsolved problems of prior generations who grappled with the same overarching questions, but they do not have answers to our problems. There are no easy solutions. Instead, there is the need for another kind of public education so that we, as a public, will be up to the challenge.

ADDITIONAL RESOURCE

Carson, Clayborne, and Kris Shepard, eds. 2002. *A Call to Conscience: The Landmark Speeches of Dr. Martin Luther King, Jr.* New York: Warner Books.

Making Space for Public Conversations

An Interview

REFLEXIVE ESSAY: *Because classrooms are places that can deaden or elevate the sprit, teaching has been a fundamental part of my commitment to critical pedagogy. To help me think through the ways in which classrooms can facilitate public conversations between teachers and students, as well as among students themselves, I invited two sociology graduate students to help me develop and co-teach two undergraduate courses. The first, "Sociology of Black Activism," co-taught with Kathryn Buford, asked students to reflect on their understandings of activism. The second, "Public Sociology," co-taught with David Strohecker, examined the intellectual and political issues of doing public sociology. This interview is taken from a conversation that I had with my co-instructors and with Meg Austin Smith, a sociology graduate student and the editorial assistant for* On Intellectual Activism, *regarding the connections among critical education, activism, public sociology, and critical pedagogy.*

Imagination is more important than knowledge.
—ALBERT EINSTEIN (1879–1955)

Meg Austin Smith: Your work has always seemed to look for ways to make space for public conversations—space for questions that look critically at power relations, at resistance, and toward hope and democratic possibilities. Could we start by talking a little bit about how you began doing the work that you do?

This interview was conducted on March 14, 2011. Special thanks to Meg Austin Smith for preparing and editing the original transcript.

Patricia Hill Collins: My life's work originated within the context of activist politics, specifically, Martin Luther King, Jr's vision of "Beloved Community." The idea of Beloved Community envisions a public space that is heterogeneous and participatory, and where we each see how we are responsible for bringing it about.

Martin Luther King, Jr. has been much misunderstood, particularly the ways in which his signature "I Have a Dream" speech has been recast as a simple individual exercise of trying not to see the color of one's skin and instead trying to see the content of one's character. This reinterpretation fits well with current arguments that the best way for the U.S. to move forward is to reject structural changes for jobs (which was also part of the "I Have a Dream Speech") in favor of individual choice to aspire for colorblindness. Yet this particular reading of King's speech privatizes our relationships to one another in ways that recast social justice initiatives such as the Civil Rights movement primarily as individual, one-on-one relationships. King's notion of Beloved Community has also been recast in terms that uphold the worldview of people who had a vested interest in keeping the status quo. Here, the notion of Beloved Community becomes redefined as a friendly, happy, harmonious community free of conflict and social inequality. The Beloved Community is a colorblind community. Because the U.S. is so far away from colorblindness, and this vision of community, King gets reinterpreted as a "dreamer," whose Beloved Community constitutes an unachievable utopia.

King's vision was far broader than these interpretations. In his "I Have a Dream" speech and throughout the corpus of his work, he develops a more sophisticated conception of the Beloved Community as a democratic ideal toward which one aspires but that one never reaches. One cannot have a Beloved Community without ensuring equal participation by all, and this includes poor people, Black people, women, and any group on the bottom of society. His is more an altruistic and radical political framework. King's vision does have elements of utopia, but it also emphasizes strategies that one might engage with to bring about such communities.

If I had to look for inspiration for my life's work, it would be this more expansive definition of Beloved Community, but it would also be tightly wedded to remaining open to a range of strategies that might bring such communities about. For example, I remain a fan of Malcolm X, primarily because Malcolm X was quite clear about saying that we are perfectly within our rights to defend ourselves and to argue on our own behalf. Just as King has been reduced to a one-dimensional icon of nonviolence, Malcolm X has undergone a similar transformation to being a symbol of violence. Toward the end of his life, like King, Malcolm X also began to argue for a broader, global sense of social justice. Although he did not use King's language of the Beloved Community, I see their commitment to social justice as being theoretically equivalent, yet strategically distinctive. Because they were both assassinated, we don't know what either one of these important Black intellectual activists would have thought had they lived.

My life's work has engaged the types of issues that confronted King and Malcolm X. It's that simple. My life's work has been devoted to fostering both the theoretical and the strategic aspects of the Beloved Community wherever I am. Sometimes I emphasize theory more than practice, or practice more than theory, but both are always considerations for me.

The phrase "Beloved Community" remains in use today. For me, the idea of Beloved Community is best reflected in contemporary social justice projects. The term social justice functions as a big umbrella that accommodates many distinct projects: racial justice, economic justice, and environmental justice initiatives come to mind. Sometimes social justice projects refer to social groups and the case for racial justice. In other cases, social issues form the core of social justice initiatives, as is the case with efforts to reform the prison system or to protect the environment from global warming. I use the language of social justice because I think that's what works now, but I see social justice as synonymous with King's sense of Beloved Community. So my life's work speaks to intellectual and political projects that can be placed under the umbrella of social justice.

My social justice work has taken different forms. Primarily, it has been intellectual, because I really do believe in the power of ideas. Not only do I see the power of the word but I also aim to use and share it through my writing and public speaking. Yet I've also had more activist phases in my life, where I could more appropriately be identified as being an activist. For example, in the 1970s, I spent six years working with the community schools movement in Roxbury, Massachusetts. Working in the schools was no picnic, but talk about a wonderful time in my life! Many people would identify those years as my "activist phase" because they understand activism as something that you do for some liberal cause when you are young. If you are lucky, you grow out of it. But they don't seem to realize that you become more effective as an activist as you see more possibilities, as you gain the wisdom of experience.

That's how I would frame out my life's work: using the power of ideas to advance social justice projects across many different social institutions. Doing the kind of work that I do, you realize that you have to create the conditions to make the work possible. You have to protect the conditions that make your work possible. You look at the conditions you are in, and those become a set of possibilities for thinking through the particular combinations of ideas and actions or praxis, not only for that point in time but also for what comes next.

Dave Strohecker: What place, in your opinion, does activist politics have in academia?

Patricia Hill Collins: Academia *is* activist politics, where struggles over the meaning of ideas constitute the primary terrain of action. I teach a graduate seminar on the sociology of knowledge whose fundamental tenet is that all knowledge is a carrier of power. What we call something shapes how we use it, value it, legitimate it, and de-legitimate it. Calling anything "activist politics" is the kiss of death in academia, because it is often assumed that one cannot be "academic," in other words, appropriately objective, and "activist," which many academics see as synonymous with irrationality. It is a particular view of the academy that separates out ideas and practice; that separates out mind, body, and passion; that separates out truth and knowledge from politics and ethics. That's a view of the world that I reject. Instead, I am comfortable with a world-view that sees objectivity and activism as linked—to be intellectual and activist is to be knowledgeable, critical, passionate, and caring, all at the same time. The term "intellectual activism" reflects this synergy.

We need to do a better job of analyzing how academia masks or hides its own political behavior. In this regard, the politics of academia resemble those of white privilege, where white privilege operates everywhere, but somehow we lack an effective language to talk about it. So I approach colleges and universities as profoundly political entities. Within the current broader political climate, the politics of academia have become much more tethered not just to the state interests but also to the corporate world. Maintaining the fiction that activism lies outside the university is naive, especially for graduate students, junior faculty, or people working in colleges and universities who lack the protection of tenure.

Meg Austin Smith: When you say that "academia is activist politics," recognizing that activist politics has to do with creating and protecting the conditions that make your work possible, are you thinking about things like peer review and processes of admission, things that really are all about protecting existing conditions?

Patricia Hill Collins: Activist politics is often the only reason why I grudgingly perform university and professional service. I do it because it's part of how I approach intellectual activism. You have to understand, even though I like my students and colleagues, I resent the constant drumbeat of requests to write letters of recommendation for virtually everything they have done or wish to do. I resent having to sit in my office drafting letter after letter, filling out numerous forms that say, "Person X is wonderful, so give him/her money," or "Person Y is wonderful, so please admit him/her to your graduate program." This is all part of an audit culture, where we are all required to measure ourselves by corporate criteria so we can rank people and fit them in the appropriate boxes. The endless surveys about virtually all aspects of our consumer experience circulated by airlines, banks, hotels, and stores seem to have the same purpose as the endless evaluative requests within academia. How is this vast amount of data actually used? Who really benefits from this perpetual audit? It angers me that some of my colleagues, many of whom are well-respected scholars, think that this kind of service work is somehow beneath them. Despite my frustration, I involve myself in processes such as writing letters of recommendation, and I write the best letters that I can for my students and colleagues because I realize it is crucial to do. I don't flail away at things I can't really change by myself. What I will do is try to massage those rules to change them if I can—that is what an insider can do.

Meg Austin Smith: How does Beloved Community connect to your vision of what *public* is? How can public sociology be a strategy for working toward Beloved Community?

Patricia Hill Collins: I envision the Beloved Community as a social group that embraces all of its members. Yet, within the space of Beloved Community, with its ethos of as social justice, there is also space for disagreement. People seem to assume that communities are happy places where no one disagrees. But to construct a vision of Beloved Community, there must be conflict and dialogue, and not running away from the conflict that might come from dialogues across differences. Communities negotiate power relations across differences. What makes a community a "beloved" community is that people within it are committed to working through these differences in power in ways that make communities fair for everyone.

The idea of a public can be coterminous with the idea of community. But not all publics or communities adhere to a social justice ethos that moves them toward King's ideal of the Beloved Community. The idea of people or a public incorporates ideas about heterogeneity. Ideas such as "public" and "community" are tied to the goal of democracy, namely, as rule by the people (who, in the U.S., are heterogeneous across categories of race, class, gender, sexuality, age, and religion) as opposed to rule by royal families, clergy, or economic elites. Public sociology tries to speak to these broader issues of democratic possibilities and democratic power relations to develop action strategies that move in that direction. This is a vision of what public could be when informed with ideas about the Beloved Community.

At the same time, I think we must be attentive to shifting perceptions of what "public" actually means. Contemporary U.S. politics seems characterized by a shrinking of respect for anything public as well as an unwillingness to commit to anything public. In *Another Kind of Public Education*, I talk about the lack of commitment to public schools, public housing, public health. Anything public is devalued in a marketplace economy. Public space is increasingly understood as stigmatized space for people who can't pay their own way. Marketplace relations that commodify and place a value on everything aggravate or even require this devaluation of the public and its associations with "free." If we were just talking about handbags, shoes, and tangible commodities, I would be much less upset about privatization. I am fine with leaving people to fend for themselves to purchase fancy handbags and shoes. But as long as we have high rates of child poverty in the U.S., I remain committed to strengthening all public institutions that support children and their families. To me, the devaluation of public institutions weakens fundamental democratic institutions.

There's a lot of discussion around public schools now—that's where these debates have moved—but I would like to use a different site to make this point. The refusal to fund infrastructure projects—water pipes; the electrical grid; bridges that are old, crumbling, and in disrepair—dramatically limits this country's ability to move forward. In the greater D.C. metropolitan area, for example, I cannot fathom why government cannot adequately fund public transportation (the Metro). It is at the hub of Virginia, Maryland, and the District. The Metro is crucial in transporting federal workers to and from work, as well as transporting the thousands of tourists and schoolchildren who visit our nation's capital. Many people ride this public transportation system, not just poor people, as is the case in many other metropolitan areas. Yet, not even a major train crash in 2009 that killed several riders and may have been aggravated by delayed maintenance was enough to stimulate public action. Despite the need, there remains a refusal to pay, one that I think persists because the system serves the "public," and the "public" is imagined to be African American, Latino, working class, young, poor, and generally made up of people who cannot afford a private automobile. Yet, the D.C. metropolitan area is also known for having some of the worst traffic in the nation. We expect private citizens to purchase private automobiles and drive them on clogged public roads that also suffer from a lack of public funding. When you talk about public transportation, you run into some barriers that occur around any discussion of public, writ large. For a democracy to cultivate its public, it has to fund its public institutions. You can't have it both ways: to have lofty ideals of democracy without funding the institutions that uphold them.

Dave Strohecker: Often, in the U.S., power is represented as being within the individual—stories about heroes or persons who have "overcome all odds" or the superhumanly beautiful or athletic or strong are constantly on TV, in newspapers and magazines, and in best-selling biographies and even fiction. You have written about this culture of individualism—or privatization—in which the success of "exceptional" individuals is used to mask persisting social problems and about how this culture often serves as a means of justifying vicious attacks on public institutions, as you were just describing. How can a commitment to "public" represent a kind of resistance to this logic? And how can it offer encouragement to re-imagine what is *possible*, even for those who benefit from this culture of privatization?

Patricia Hill Collins: I think the response is to pick the public institution you are going to commit to and just do it. Just go there. Committing to a public institution is one way of advancing broader goals of social justice. Not everybody wants to do this. In my case, I chose public institutions of higher education and have worked in this area for more than thirty years. I have not always attended public institutions as a student, but without access to my 12 years of quality public education provided by the Philadelphia public schools and the expansive holding of the Free Public Library of Philadelphia, I would have been unable to compete for college scholarships, let alone attend college and find good jobs. So I have realized the importance of public institutions for upward social mobility, not only in my own life but also for all those who want to better themselves and their families.

Institutions like the University of Maryland and the University of Cincinnati are special places that should be valued more than they are for the important work that they do as public institutions. One important function of public institutions of higher education is that they provide educational access for students from heterogeneous backgrounds. That's one reason why I like public institutions—their demographics often reflect those of the general public from which they draw their students. I like teaching at public institutions of higher education because that's where I find sizable numbers of students of color, women, LGBT students, immigrant students, returning students, and not just a few token members of these groups. I like working with sufficiently large enough populations so that I can see the heterogeneity *within* various groups, among African Americans, for example, and not just stereotype African Americans based on conversations with the few individuals who happen to enroll in a given course. Public institutions are pressured to measure their performance using standards that have been developed for private institutions. Do not get me wrong—I value private institutions of higher education as well—but one reason why private institutions achieve excellence is that they have sufficient funding. If public institutions were funded to the same level as private ones, think how different that would be for the populations we serve.

I know many people who are committed to public education and public institutions of all sorts—I am not the only one. One disappointing dimension of my teaching over the past several years is how often people around me do not think that activism and political resistance are viable options within and/or against public institutions in their everyday lives. Activism is episodic, namely, something you do when your real work is done, or every couple of years, when an election is held. Students often do not see public institutions as being important venues for sustained and long-term activism, for example, becoming involved in the admissions process or being an active lifelong member of the alumni association. In *Another Kind of Public Education,* I aim to refute these views by providing domains of framework in ways that catalyze a language of resistance. With their focus on community, activism, and public, both courses drew from that framework as an organizational scaffold for the material.

Dave Strohecker: By helping students learn to question assumptions and think reflexively about where they are coming from when they form their questions, you really listen to students and students' ways of questioning in (and out of) the classroom. This helps to break down the idea of a student–teacher dichotomy—it helps students see the teacher as a learner and helps students see themselves as both learners and teachers. With the "Public Sociology" and "Sociology of Black Activism" classes, what are some of the things you have learned about doing public sociology with students? Are there particular strengths or weaknesses they have helped you see about public sociology as a way of knowing and a way of questioning?

Patricia Hill Collins: We had great students in both courses. As individuals, they had interesting lives and I learned much from them concerning what it's like to be in one's early twenties in contemporary America. Collectively, however, one thing that stood out for me was how rusty the students have become in exercising their imaginations. Anyone who has spent time with small children knowsthat they routinely ask big questions, propose outrageous hypotheses, and are not shy in testing out their ideas. I think the undergraduate students in both courses were more passive than I would have liked in how they learned. The skill set of passivity that may have served them well in high school and in large lecture classes often maladapted them for the demands of our courses. They needed far more practice in problem solving and imagining new ways of living their lives than I initially expected. It's not that the students were resistant to ideas about activism and thinking for themselves, but rather, they initially were quite skeptical that exercising their imaginations would be worth it.

Another striking thing for me was how little our students knew about how the world worked. Students in both classes often had a minimal grasp of history. So they tended to develop solutions to problems that were new to them, but that were not necessarily new at all. Curriculum content had to fill in gaps in their knowledge, an ironic thing, given the explosion of information that surrounded them. Once they were armed with information, they often asked themselves, "Why don't I know about this?" We had students in both classes who were predisposed to wanting to change the world, make a difference, resist, and bring about a Beloved Community. But I saw a significant disconnect between their ability to imagine such communities and to draw from past wisdom in crafting solutions for contemporary social problems.

Dave Strohecker: How do you think public sociology can reinvigorate or spark imagination?

Patricia Hill Collins: To be honest with you, I don't think public sociology as a content area or field of study can do it. Instead, I think that we need solid curriculum materials that teachers can use to introduce new ways of viewing the world. For example, since the 1990s, Margaret Andersen and I have been co-editing *Race, Class, and Gender*, an anthology of readings designed primarily for undergraduate classrooms. We revise our book every three years so that we can trace how this important field of study is unfolding. Via this project, we do public sociology rather than just talk about it. I also think we need critical pedagogy across a range of disciplines that helps students develop skills of critical thinking and imagination. What came out of teaching both courses for me had less to do with the content of either course than with a renewed understanding of how important the process can be. It's far more difficult to cast a critical eye on your own teaching, and on areas of expertise in which you have a vested interest, and to encourage students to criticize them.

Course content such as that in "Sociology of Black Activism" and "Public Sociology" lends itself to the kinds of issues we have been talking about today. The bigger question is providing a critical pedagogy, regardless of content. We do not serve students well by trying to entertain them with videos (we can certainly make effective use of videos as teaching tools) or by feeding them cookies, cupcakes, and pizza to improve our teaching evaluations. Media is a great supplement for teaching—our Sociological Cinema project fielded by University of Maryland sociology graduate students speaks to that—but it is no substitute for good teaching. If I could do a little teachable moment here, let me say more about process.

Critical pedagogy rests on a three-legged stool. First, as instructors, we have content to deliver. We want people to leave our courses knowing something they didn't know before. The content of "Public Sociology" and "Sociology of Black Activism" lent itself to critical pedagogy. Neither course was required, so the students who took these courses tended to be motivated. Both courses provided historical and contemporary material that held students' interest because, while not necessarily new to us, the content was new for students. For example, I was surprised at how much the students in "Public Sociology" enjoyed reading books like Barry Glassner's *The Culture of Fear: Why Americans Are Afraid of the Wrong Things* as a bestseller of public sociology; Charles Fishman's *The Wal-Mart Effect*; or Nicholas D. Kristof and Sheryl WuDunn's bestseller *Half the Sky: Turning Oppression into Opportunity for Women Worldwide*. Our students often read these books not just to unpack the arguments of the authors but also to gain information. I was similarly taken by how much the students in "Sociology of Black Activism" enjoyed our approach to activism as being grounded in music and the arts. They liked hearing the music of Nina Simone—it opened their eyes to a view that mass media is not necessarily all about entertainment and that popular culture can be a legitimate and important site of activism.

Second, we have a skill set that we want students to practice throughout a course. Teaching critical thinking is far more complicated than "teach them how to think." What does that mean? Norris Sanders' classic book, *Classroom Questions: What Kinds?*, identifies components of critical thinking that range from skills of simple translation, to application of concepts, to analysis, to synthesis, to evaluation. Critical pedagogy pays attention to these dimensions of critical thinking, trying to help students develop skills that are appropriate for them. For example, if a student cannot translate from one language to another, for example, from academic language to his or her own words, how can we expect that student to understand complicated work? Students in both courses found certain readings difficult because they had not had sufficient practice in translating this kind of material into their own words. This is something I grapple with now in teaching social theory on the graduate level. How do you analyze something if you haven't translated it? How do you evaluate something that you don't understand?

The third leg of critical pedagogy's three-legged stool involves something called "affective learning." How students feel in class shapes so much of how they receive content as well as their ability to develop critical thinking. Emotions matter for students and teachers alike. Social inequalities become important here via all the classroom practices that create privilege and penalty in the classroom, with all the feelings of empowerment and hurt that go with them. When we set up our classes such that some people dominate classroom discussions and others never say anything, we are actually teaching inequality and the emotions that it engenders. Social hierarchy is quite crucial to how students feel about learning, regardless of content and critical thinking.

These three things are crucial, and neglecting any one of them topples the stool and can sink what otherwise might be a well-planned course. In both classes, I was able to revisit these pedagogical issues of content, skills, and affect because I co-taught them with two of you. I had another set of eyes, hands, and ears, as well as an additional heart, in the classroom, and that made an important difference. If you are co-teaching, you must have dialogue, you must collaborate, and you must see what each person brings to the table, so I think that is a very important piece of critical pedagogy as well.

Kathryn Buford: I agree that we need to meet students where they are, and for "Sociology of Black Activism," we did get students who were predisposed to want to do "good"—somewhat of a social justice mindset. But also I think students were coming to that class to forge or refine an activist identity, or an anti-racist identity. One of our students, "Lisa," came to me to discuss one of the assigned readings. Lisa was grappling with Audre Lorde's text from *Sister Outsider* where Lorde calls out some injustices and hypocrisies in the feminist movement, particularly with white women. As a white female student, Lisa came to me, trying to get me to help her work through some of those issues she was having, such as: How is my identity associated with privilege? How can I be an anti-racist activist? How can I reconcile my commitment to helping this community without necessarily knowing exactly how to do this? She really took Lorde's critique of white feminism to heart. And I felt like she was wondering what her place was in, not just anti-racist activism, but black empowerment. In conversations that I had with her outside of class, I sensed that maybe she wanted me to help her resolve issues she was having with that, but I didn't know what to say; it kind of caught me off-guard. I realize I never brought this to you, but I'm wondering how you would have handled this. Had you anticipated students grappling with these concerns?

Patricia Hill Collins: I think that she was asking the very important question of how to be an ally if you are in a position of privilege. In this case, Lisa's questions concerned the uses to which white privilege could be put, because race was one theme of our course. Because she was white, she wanted to know how she could bring the power of whiteness to an anti-racist struggle. Fortunately for Lisa, there is a tradition of engaged scholarshipthat might help her. A classic work such as "White Privilege: Unpacking the Invisible Knapsack" by Peggy McIntosh (reprinted in *Race, Class, and Gender: An Anthology,* 8th edition) provides a template for all the places that white privilege might be named and challenged. Social science studies of whites involved in racial justice activism, for example, Mark Warren's important study *Fire in the Heart: How White Activists Embrace Racial Justice,* would be excellent suggested reading for Lisa.

But the overall issues that she raises are much broader than race. Being an ally requires learning how to form working relationships across differences in power. Depending on what kind of privilege you have (race, class, gender, sexuality, age, or citizenship status), how can you be an ally to people who are disadvantaged by your privilege? How do you respect their space to do what they need to do, but without having your privilege take over? Men who are upset by the treatment of women; affluent people who are concerned about poverty; straight people who are offended by the discrimination that LGBT people routinely confront; and American citizens who think that immigration policies penalizing undocumented Latino, Asian, and African immigrants are flawed, all face this theme of how to be an allies from positions of privilege. These issues of forming relationships across differences in power are just as germane to classroom dynamics among teachers and students as they are in politics of race, gender, or economic class. She was really sensitive to thinking through those issues, and she was in the moment of thinking it through. I think she was thinking that, once she thought it through, she could just move on and be a really terrific ally.

The first thing we needed to do was to acknowledge the importance of her questions—to clap for her for raising them. White students like Lisa often receive little affirmation for taking difficult stances. That's the first thing. So often, getting people to the point where they can see their own privilege is difficult. They can see their own penalty, but not necessarily their privileges. For example, Black men do not want to examine how their gender privileges them in many situations (it penalizes them in others). Instead, they want the moral benefits that accrue to identities of being racially disadvantaged. Similarly, heterosexuals deny their heterosexual privilege regarding marriage, taxation, adoption, and police protection from hate crimes. Given this climate of denial, it is important to acknowledge the courage attached to that student's question.

I would caution you about one downside of being an African American professor. When it comes to anything concerning race, you end up with everybody on your doorstep. Students do not just learn racial content or develop skills of critical thinking by reading books by African American and African Diasporic authors. Instead, courses like "Sociology of Black Activism" can catalyze deep feelings and emotions in students. This is what makes such courses exhausting and exhilarating to teach. Lisa had needs, but each and every other student in that course had similar questions and needs. White students like Lisa might ask how they might become allies, yet a more typical response among white students is to struggle with the meaning of white privilege in their own lives. Black students tend to express a different set of issues that can develop into demands. The material can be just as new for them as for white students, yet their emotional reactions may differ. I have encountered Black students who have shown up in my office, extremely angry, often not knowing who they should be angry with or even why they are angry. Other Black students have heard material about racial oppression so many times that it leaves them dispirited.

I decided to call the class "Sociology of Black Activism" because I wanted to focus on *activism,* not oppression, on problem-solving *actions,* whether they were successful or not. This focus avoids the trap of overwhelming students with oppression information, leaving them informed but curiously disempowered. Instead, the focus is on studying people who have harnessed the power of their emotions to the critical task of bringing about social change. The knowledge becomes a vehicle for practicing critical thinking skills. Such people need not be victorious. Just knowing that they exist is often enough.

Kathryn Buford: In a similar sense, when we began that class, I wasn't thinking there was something particular I wanted Black students to get out of that class, but when we finished it, I think subconsciously there was—I did want Black students to understand the Diaspora, understand that the Black community is global in scope. What are the implications of wanting black students particularly to get that message out of the class? When you were teaching "Sociology of Black Activism," did you have in mind something you wanted particular students to take away?

Patricia Hill Collins: Absolutely. Let me say a bit more about how the classroom community itself had to consider how content, critical thinking, and emotional learning worked together in the course as well as how students from diverse backgrounds might experience that classroom.

For "Sociology of Black Activism," the dynamics of the classroom were crucial. Teaching the course to racially homogeneous classes of white or African American students would have produced different dynamics. Both classroom settings would have had value, but they would have limited our ability to do certain things and enhanced our options in other areas. In our case, we had a heterogeneous mix, but making sure that we had built as much diversity into the class as possible involved decisions that I made before the first student walked through the door.

Developing the course as a dual-listed offering by both Sociology and African American Studies drew majors from each field. From the beginning, the course enrolled students with different expectations about what they wanted from the course that stemmed from their respective majors, as well as a skill set that said that they were not simply shopping for a diversity experience but also could bring some knowledge of their own to our discussions. We enrolled some African American students who were Africana Studies majors but also a sizable segment who were sociology majors. I was quite happy with the demographics of the course. I couldn't have asked for a better group of students.

When it comes to understanding how students experienced the classroom, we can't underestimate the agendas students bring for why they enrolled in the course. Some students come to be exposed to new knowledge, some students enroll to understand questions that they already have on their minds, and some students sign up because they want to develop action strategies for things that they already think they understand. I see students as distributed along a continuum ranging from extremely passive learners—those who sit and wait to be taught information, to extremely active learners—those who are already involved in activist activities and want more. Our classroom process was designed to disrupt the assumptions that students had, regardless of where they were positioned along that entire continuum.

I saw no significant substantive differences between the concerns of the white students and those of the Black students, save those of our earlier discussion of the role of white allies within Black activism. We had students distributed across all three groups, with varying reasons for taking the course. That's not to say that there were no differences, only that I'm not sure that they map well onto the assigned race of the student. Recall that the "black" students within "Sociology of Black Activism" were themselves quite diverse, with some from immigrant families from the Caribbean and African nations and others African Americans of quite different social class backgrounds. The students from Africana Studies who were of African descent seemed more attuned to thinking about action strategies and thought of activism not simply as an academic area of study. The students from sociology also were interested in action strategies, but they seemed more interested in understanding the Diaspora, perhaps because this had been underemphasized in prior courses. Moreover, some of the sociology students were on a research track and had to think about how action strategies and activism fit in with that path.

I would love to see Black students become much more proactive as leaders, more outspoken when it comes to race, and I would love to see them take on many of the issues of anti-racist struggle, but I do not see them as the only people doing that, nor do I see engaging in activism as a requirement for every Black student.

I am much more interested in seeing all of my students, regardless of their backgrounds, learn to think for themselves. When they do so, they move toward becoming leaders. I am sharing my ideas about my life's work because I hope that my experiences and analyses might be helpful in developing such leadership. If there are no people to replace me, well, then that's it. It's that simple. When I turn around and look back, I want to see people behind me who have a comprehensive knowledge about how the world works, who can think and problem solve, and who are passionate about what they think and do. Via my scholarship and my teaching, I do everything I can to expose students to the range of choices they have, but I will always say that. Your choice.

Dave Strohecker: Is that where you would like to see public sociology go?

Patricia Hill Collins: I certainly would like to see public sociology go in this direction, yet I am of two minds about the future of public sociology writ large and how it might connect with the ideas I've discussed thus far. Public sociology has provided an important set of tools for my life's work. When I read and reread works such as C. Wright Mills' *The Sociological Imagination*, I see public sociology's promise. I think we are in an interesting historical moment when the public looks more favorably on sociology, with public sociology the type of sociology they encounter. At the same time, I wonder: Will this excitement and engagement persist? Is public sociology another academic fad?

One way to address your question is to focus on the "Public Sociology" course. I think talking about the course will answer that question better then talking about public sociology in the abstract. I think the future of public sociology will be worked out through courses such as "Public Sociology," or by evaluating similar action strategies. What's happening in some classrooms is instructive. One concern that I have is that many instructors conflate public sociology with service learning, a worthwhile endeavor, but something that is far narrower than the expansive ideas of public sociology. So the students go out into the public and they do good, and then they come back and they write it up. It becomes almost a way to boost the sociology curriculum so that students get some skills that help them with their careers, that make them more competitive and, hopefully, more informed. Service learning asks students to support agendas that are crafted by others. Public sociology helps them to imagine and bring about new agendas via collaboration with specific publics (communities).

By requiring public sociology projects, in "Public Sociology," we asked our students to do something that was more difficult. They had no models of public sociology projects to follow. Instead, they had to create them. In doing so, they drew from skills of traditional research projects, for example, identifying a research question, researching relevant literature, preparing a methodology, executing the project, and writing up its findings for a scholarly audience. Yet we asked them to focus on the ways in which public sociology differed from a traditional research paradigm. They engaged traditional sociology through processes of acceptance and critique.

One of the most significant differences between public sociology and other forms of sociology concerns the relationship of all aspects of research with a specific or imagined public. It was challenging for our students to think about working in dialogue with their chosen publics to create projects that their publics would find meaningful. They had to make the conceptual shift from thinking they would learn useful information in college and take that knowledge back to their home communities or political projects to "serve" them. This is the standard disciplinary knowledge taken to an applied setting model, one where scholars talk down to the public. Instead, we asked them to consider how they would identify intellectual and/or political objectives *with* and not just *for* their chosen public. In "Public Sociology," we asked them to consider questions such as: Who's the audience for your public sociology project? Who is your imagined public? What are the best ways of determining good questions that are important to them? How will you share your findings with your public?

To address these questions, our students had to make connections between the sociological material of the "Public Sociology" course and their everyday lives. That is how undergraduates encounter sociology, and when they are happy with sociology, this type of engagement is what they are doing. I wanted them to position their public sociology projects in that space. Undergraduate students are front-line actors of public sociology, but often do not realize it. We wanted them to become lifelong sociologists and to take this public sociology sensibility into their worlds long after they ceased being sociology majors.

ADDITIONAL RESOURCES

Andersen, Margaret L., and Patricia Hill Collins, eds. 2013. *Race, Class, and Gender: An Anthology,* 8th edition. Belmont, Calif.: Wadsworth/Cengage Learning.

Duncan-Andrade, Jeff, and Ernest Morrell. 2009. *The Art of Critical Pedagogy.* New York: Peter Lang Publishing/USA.

North, Connie. 2009. *Teaching for Social Justice: Voices from the Front Lines.* Boulder, Colo.: Paradigm.

Sociological Cinema: Teaching and Learning Sociology through the Web. http://www. thesociologicalcinema.com/index.html. Accessed June 26, 2012.

IV

Racial Politics

Coloring Outside the Color Line

REFLEXIVE ESSAY: *I first presented the ideas in this essay as part of a panel discussion on race at the 2005 American Sociological Association's annual meeting in Philadelphia. I was born in Philadelphia, not far from the conference hotel, and I approached the session not solely as a theoretical abstraction but also though my own lived experiences. Because the specific setting was so important to the essay's arguments, I have maintained its original, spoken word feel. When I drafted these ideas, I could not have imagined that Barack Obama would be elected to the Presidency in 2008. Given the changing contours of racial politics since I delivered this talk, I have updated the essay in light of my current thinking about race but still keeping the immediacy of the place and time where I shared these ideas.*

AS WE MEET in Philadelphia on the 100th anniversary of the American Sociological Association, it seems fitting that I compare two stories about race, public education, and Philadelphia that have special meaning for me. The first concerns my futile search for African American history as a student in the Philadelphia public schools. During my twelve years of public school education, little mention was made of African Americans, save entries such as that in my sixth-grade history book. There Black history was collapsed into the slave experience, and the slave experience was further filtered through the lens of what whites wanted to believe about racial hierarchy and, by

---

I would like to thank David Strohecker at the University of Maryland for his assistance in locating statistical information for this essay. I include additional endnotes so that readers might locate updated information. I also encourage readers to consult the Note on Usage for a discussion of the politics of capitalization of "black" and "white."

implication, about the African Americans who routinely occupied the bottom of this hierarchy. There it was, one sentence: "The slaves were happy because they sang all the time." When I describe this unfortunate depiction, the audience often gasps. "How backward," I suspect they are thinking. "I'm so glad that America has moved beyond such blatantly discriminatory practices."

But has it? This brings me to my second Philadelphia story, one that speaks to early-twenty-first-century racial realities. In 2005, the Philadelphia public schools voted to make one course in Black history mandatory for all high school students. Defenders of the decision argued that the Philadelphia public schools needed to include more Black history in a spirit of reparations for the damage done to generations of public school children who, like their teachers and many college professors, remain stunningly ignorant about African American history and culture. Everyone would benefit, they argued, even white kids. However, criticisms were raised by white Philadelphians when the School Reform Commission unanimously passed this measure. Many white students and parents did not see how understanding "their [Black] history" would benefit them.[1]

To me, this was amazing. The Philadelphia public schools were still trying to address the issues of exclusion that I faced more than forty years earlier. Yet times had changed. Since I attended school in the 1960s, the white population of the city had steadily decreased—by 2005, whites made up approximately 40 percent of the city's population. During this same time, white parents virtually abandoned the school system, an immense school district serving more than 200,000 students in forty-three neighborhood and magnet high schools. By October 2005, African American students comprised 64.4 percent of the Philadelphia public schools, with Latino students a distant second at 15.8 percent.[2] As of the 2003–2004 school year, fewer than 15 percent of the students in the Philadelphia public schools were white.

Philadelphia is a textbook case of white flight from urban public schools. Social science research consistently points to how whites perceive racial tipping points in schools. Having a few African American children is acceptable, and even desirable if parents believe that their children benefit from having one or two Blacks as friends. Yet, when too many African American children seemingly populate a school, white parents believe (although most won't admit it) that their children's education will suffer. So whites leave en masse: for the suburbs, for private schools, for Catholic schools, for home schooling, for anyplace

---

[1] Janofsky, Michael. 2005. "Philadelphia Mandates Black History for Graduation." *The New York Times*, June 25. http://www.nytimes.com/2005/06/25/education/25philly.html. Accessed April 27, 2011.

[2] The demographics of the Philadelphia public schools were recorded in 2009 as 62 percent African American, 17 percent Latino, 13 percent white, 6 percent Asian American, and 1 percent other. This information was gathered by the Pew Foundation's Philadelphia Research Initiative in 2010. http://www.pewtrusts.org/uploadedFiles/wwwpewtrustsorg/Reports/Philadelphia_Research_Initiative/PRI_education_report.pdf#page=8. Accessed June 26, 2012.

that has not tipped toward too many Black kids. Given the historical trends and current demographics of the Philadelphia public schools, why object to requiring only *one* Black history course in this particular system?[3]

Opponents of the decision argued three things. First, because racism is now a thing of the past, *separate* courses on Black history are no longer needed because Philadelphia public school students live in a post-racial society. Debates about the realities of racism and remedies to it, in this case, the action strategy of requiring a separate Black history course, were more appropriate in prior eras. No one refutes the existence of Jim Crow segregation in the past, yet that particular racial formation, a "color line" of racial segregation, seemed, to many white parents, an anachronism. Thus, when African Americans ask for Black history courses, they reinforce past patterns of racial separatism, thus *creating* racism in the present by constantly bringing it up.

Second, those opposed to adding one Black history course ask, "If the Philadelphia public schools add one class on African Americans, wouldn't the district have to add similar courses for everyone else?" "We've been oppressed too," other groups quite rightly claim. The school district would need courses on Puerto Rican history, Jewish American history, Irish American history, Italian American history—all groups that have long and distinguished histories within the city of Philadelphia that also merit more sustained treatment in the public school curriculum. It would also need to develop courses for all of the new immigrant groups, such as Dominicans, Vietnamese, and who knows who else. The process would quickly become unmanageable and nonsensical. Moreover, how would the school district pay for all these courses whose efficacy remains unproven?

A third objection is related to the second. Wouldn't it be *unfair* to all the other students whose histories have also been excluded to single out African Americans for *special* treatment? Even if the district required the course to be taken by everybody, given the demographics of the district, African American students would be those most likely to take the Black history course, and the course might be seen as being created for them. Why should Black history be singled out? Doesn't that give African Americans special treatment? African Americans have already received their fair share of special treatment through affirmative action and anti-poverty programs. African Americans occupy visible positions of power—Condoleezza Rice, Oprah Winfrey, and Maxine Waters are three powerful African American women whose achievements prove that the American Dream is possible for everybody. Without a compelling reason to

---

[3] The National Center for Educational Statistics has a series of tables, maps, and figures outlining demographics for U.S. public schools. http://nces.ed.gov/surveys/sdds/index.aspx. Accessed June 26, 2012.

The Pew Foundation has some figures from 2009; see note 2.

The School District of Philadelphia also posts demographic data on its website. http://www.phila.k12.pa.us/about/#enrollment. Accessed June 26, 2012.

do so, that one Black history class might aggravate race relations by singling out African Americans as unfair recipients of special treatment.

Adjusting the Color Line: How America Has Changed

Given the persisting reality of racism, especially for African American school-children who attend racially segregated, inferior Philadelphia public schools down the street from our fancy downtown hotel, we must ask ourselves about the substance of these objections. Arguments against Black history that claim that "racism is past," that "we're oppressed too," and that a policy of "no special treatment for Blacks" may have some validity. Opponents of adding the one Black history course suggest that focusing on race and Black people will slow down efforts to move beyond racial segregation and toward a post-racial society. They quite rightly point out that Black people are not the only people of color in America and that the concept of a color line organized via a black/white binary fails to capture these nuances.

I agree that it is time to challenge prevailing notions of racism and of the color line of racial segregation, but not for the reasons routinely given to block offering Black history courses. Within contemporary racial politics, color still matters. After all, the Philadelphia public schools are racially segregated. Children attending those schools do not yet live in a post-racial society. Poor and working-class Black children typically live in racially segregated neighborhoods. Their racially segregated schools fail to prepare them for good jobs, and home addresses in racially segregated neighborhoods often serve as indicators to employers not to hire or even interview them. When it comes to patterns of Black urban poverty, one would be hard pressed to make the case that a post-racial society has arrived. At the same time, many middle-class Black kids neither live in racially segregated neighborhoods, nor attend racially segregated schools. Like their less fortunate counterparts, however, they do experience similar harassment by the police and similar risks when others see them as being in the wrong place.

In this context, we must ask several questions. Why have these arguments of "racism is past," "we're oppressed too," and "no special treatment for Blacks" emerged at this time? What purpose do they serve? And what makes these arguments so attractive to academics and the general public alike? I suggest that two contemporary social phenomena shed light on this historic moment where the possibility of one Black history course can raise such strong feelings.

Changing Demographics

In *The Souls of Black Folk*, William E. B. Du Bois proclaimed that the problem of the twentieth century would be the color line. Describing the racial order before the massive European immigration of the early twentieth century, Du Bois conceptualized the color line in the context of racial segregation, of which

race relations between African Americans and the ever-changing white majority constituted the dominant racial formation during his lifetime. Moreover, for
Du Bois, the color line was never solely a matter of race. Instead, racism was a
fundamental dimension of class exploitation that kept people who were racialized as "black" poor and disempowered. For Du Bois, the color line served as a
powerful metaphor for the race/class politics of segregation that formed such an
essential feature of American political, economic, and social life.

We live in different times, where Du Bois's color line is being redrawn. Currently, the growth of Latino and Asian populations, resulting from immigration
and high birth rates, fosters a rethinking of the deeply entrenched nature of
racial hierarchy within American society. Interestingly, the histories of Latino
and Asian populations in the United States have also been affected by racial segregation. They too experienced a distinctive version of the color line, demonstrating its robustness as a construct in explaining American racism. Currently,
race and class hierarchies in the United States are still present, yet the massive
changes brought about by immigration mask their organization and effects.

The substantive growth of racial/ethnic populations that are not identifiably
white has dramatically changed the racial demographics of the United States as
well as those of the Philadelphia public schools. By 2009, Latino students measured 17 percent of the school district's student population. This is an important shift, yet the presence of Latinos in the Philadelphia public schools does
not mean that Latino students will receive a better education than their African American counterparts. Rather, it is more likely to suggest that white flight
will target *both* Blacks *and* Latinos who cannot escape attending this urban
district. These changes in this one district mirror larger demographic changes
of the United States as a whole, where the Latino population has continued to
grow. The U.S. Census recorded the Latino population of the United States as
9.6 million in 1970, but it has since skyrocketed to 35.3 million in 2000, and it is
predicted to reach 73.0 million by 2030 and 102.6 million by 2050.[4] Blacks and
Latinos may experience different, yet interconnected forms of racism, suggesting that the color line has not disappeared into post-raciality, but rather that it
is being reconfigured.

Given these demographic trends, the United States is in the midst of a period
of *color adjustment* of its color line. Racial segregation still works, but not the
way it used to. The presence of Latinos, Asian Americans, and Muslim Americans who do not fit within traditional racial categories of "white" or "black"
suggests that it is time to develop more sophisticated analyses of contemporary
racism. Toward this end, we cannot simply insert new groups into old models,
hoping that the analyses still fit. U.S. society is adjusting to new racial realities

---

[4] Data on the Hispanic population of the United States are available from the U.S. Census Bureau. http://www.census.gov/population/www/socdemo/hispanic/hispanic.html. Accessed
June 27, 2012.

that combine past forms of racial segregation with emerging forms of racism that are effective within desegregated settings.

We need to remember that, regardless of how a color line is configured and adjusted, racism is a system of power that distributes social goods such as schooling, housing, and jobs in ways that produce racial inequalities. Questions of racial classification and identity have never altered the fundamental character of American racism that places varying segments of Blacks, Latinos, native peoples, and Asians at the bottom of the social hierarchy. Racial classifications have proven to be malleable over time, yet racial hierarchy itself has proven to be, in the words of Charles Tilly, "a durable social inequality." Why should we expect anything different now?

Individualism and the Scrutiny of Racial Identities

The growing number of people who readily identify themselves as biracial or multiracial constitutes a second social phenomenon that shapes why reactions to a mandatory Black history course might have been so strong. Because definitions of "black" are no longer taken for granted, the question of what constitutes a "black" history course becomes similarly suspect. Because the United States is in a period of color adjustment, the stark racial categories of the past, with strictures such as the "one-drop rule," no longer fit. Many people now occupy racially ambiguous categories, making it difficult to figure out where they "belong." Because "blackness" is so contextualized and nuanced, any one course dealing with Black history would need to be as well.

Two groups have gained increasing political power in drawing attention to racial identities, each having heterogeneous responses to this question of racial identification and both rejecting prevailing understandings of the white/black binary as descriptive of America's color line. Black biracial and black multiracial individuals (those who are visibly and/or culturally of African descent) quite rightly ask where they fit within the new multiethnic America and, by implication, within the one Black history course. This is a reasonable question and most certainly is not new. Du Bois's observation about his "racial twoness" still stands as one of the most powerful statements of a biracial individual (by today's standards) who understood how his very existence challenged prevailing racial norms. Du Bois was not supposed to exist, yet he did. Du Bois was supposed to accept his status as a derogated mulatto, yet he didn't. Instead, he devoted his entire life to studying and fighting racial injustice.

We must ask whether contemporary people with his biological make up encounter racism in the same way. As I argue here, everyone experiences a new racism and biracial individuals are no exception. What is different, however, are the new social conditions that produce black biracial and black multiracial identity as well as the power of those in these categories to make their issues seen and heard. Du Bois was biracial during a time when biracial meant "black" because the children of African American mothers and white fathers assumed the status of their mothers. Categories such as Black American, African American, and Negro included biracial individuals, creating African Americans as a population that is inherently hybrid and inclusive toward multiple shades of the rainbow. Race was not a biological classification but rather a pragmatic recognition of the power relations that created the racial category of "black" and the ethnic identification of African American or Negro. Black people as a collectivity, the capitalized "Black people," emerged within this history.

How one related to biracialism was reflected in one's ability to "pass" as white as well as how those individuals who chose not to pass identified with those who could not. Under racial segregation, many of the major African American Civil Rights leaders were "race men" or "race women," light-skinned and highly educated individuals who, like Du Bois, placed their skills in service to social justice. Others became the face of a "mixed" category, the "tragic mulattos" of American literature who could not reconcile their in-between, borderland identities. The fact of "blackness" was not optional. What mattered was the way in which individuals negotiated their racial identification within the context of a strict color line. "Passing" made sense in a context where white supremacy granted those who were categorized as white privileges that were denied to everyone else.

Black biraciality means something completely different in the early twenty-first century, primarily because the social context concerning interracial dating and marriage, as well as the removal of signs of strict segregation, is so different. It still involves choices about "passing," for those who can "pass" as white, and it also involves choices about one's relation to "blackness." One significant difference is that growing numbers of black biracial children have white mothers and African American fathers. In short, *how* black biracial people get their "whiteness" is very different than in the past. The fourteen-year-old African American girl in Virginia who gives birth to a biracial baby after being raped by a white man passes on to her child a biraciality that reflects the power relations of a given place and time. That young rape survivor was my grandmother, and her biracial child was my father. Despite the fact that he could pass for white in the right light, my dad lived eighty-nine years as a proud "black" man, sixty-two years of them in Philadelphia. He married a brown-skinned Black woman, making it clear that he thought Black women were beautiful. His conception of Blackness stemmed not from biological categorization, appearance, or the changing categories of the U.S. Bureau of the Census, but rather from political stances that defined blackness as a political identity. In hindsight, I can see how his politics reflected not just his analyses of race and class but also those of gender. He never called himself "biracial." It was not important for him to do so because embracing a racial identity as mulatto or biracial promised little for his empowerment as an individual or for African Americans as a collectivity. Like Du Bois and so many others, my dad's very existence was evidence of the unjust racial hierarchy and the gendered nature of racism that relied on rape as a tool of racial rule.

This leaves me wondering about early-twenty-first-century patterns of black biraciality and the political implications of the emergence of this language at this particular time. Media figures such as Halle Berry, Alicia Keys, Mariah Carey, Dwayne "The Rock" Johnson, and Tiger Woods represent a less politicized form of black biraciality that isn't necessarily linked to anti-racist politics. I remain fascinated by the proliferation of brown-skinned, curly-haired "black" people on television shows as a new form of beauty. I also wonder about the body politics of the academy, where light-skinned and openly self-identified "biracial" individuals have a leg up over ordinary, domestic African Americans. One major shift in the contours of black biraciality concerns its current patterns—black biracial individuals are much more likely to be the children of white mothers and African American fathers than the reverse. Intersections of race and gender raise entirely different questions about the racial identification of children who are raised by white mothers who can pass on the financial and/or cultural benefits of whiteness. I am left wondering whether, instead of being the "tragic mulattos" of the past, contemporary black biracial individuals have greater choice in performing an "optional blackness" from one context to the next that resembles the "optional ethnicity" of their white counterparts described by sociologist Mary Waters in *Ethnic Options*.

Immigrant groups of color also highlight issues of racial identification, yet in a different way. Immigrants from Latin America, the Caribbean, Asia, and continental Africa quite rightly ask, "Where do I fit within the United States' racial hierarchy?" Most clearly are not white—any Latino doing the service jobs that are so essential to the functioning of this country can tell you that. At the same time, they are not black, nor do most of them want to be. New immigrant populations have to figure out how to position themselves within longstanding patterns of first- and second-class American citizenship that were also defined by the white/black color line. No natural alliance exists between any new immigrant group and African Americans, nor does a clear path to whiteness exist for any group that cannot be phenotypically classified as white.

No More Black History:
A Convergence of Opinion?

The push to eliminate race as an artifact of the past creates a dilemma for African Americans. Collectively, the three arguments against the Black history course all stem from the belief that, because the appearance of race in America has changed so dramatically, the substance itself has changed. Using the evidence of multiracial America to refute the existence of the white/black binary, at best, only carries surface-level plausibility. Arguments of "racism is past," "we're oppressed too," and "no special treatment for Blacks" fail to address the persistent nature of institutional racism in America. These arguments also serve to mask the real issue, namely, the convergence of liberal and conservative thinking about race in the post–Civil Rights era.

This desire to imagine a new America that is no longer shackled by past racial practices affects liberals and conservatives alike. The "racism is past" argument finds conservative and liberal advocates. Conservatives argue that a colorblind, fair American society has already been achieved—African Americans simply need to fix their families, learn to work hard, and take advantage of the opportunities that already exist. Surprisingly, many liberals buy into the "racism is past" argument, but often through a convoluted analysis that wishes to see the ideal in the real. Liberals often wish so badly for American society to be colorblind that, through conceptual misrecognition, they inadvertently perceive American society as already there, in effect, grafting the colorblind ideal onto the realities they perceive around them.

Black biracial and new immigrant populations occupy distinctive positions within these changing social relations that equate the white/black binary with the color line and then bash both as antiquated. Many black biracial individuals don't feel oppressed, don't see themselves as oppressed, don't want to be oppressed, and use their own optional racial identities as proof that American society has moved on. Many were raised in middle-class environments and, like their African American counterparts, share the dilemma of figuring out what that means. Still other black biracial individuals see little contradiction between being biracial and being African American—this is a continuation of historical understandings of African American identity that see race not as a biological, blood quantum process, but see racism as a system of power.

Regardless of their individual identifications, black biracial individuals can become very useful in the politics of multiracial America that now highlights skin color, yet erases its connections to hierarchies of power, such as racism. Black biracial individuals face the additional issue of negotiating their growing visibility as the go-to "blacks" on matters of race in higher education, corporations, and symbolic positions within government and the media. Such individuals need not be "tragic mulattos," but it would in fact be tragic if they mistook their own acceptance within American social institutions as evidence that American society was in fact post-racial.

New immigrant groups face a different set of issues. Dominicans and Haitians, for example, can claim with moral certainty, "We've been oppressed too." Yet the site of oppression is typically a far-off land, where American citizens, who are notoriously uninformed about world affairs, cannot see the connections between U.S. foreign policy toward Haiti and the Dominican Republic and new immigrant populations within the United States. The "we've been oppressed too" argument holds merit, yet the response to it can be a facile slip back to the "racism is past" frame or the "no special treatment for blacks" trope. Rather than developing a more robust analysis of how racism actually operates, replacing one group for another as the benchmark experience for examining racism—substituting Latinos for Blacks or Haitians for any group of color holding American passports—obscures more complex analyses of racism. When combined, these arguments converge on their agreement that Black people, along with native peoples, are poster children for *historical* racism. As with the sanitized history of Native American genocide that supports contemporary practices of reserving Indian mascots for universities and sports teams, African Americans who persist in talking about racism, or worse yet, want to have required courses in it, are now perceived as the problem. "Get over it," we are told—"Can't you see that progressive young white people love hip hop and conservative old white ones respect Colin Powell and Condoleezza Rice?"

The stage is set for a convergence of opinion concerning the "no special treatment for blacks" point of view. Again, this perspective pervades conservative and liberal arguments about race in America. Conservatives are more likely to embrace the paternalistic argument that "special treatment" has harmed African Americans and that we help them by withdrawing race-based policies that were designed to remedy past discrimination. In contrast, many liberals wish to avoid talking about race at all, staking their claim on the high ground that attending to class issues will, over time, erase any racial disparities. Surprisingly, the "no special treatment for Blacks" point of view can also be heard from potential allies—Latinos and Asians ask why African Americans should receive what they perceive as being "special favors." As two groups that also suffered from racist treatment, the invisibility of this history can foster contemporary resentments.

Rethinking the Color Line

When it comes to racial theory, embracing a more complex notion of the color line means that we must start in a new place with a new set of assumptions. First, *there never has been a white/black binary.* Continuing to use this language means that we persist in stuffing a complex racial history into a very limited conceptual category and setting up a straw man that obscures more than it reveals. As Elizabeth Martinez points out, the longstanding presence of Latinos in the United States refutes this notion of a rigid black/white color line. Latino populations have resisted racial categorization, thus illustrating the constructed and contested nature of the social construction of race.

While the categories of race may shift in response to changing political and economic conditions, the fundamental belief in race as a guiding principal for viewing segments of the American population remains remarkably hardy. For example, in the 1920s, certain groups of white immigrants (such as Irish or Italian immigrants) were defined as being part of a distinctive race. As David Roediger shows in *Working toward Whiteness: How America's Immigrants Became White: The Strange Journey from Ellis Island to the Suburbs*, these groups have been folded into the social construction of whiteness as a racial identity (ironically by rejecting white identities). Similarly, lighter-skinned blacks were classified by the Bureau of the Census as a separate racial group, that of "mulatto." With the growth of Jim Crow segregation, mulattos disappeared, to be replaced by the more rigid racial category of "Negro." But today, the category of "multiracial" reappears during yet another period where racial meanings are contested within hierarchical power relations. Rather than recasting this history of changing racial categories into the logic of linear progress, for example, viewing America as less racist than in the past because the Census recognizes more racial categories, the emergence of new racial identities and categories are better understood as part of an ongoing color adjustment about the meaning of race.

Second, what we have in the United States is a racial *hierarchy,* with a dynamic color line used to make people toe the line. This fundamental hierarchy persists yet racial theory may not be up to the task of explaining why racial inequalities persist in America. In the 1980s and 1990s, a subtle substitution occurred within racial theory, one of replacing more politicized language with less contentious terms. For example, the term "race" replaced "racism," "inequality" replaced "oppression," and "color" replaced "black" and "white." Black people suffered demotion from a capitalized "Black" to a small "black" that better paralleled the small "white" of white identity politics. "African Americans," "Black people," and "Blacks" disappeared in a language riddled with seemingly polite euphemisms of "inner-city neighborhoods," "urban contemporary music," and "welfare queens" of public policy. Seemingly, it became much easier to engage in polite discourse about whether "race" is real or whether the "white/black binary" suppresses African American individuality than to confront structures of white supremacy that enabled whites to abandon urban public schools and demonize Black kids in the process.

The fact that many academics were quick to embrace the idea of a white/black binary as synonymous with American racism shows how out of touch scholars can be with events, such as those occurring right down the street here in Philadelphia. They saw racism through the prism of a color line and when it went away, they thought that racism disappeared with it. Like many in the American public, academics embraced color, now denuded of political associations. There is nothing wrong with celebrating color in one's individual life, but having friends, loved ones, colleagues, and children of color is no substitute for hard-hitting analyses that speak to the persisting inequalities such as those faced by children in the Philadelphia public schools. We must reorient the racial continuum from its current status as a benign *horizontal* line, where talk of centers and margins, metropoles and colonies inadvertently recenters attention on the center. Instead, the color line may be more profitably thought of as a *vertical* measuring stick—with whites clustered on the top, Black people and native peoples clumped on the bottom, and all other groups arrayed in between. A vertical color line points to social hierarchy, challenges of upward social mobility, and the politics of slope that are provided by changing opportunity structures. The erosion of public institutions of all sorts, especially urban public schools, has tilted the opportunity such that people on the bottom find it increasingly

difficult to get ahead. Too steep a slope characterizes a slippery downward social mobility that seems to shape the fate of not only of racial/ethnic groups
today, but a growing portion of the population that thought its place in the center was secure.

This leads to a third and final key point for developing racial theory, namely,
how different individuals and groups now strive to position themselves within a
changing mosaic of contemporary American society characterized by a shape-
changing, vertical color line. The essential categories of white and black have
shrunk, creating a much larger and seemingly elastic border between them.
Focusing on the middle should not detract from the ends of the racial hierarchy—whites on top, hypervisible Blacks and invisible native peoples on the
bottom, and everyone else jockeying for a place in between. In this context, as
individuals and as social groups, we're also all learning to do a quick and more
complex form of racial calculus. Similar to the logic of racial segregation, when
skin color served as an essentialist marker of the attributes, morals, and intelligence of the person who was classified as white or black, now we practice new
racial taxonomies. We learn to see a person, give that person a provisional racial
classification (e.g., white, black, native), and then test the accuracy of that classification by getting additional information (e.g., facility with standard American English, style of dress, hair texture, the type of car s/he drives, visible signs
of wealth). Armed with this additional data, we can then further classify that
person with designations of honorary whiteness (even though s/he may be visibly of African or native descent), or social blackness (even though s/he may
have white skin).

In this context, as Troy Duster's book *Backdoor to Eugenics* reminds us in his
chilling analysis of race and genetics, biological classifications of whiteness and
blackness still have tremendous power. Ask any dark-skinned African American teenage boy why the police stopped him or ask any dark-skinned African
American woman why the man in the car passing her hollered out "$50" and
it is clear that racial discrimination based on appearance lives on. Better yet,
keep reading Douglas Massey and Nancy Denton's *American Apartheid* on the
resegregation of neighborhoods or Gary Orfield's work on the resegregation of
American public schools to get a sense of the persistence of anti-black sentiments within American society. Virtually none of the whites whose seemingly
individual decisions to move away from African Americans and who inherently contribute to resegregated neighborhoods and schools admit to harboring
any anti-black sentiment. Many have African American friends and may have
black biracial members in their own families. It's all about money, property
values, location, finding the right school for a gifted child, and a list of other
euphemisms. This belief in black inferiority, the hallmark of American racism,
helps to explain resistance to that one lone Black history course that most likely
would be taken by African American students. Why waste money on something that will always be second best?

Can't We Get Just *One* Black History Course?

So how do we make sense of these vignettes of the absence of Black history during my schooling and arguments against adding one Black history course to the Philadelphia public schools? Perhaps in the abstract, the objections to the one Black history course make sense, yet are they reasonable in the context of the specific history of the Philadelphia public schools? Ironically, Du Bois points us in the right direction here. Du Bois is typically admired for his book *The Souls of Black Folk,* the volume where he introduces the idea of the color line. Yet for the needs of the children of the Philadelphia public schools, his other works might be more beneficial in building the curriculum that all American children might need. Works such as *The Philadelphia Negro,* a sociological structural analysis of how race, poverty, and urbanization affected the African American population of Philadelphia, or *Black Reconstruction in America 1860–1880,* a study about the failed policies of Reconstruction that have doomed America to relive its racial past over and over, constitute solid starting points for a more analytical form of Black history. Rather than celebrating Black heroes, the kind of Black history that Du Bois achieved provides tools for seeing how race, class, gender, and citizenship status have been core themes not just in explaining African American history, but that of the United States. When the public schools do decide to incorporate this kind of Black history, let's hope that the full complexity of Du Bois's intellectual activism is part of the core curriculum. Better yet, let's hope that that by the time that you read this essay, the course is already being taught.

ADDITIONAL RESOURCES

Du Bois, William E. B. 1979. *The Souls of Black Folk.* New York: Dodd, Mead.
Hale, Janice E. 2001. *Learning White Black: Creating Educational Excellence for African American Children.* Baltimore, Md.: Johns Hopkins University Press.
Martinez, Elizabeth. 1998. *De Colores Means All of Us: Latina Voices for a MultiColored Century.* Cambridge, Mass.: South End Press.
Takaki, Ronald T. 1993. *A Different Mirror: A History of Multicultural America.* Boston: Little Brown.
Tilly, Charles. 1998. *Durable Inequality.* Berkeley: University of California Press.
Waters, Mary. 1990. *Ethnic Options: Choosing Identities in America.* Berkeley: University of California Press.

16

Are We Living in a Post-Racial World?

REFLEXIVE ESSAY: *I first presented the ideas in this essay as part of an opening plenary panel at the 2010 annual meeting of the Association of Black Sociologists (ABS). I really liked the conference title, "Repositioning Race Through Prophetic Research, Teaching and Service," because it helped me outline my thoughts about contemporary racial theory and practice. Several months later, I was invited to deliver a public lecture on the topic "Are We Living in a Post-Racial World?" In contrast to the ABS theme, I immediately disliked the title—wasn't it clear that the talk could be summed up in the word "no"? As I prepared for the talk itself, I realized that my annoyance at confronting this question got to the heart of some of arguments that I initially presented in at the plenary panel some months earlier. This essay draws from both of those events.*

ARE WE LIVING in a post-racial world? When I focus on social problems that disproportionately affect Blacks and people of color, I answer, "Of course not." Let's start with the obvious. Why is it that when I walk the streets of downtown Washington, D.C., or attend conferences in San Francisco (where I was American Sociological Association president in 2009), the majority of homeless people I see are African American? Is this just bad luck, misfortune, their own flawed values, or something else? Is being a sociologist such a curse that I am forced to see racial disparities everywhere I go, even when I don't want to see them? In a truly post-racial world, we would see "equal opportunity" homelessness—a post-racial homelessness, if you will.

Are we living in a post-racial world? Of course not—I am dispirited by seeing the faces of the same "black" criminals, the granddaughters and grandsons of the "black" criminals that, three decades ago, catalyzed Angela Davis to make her groundbreaking arguments about the prison industrial complex. The criminals are hidden away and made into entertainment by our media, yet most people know that U.S. prisons are full of young Black and Latino men, with the young white men who are locked up alternately cast as a beleaguered minority who fall prey to white supremacist dogma for reasons of protection.

Are we living in a post-racial world? Of course not—just look at the drop-out rates for African American and Latino kids in the United States. And this is a country where school is free and mandated by law to be paid for with public funds. It breaks my heart to see all that talent lost. It breaks my heart even more to realize that sometimes I am afraid of those same children who quite rightly have figured out that this seemingly post-racial world has no place for them. Unlike the criminals, the legions of kids who are pushed out of school before they are swept up in the punishment industry do not garner the same degree of press in reality television. But then maybe their schools are already part of the punishment industry—we only call them schools.

Are we living in a post-racial world? Of course not—has anyone checked global patterns of HIV/AIDS lately? This public health issue touches millions of people, but what is overlooked are the racial patterns whereby race and poverty bundled together mean that one's risk of exposure to and dying of HIV/AIDS is directly related to resources. Class, race, gender, sexuality, and citizenship collectively determine who is at highest risk. Can we pull out the "race" piece and, with a straight face, argue convincingly that we are living in a post-racial world because AIDS is really just about poverty and sexuality?

Are we living in a post-racial world? Of course not—take a look at the globe—we have a pristine correlation between race, wealth of nations, and the legacy of the colonial past. Compartmentalizing the world into nation-states resembles arguments about poor Black and Latino, affluent white, and racially integrated "changing" neighborhoods in your local metropolitan area that are evaluated through racially unmarked language about good and bad neighborhoods. Race and class are so tightly bundled together as intersectional systems of power that their interactive effects yield social inequalities. Who would you rather be—a white, affluent Norwegian citizen, a poor black citizen of Haiti, or an undocumented Latino immigrant living along the U.S. border in Arizona? Compared with the life expectancy of populations in Scandinavia and Canada, people living in Africa are poor, with many starving, living with civil wars, the presence of child soldiers, and rates of rape that stem not from the cultures of the people involved, but from the legacy of myriad expressions of colonialism. The West seems to care more about preserving the gorillas in the mist than the people living with environmental pollution along oil pipelines in the Niger delta. Norway, Haiti, the Mississippi delta, Nigeria, the United States—can we see the patterns?

Are we living in a post-racial world? It all depends on where you stand because where you stand gives you a distinctive angle of vision on what you can see and what remains invisible to you. It gives you a particular angle of vision on this question as well.

My overarching concern lies less with the theoretical framework arguing that race is socially constructed. More than fifty years of racial research
aimed at refuting the core premises of biological race on which the Nazi state
constructed its horrific social policies has refuted ideas about race as a real
phenomenon. Yet race is real in its effects. The world is clearly racially constructed—that's the legacy of the racism of the past. The question is whether
the racial disparities that I pointed to in the beginning of my talk are evidence
of *racism*. Is racism real today, and if so, how do we talk about it? What do we
do about it?

In the remainder of this essay, I argue that racism persists, but that we often
have difficulty analyzing or, in many cases, even seeing racism as a system of
power. Because systems of power are dynamic and ever-changing, they can
change form and shape. Racism is but one case of the changing-same nature
of power relations. In response, our analyses of racism and the implications
of analyses for anti-racist practice must be similarly dynamic. This essay has
three parts.

First, I unpack the initial question. If instead we ask, "Are we living in a
post-*racist* world?" we see the limits of the first question. This slippery linguistic slope that academia began in the late twentieth century, moving away from
terms such as "racist," "racism," and "oppression," to the more benign substitutes of "race," "racial," "inequalities," and "disparities," shapes the types of
questions we ask. My goal is not to chastise anyone for asking the question, "Are
we living in a post-racial world?" Rather, the challenge lies in unpacking the social, intellectual, and political context that enables this question to emerge in
the first place. If we successfully unpack the question, we can mine it for what's
useful, leave the rest behind, and move on to ask different questions.

Second, I briefly present an overview of the domains of power framework
that I have used to analyze power relations. I suggest that this framework can
be helpful in assisting us in thinking through the shift from color-conscious
to colorblind racial formations. My goal is to go beyond our current racial theories, suggesting that, when it comes to analyzing contemporary patterns of
racism, many of our theories suffer from what one of my students calls the
"Grandpa fallacy." In her words, we engage in the Grandpa fallacy when, like
her Grandpa, we look at the past and argue that everything was better (or worse)
then. When it comes to making sense of racism, it seems to me that contemporary racial theory can be divided into *post-racial* and *anti–post-racial* camps
and that each has its own variation of the Grandpa fallacy. The post-racial camp
looks back and proclaims that racism was much worse in the color-conscious
era, and that today's ostensibly colorblind formation is better. Some even go
so far as to argue that racism has in fact disappeared (e.g., we are *post* racism).
Not to be outdone, those in the anti–post-racial camp (are these prefixes really
necessary?) look back with nostalgia on the past. "The kids were better—the
boys kept their pants pulled up, the girls kept their dresses down, they went to
church, and none of them used foul language," they proclaim. Anti-racist pol-

itics were better too—African Americans were unified and stuck together in fighting the enemy. Hell—even racism itself was better! It was clear, we knew what it was, we knew it when we saw it, and we fought it heroically.

I want to respond to the Grandpa fallacy advanced by both camps by suggesting that we need an analysis of *contemporary* racism that does not uncritically apply racial theories developed in response to past racial formations to talk about the present. My response has been to develop a language for talking about power relations that we can all use. My domains of power framework should help us analyze colorblind racism as a distinctive form of racism in contemporary society.

Third, I conclude the talk by asking you to think with me about how a more robust racial theory might help catalyze more effective anti-racist praxis. Railing against the evils of racism does not mean that we really understand its nature. Anti-racism strategies that lack an incisive analysis of racism itself can only hit the mark by accident some of the time. No wonder we so often talk past one another.

Unpacking the Question

When it comes to unpacking the social, intellectual, and political context that has catalyzed the question, "Are we living in a post-racial world?" I see three sets of issues: First, whose question is this? Second, why this particular question? Why now? And third, what questions should we be asking? Let me take each in turn.

First, whose question is this? The query "Are we living in a post-racial world" feels a bit like that question raised by kids on a long car ride—the adults are trying to follow the map to find the elusive beach house or hotel, and the kids keep asking, "Are we there yet?" Because they have never seen the journey's endpoint, they lack the ability to know whether they are there or not. What they don't realize is that those of us driving the car have never visited the elusive post-racial world either. We rely on the maps crafted by those who came before us, engaging in course corrections when we realize that the bridge is out, the traffic is too heavy to continue, or the route that we thought we would be taking is under construction. To us, the kids' questions seem intrusive, but their queries also reflect a cognitive style of conflating an imagined or ideal destination with the actual reality of the passing scenery. The kids keep asking, in the hope that the answer will miraculously be "yes," because they want to believe that we have arrived.

In a similar fashion, the question "Are we living in a post-racial world?" conflates the *ideal* of a race-neutral, colorblind society with the actual and rapidly changing society in which we now live. We want so desperately to arrive at Martin Luther King, Jr.'s destination of a place where our children can be judged by the content of their characters and not the color their skin that we imagine ourselves already to have arrived. But what would this destination look like? Can we honestly say that early-twenty-first-century U.S. society is race neutral? Can we honestly say that race has no meaning anymore?

"Are we living in a post-racial world?" This is not is a core question raised by Black people, Latinos, and the people of color who disproportionately experience the social problems that I identified earlier. People who have long suffered the effects of racism and other forms of social injustice possess a long institutional memory that grants them the skills to recognize the car of racism headed toward the ideal of a socially just, race-neutral world. In my case, I've been on a journey doing anti-racist scholarship and activism my entire life—not just my professional life, my entire life. I don't see racism as a cardboard, one-dimensional filter where we can colorize ostensibly normal practices and call the result "racial." Instead, I see racism as an ever-changing system of power relations that works with and through gender, class, sexuality, age, ethnicity, citizenship, and other similarly structured systems of power. Despite my chagrin in thinking about how deeply entrenched social problems actually are, I have to remind myself not to blame the new kids in the car—how can they possibly know how tired I am? Some of them are so young that they don't even know that they are in a car, let alone that it is still moving.

When it comes to unpacking the social, intellectual, and political context that has catalyzed the question "Are we living in a post-racial world?" a second issue is, why this particular question? why now? In many ways, the question "Are we living in a post-racial world?" is eminently reasonable because several important changes in contemporary society mean that we are living in a greatly changed world.

When it comes to race, the world is quite different. Just look around—the race relations we encounter on a daily basis look quite different than those of the pre–Civil Rights era. We are in the in-between space between the racial segregation of the mid-twentieth century, the form of color-conscious racism that divided the world into clear boxes and sorted people accordingly, and the ostensibly post-racial world of the early twenty-first century. In the United States, segregation took the form of separate schools, housing, neighborhoods, jobs, and even cemeteries. The Civil Rights and Black Power movements took aim at racial segregation, experiencing success in changing the ideological context that had so long been based on assumptions of black inferiority. In contrast, the contemporary period seems remarkably integrated. The multi-racial, multi-ethnic audiences that I routinely address could not have existed fifty years ago. I certainly would not have been a keynote speaker for Black History Month. When you look around, the world looks entirely different. Seeing is believing— but can we trust what we see?

One major reason why the world looks and feels so different to those of us living in the West is that new communication technologies have created possibilities for relationships that were unimaginable two generations ago. Mass media representations have invited us to be savvier about the music, dance, and cultures of peoples from all over the globe. Social networking sites put us in touch with all sorts of people we may never meet in everyday life. Those of us who have access to these communication technologies and to new transportation technologies that enable us to travel to all parts of the globe can easily develop the habit of not seeing the barriers, borders, and boundaries, primarily because they no longer circumscribe our lives to the same degree.

I see connections between the growth of digital networks and the ability to imagine a post-racial world. Here, the growing significance of new communication technologies that are radically remaking the globe provides a new space for negotiating longstanding issues of race. Media representations and social networks enable people from all sorts of backgrounds to see, hear, and get to know one another, or at least to imagine that they do. Considering how many of these people coming from such different backgrounds, both within the United States and around the world, used these social networks and digital media to establish and develop support for Barack Obama, it's not unreasonable to see the online world as a form of racial integration.

Barack Obama himself has come to serve as the signpost for the post-racial camp, meaning that the election of President Obama marked an ultimate endpoint, much as the 1989 fall of the Berlin wall signaled the end of a divided Germany and the beginning of a post-Soviet era. Naming such an endpoint suggests that there is some dividing line. Before this event, before Obama's election, there was a past that was racial (whatever that means), but now that we've reached this historic election, the present is not. And if there's no race in the present, there is no need to discuss it. Doing so would only create (or re-create) race—and racism.

If we could live completely in virtual reality and the world of discourse that is totally of our own making, watching our own YouTube videos of the world, reassured by the media representations and the election of Barack Obama that race has been transcended, then I understand how it could feel as if the world is truly post-racial. Yet, despite all those avatars playing games in cyberspace as I speak, none of us is a virtual being, living in a virtual world. As a sociologist, when it comes to understanding racial inequalities and the links to racism, I'm more likely to be a follower of Madonna—"I'm just a material girl living in a material world." When someone pulls the plug on our electricity and our computer screens go blank, we realize the virtual world is no substitute for or protection from the real one. Sure, I can imagine that one day I'll hang out with Barack and Michelle Obama at the White House, but how likely is that ever to happen? (Especially if I keep giving talks like this.) I can imagine myself living in a post-racial society because of the combination of dramatically changed opportunity structures since my childhood—I am currently living a lifestyle that my parents could never have even imagined for either themselves or me—and my rich virtual world organized through multiple e-mail accounts. But when I turn off my computer, put my BlackBerry or iPod Touch into my bag, and walk out into my neighborhood, who I am, where I live, what I'm wearing, what I had to eat, and how I look matter greatly. Despite the fact that so many of us in the United States are so busy staring at our smartphones while walking down the street that we cannot see actual social relations around us, contemporary racial practices are real, not virtual. My world is organized via racialized structures of meaning, not of my own making, yet amenable to my influence.

To sum up thus far, the question "Are we living in a post-racial world?" stems from contemporary conditions, including the election of Barack Obama and the explosion of new communication technologies and their effects on how we view reality. Barack Obama's election serves as the period at the end of the sentence of desegregation, the endpoint that marks the beginning of post-raciality. Yet, might his election equally suggest just another stop along the road to the ideal of race neutrality and colorblindness? In this context, we *must resist the question itself.*

This leads me to my third theme, namely, what questions should we be asking? The Civil Rights and Black Power movements, the two major social movements that provided the theoretical frameworks for racial theory and anti-racist practice, spoke to a specific time and place. We must start in a new place, even if that requires raising some uncomfortable questions: Are our racial theories talking back to a racism that no longer exists? In what ways, if any, are our responses to this imagined racism effective, ineffective, or irrelevant?

Racial Theory for a Seemingly Post-Racial World: The Domains of Power Framework

People who are committed to social justice, especially those coming of age in the early twenty-first century, need a new language for analyzing the new colorblind racism of a seemingly post-racial world. Our era marks a shift from a color-conscious period of past patterns of racial segregation to a yet-to-be-achieved social ideal of racial integration. The result is an imperfect racial desegregation, where some aspects of society are clearly fairer than they were before, while others are not. In this context, we need analyses that will help us see the contradictions raised by this in-between space.

Toward this end, I propose a framework for how we might think about power relations that, in this case, might be used to help us think through racism as a system of power. I focus on colorblind racism during the post–Civil Rights era because it constitutes an especially deeply entrenched version of America's struggle with social inequality. Although the contours will differ, the framework that I discuss here, as well as the strategies for practicing resistance that it might catalyze, can be applied to any form of social inequality. In addition to race, gender, ethnicity, class, religion, sexuality, and ability all have distinctive structures of power with their own individual histories. By analyzing race, I do not privilege it as the most fundamental or the most important type of inequality. Rather, these systems of power draw strength from one another, both in structuring social inequalities and in fashioning strategies for change.

Racism as a system of power is organized via four domains: (1) A structural domain of power that shows how racial practices are organized through social institutions, such as banks, insurance companies, police departments, the real estate industry, schools, stores, restaurants, hospitals, and governmental agencies. This is the structure of racism as a system of power, the way it's organized without anybody doing anything. This is the structure we're all born into. And these would be the structures left after us when we die. (2) A disciplinary domain of power where people use the rules and regulations of everyday life to uphold the racial hierarchy or challenge it. The disciplinary domain is often organized through bureaucracies that rely on practices of surveillance, but it need not be. (3) A cultural domain of power that constructs representations, ideas, and stories about race and racism. The practices of this domain manufacture the ideas that either justify racial hierarchy or challenge it. (4) An interpersonal domain of power that shapes the everyday social interaction among individuals. The interpersonal domain is the on-the-ground workings of racial practices from the structural, disciplinary, and cultural domains: one-on-one encounters and personal choices. This domain involves ordinary social interactions where people accept and/or resist racial inequality in their everyday lives.

Under color-conscious racial formations, the structural and interpersonal domains of power were far more visible in organizing racial inequalities than the disciplinary and cultural domains. The legal structures that upheld racial segregation shaped the contours of the structural domain. In the interpersonal domain, each individual was overtly conscious of where he or she fit within the racial order. Whether regulating rules of racial etiquette or monitoring individuals' behavior, the color line shaped everyday social interactions. The disciplinary and cultural domains were equally important, but far less visible. Under color-conscious racial formations, this question of a post-racial society would have been nonsensical. In contrast, despite the continued influence of the structural and interpersonal domains, contemporary color-blind racial formations rely far more heavily on disciplinary and cultural domains of power. The disciplinary and cultural domains are growing in significance in the contemporary period, yet may not be adequately recognized.

It is important to stress that all four domains have organized power relations in both periods. While some domains may be more visible than others, all four domains are equally necessary for racism as a system of power to function. Yet, how power is organized shifts across time and space. Asking "Are we living in a post-racial world?" is one way to mark the transition from color-conscious to idealized colorblind racial formations. In most people's minds, especially if they conflate the ideal of a colorblind society with its achievement, the first three domains—the structural, the disciplinary, and the cultural—often disappear. As a result, people understand racism as a phenomenon that is confined to the interpersonal domain. This logic fosters a belief that if individuals could rid themselves of racist beliefs, racism would disappear. This is an attractive idea, yet for those on the bottom, changing society one person at a time would be so slow that it might not feel like change at all.

Colorblind racism relies on structural and interpersonal phenomena, yet the growing visibility and significance of the disciplinary and cultural domains creates space for seemingly contradictory practices to emerge. Populations can be disciplined *both* to hold on to old ways of racial thinking and racial behavior *and* to embrace new ways of thinking and acting at the same time. Stated differently, people can go willingly to their assigned places in the racial hierarchy, yet learn new ideologies of colorblindness that limit their ability to see racial hierarchy at all. Thus, it is comprehensible for a Nigerian immigrant who is of African descent to claim that America is not racist because the whites he or she encounters as a cashier in a big box office supply store do not discriminate against him or her. He or she sees dreams of being an assistant manager and then a manager one day. Yet, this same individual may also return home to a working-class, disproportionately African American and Latino neighborhood whose designated high school is a well-known major dropout factory. His or her children attending the public schools and searching for their own jobs may experience a different reality. Conceptualizing racism solely through the lens of the interpersonal domain and ignoring the sedimented, past-in-present practices that shape the structural domain enable both of these ideas to be "true."

We need to understand how people negotiate colorblindness, where racial hierarchy (as measured by the criteria of economic exploitation and political disenfranchisement) is replicated, even as structural policies and disciplinary practices exclaim that racism is forbidden. Consider, for example, the events surrounding a 2011 webcam video filmed by a white female UCLA student. The student stated that her intention was to air what bothered her about "these hordes of Asian people that UCLA accepts into our school every single year." After she posted the video on YouTube with the title "Asians in the Library," it went viral. Reposted and reported on personal blogs, social networks, news sites, and traditional media outlets, the video traveled widely through the cultural domain. The unwanted attention prompted the chancellor of UCLA to issue an official position for the institution, condemning the "hateful and ignorant" views the student expressed. In other words, the structural domain was responding to the cultural domain. The chancellor's response also illustrated how prevailing practices in the disciplinary domain uphold colorblind racism, namely, the practice of visibly decrying overtly racist statements that would tarnish veneers of "tolerance."

Moreover, this example illustrates how each of these domains shapes (and is shaped by) the interpersonal, by individuals' responses to the video. Many people truly *are* disgusted by the anti-Asian sentiments expressed by the student, and these folks, along with others who wouldn't want to be mistaken for racists, went online to share their disapproval of the video itself as well as the ideas and behaviors of its creator. For many, asserting hatred of the video was a means of absolving themselves from examining how they too might have been implicated in the social relationships that fostered and encouraged the perspectives of this young woman. Thinking that it is enough to say, "I'm a nice person, and I hate that video," is an idea not so different from the one the UCLA student had when she offered her own disclaimer at the outset of her rant: "I don't mean this toward any of my friends. I mean it toward random people that I don't even know in the library." These disclaimers flatten power relations to the interpersonal: *So long as I make it known that I am a nice person, I can't be a racist, and my behavior can't harm others.* Reducing racism—and anti-racism—to the interpersonal domain enables a willful blindness to the ways in which racism permeates everyday life. If we focus only on overtly racist institutional practices and/or the overtly racist hate speech of individuals, then we are talking back to a racism that no longer exists in the same way.

Practices such as condemning highly visible and overt expressions of racism (while ignoring race as a system of power) can encourage blindness to global and local racial patterns, thus contributing to sites of domination. Yet, developing action strategies within and across all four domains of power also catalyzes resistance. That all depends on how power holders in these domains use their social locations in working for or against social justice.

Racial Theory and Anti-Racist Practice

Continuing to hammer away at forms of racism that no longer exist can make racial theory seem out of date and out of touch. People who have come to adulthood two generations removed from the Civil Rights and Black Power movements quite rightly ask whether racism is real and, if it is, what do we do about it? Rosa Parks got her seat on the bus—now what?

Understanding the dynamics of racism through the domains of power framework sets the stage for developing pragmatic strategies for practicing resistance and catalyzing change in an ostensibly post-racial world. One core feature of the domains of power argument is that racism is simultaneously situated and resisted *within* each domain as well as *across* all four domains. Because each domain is an analytically distinct entity, each has its own characteristic set of questions that help us think about how racism is embedded and how it is routinely resisted *within* that domain. Taking, for example, the earlier discussion of Blacks and Latinos incarcerated in the U.S. prison system, for the structural domain, we might ask, "How does the legal justice system or the media help reproduce racism, and how does anti-racism manifest itself within these particular social institutions?" Because the disciplinary domain examines the dynamics of how racism operates, we might concentrate on examining how the rules of racism work and how they might work differently, if at all. Questions might include how some lawmakers interpret how those labeled felons can exercise their voting rights. For the cultural domain, the space of ideas and ideology, we might analyze the content of newspapers that routinely circulate images of black male criminals and pretty white victims. Questions such as how racism is justified, what kinds of images uphold it, what kinds of arguments criticize it, and what kinds of anti-racist society we might imagine belong in this domain. Because people live with racism in their everyday lives, we might ask how individual men and women from all social classes, ages, and sexualities embrace their racial identities in ways that foster domination or emancipation. Why would you fight for social justice if all around you were signs saying that justice has already been achieved and that those who are punished are individuals who have failed and done wrong?

We must take into consideration how the disciplinary and cultural domains are organized differently in the context of an ostensibly post-racial world. The disciplinary domain has changed dramatically. In the mid- to late twentieth century, bureaucracies and formal processes of certification (like diplomas and licenses) were the primary methods of regulating who would be allowed to do what. Increasingly, these methods operate in conjunction with surveillance of web-based social networks that make it possible to police a person's digital trail of status updates, photos posted, friends contacted, and sites visited. Where once resistance to disciplinary methods was characterized by uprisings of those who did not have access to rights, let alone those formal processes of certification, now resistance may be both controlled and empowered by these digital capabilities. But to ask whether emerging practices in the disciplinary domain are *either* sites of control *or* sites of newfound freedom misreads current power relations. The power preserved in the disciplinary practices of nation-states persists, along with a new web-based logic of social networks ushered in by global interdependence. It is not one or the other, but rather newly complicated relationships that include both. Resisting oppressive disciplinary power means negotiating these relationships. From high school students and undergraduates who use social media activities as a means of resisting disciplinary practices that ask them to store up certain facts and ways of thinking but not to question or criticize them in light of their own lived experiences, to the Twitterers in Tahrir Square who allowed protesters to organize and reorganize on a Tweet-to-Tweet basis until they brought about a revolution, there are new possibilities and new actualities of discipline and resistance.

The cultural domain becomes especially important in an ostensibly post-racial world. Schools and mainstream media aim to convince dominant and subordinated groups alike that racism is dead and buried, that the world is finally fair, that global market forces have nothing to do with race or other so-called identity categories, and that we should make ourselves willfully blind to the racial face of the social inequalities around us. The post–Civil Rights generation is two generations away from the major mid-twentieth-century social movements that reshaped the globe. New communication technologies and legal structures have enabled new types of relationships, virtual and real, to emerge. Moreover, the post–Civil Rights cohort has no lived memory of events that have catalyzed their freedoms and, for increasing numbers, their parents have no lived experiences either. In the context of global communication media, the musings of senior scholars about the Civil Rights and Black Power movements or struggles for decolonization are just as virtual as YouTube videos of Nicki Minaj and Michelle Obama. This situation suggests that we need racial theories that are not only adequate to explaining this new social world but also far more attentive to the workings of the knowledge industry in shaping how people consume information of all sorts. If knowledge is, in fact, power, then we need to be more attentive to how this knowledge/power process works.

Racism in an ostensibly post-racial world is neither a top-down phenomenon, whereby people simply go along with laws and policies of discrimination, nor a grassroots phenomenon, whereby individual men and women engage in racist name-calling or racially discriminatory behavior. Anti-racist resistance is neither solely social movement actions to boycott, picket, sue, and/or protest racially discriminatory practices and organizations, nor is it restricted to complaining about the racial stereotyping on television. Individually and collectively, racism is produced and resisted *within* each domain of power as well as *across* all four domains.

By starting in the now, and assuming that various expressions of racial theory have some contribution to make, we can explain the now with fresh eyes. Do not aim to fit it into some preexisting narratives, especially an historical narrative that limits imagination by manifesting itself as a script to follow. No more Grandpa fallacy thinking that retards possibilities for cross-generational coalitions. Moreover, it should be clear from this talk that one cannot simply resist *within* the contours of the question—it's been framed out and can lead to reformist responses, primarily because the terms of debate have already been established.

I have learned to ground my analysis in specific social issues that disproportionately affect African Americans and, by implication, people who experience social injustices of some sort. The social issues with strong impact on African Americans—mass incarcerations, homelessness, inadequate housing, poor schools and bad education, and poverty—are not peculiar to African Americans. When it comes to anti-racist activism, grounding theory and practice in actual social issues and then tracing how they affect different groups has the potential to build the broad-based coalitions needed to address the social issues of the ostensibly post-racial world. Yet, how can we address these important social issues without taking racism into account? The implication of believing that we live in a post-racial world is the misguided belief that we can do away with global poverty, homelessness, educational disparities, HIV/AIDS, and similar social issues by ignoring the possibility of racism. And in our misguided belief, we leave far too many people to suffer.

ADDITIONAL RESOURCES

Alexander, Michelle. 2011. *The New Jim Crow*. New York: New Press.

Alonso, Gaston, Noel S. Anderson, Celina Su, and Jeanne Theoharis. 2009. *Our Schools Suck: Students Talk Back to a Segregated Nation on the Failures of Urban Education*. New York: New York University Press.

Omi, Michael, and Howard Winant. 1994. *Racial Formation in the United States: From the 1960s to the 1990s*. New York: Routledge.

Roberts, Dorothy. 2011. *Fatal Invention: How Science, Politics and Big Business Re-Create Race in the Twenty-First Century*. New York: New Press.

The Ethos of Violence

REFLEXIVE ESSAY: *This essay comes from my broader project of investigating racism, sexism, class exploitation, and heterosexism as intersecting systems of power. I contend that intersecting systems of power share points of connection or overlap of practices and ideas that enable their interconnections. Stated differently, they have saturated sites of intersectionality, where certain practices or ideas serve as a sort of conceptual glue that links the systems together. These saturated sites may be so taken for granted that they are rarely questioned and can operate as seemingly natural entities. Violence is one saturated site of intersectionality that reappears across all forms of oppression. Here I sketch out a more complex understanding of violence with an eye toward thinking through these interconnections.*

IN 1963, AFRICAN AMERICAN intellectual Malcolm X responded to the assassination of President John F. Kennedy by noting, "Violence—the chickens came home to roost." Malcolm X was routinely castigated for his point of view. Some misunderstood him, thinking that he was happy that the President had been assassinated as payback or retaliation for violence visited on Black people. In this "eye-for-an-eye" frontier model of justice, violence is justified. When your enemy hurts you, you are justified in going after all that he holds precious, no matter how innocent. This interpretation carried weight with many Americans who believed, despite the fact that Malcolm X called only for self-defense and never advocated violence, routine media links that com-

---

I gave an original version of this talk at Wooster College as part of their annual Martin Luther King, Jr., Day celebration. I delivered the revised version included here at Ithaca College in 2012 as part of the Center for Culture, Race and Ethnicity series on Black men.

pared Martin Luther King, Jr., as upholding the banner of nonviolence (also much misunderstood), by default establishing Malcolm X as his other, namely, the prophet of violence. It didn't help matters that, because J. Edgar Hoover declared King an enemy of the people, by extension, Malcolm X was considered an even greater threat. In this context, few took kindly to Malcolm X's blunt response to Kennedy's assassination.

Despite the response, I think that Malcolm X was misunderstood. His words eerily apply to a series of events that are linked across time and space in a sad necklace of visible acts of violence that break through the seeming calm of everyday life. Gun violence gets the public's attention, yet its patterns often go unrecognized. When, in 2011, Jared Loughner emptied the magazine of his 9 mm semi-automatic Glock on U.S. Representative Gabrielle Giffords' Congress on Your Corner event at a grocery store in Tucson, Arizona, killing six and injuring thirteen, a mere fourteen months had passed since Army psychiatrist Nadal Hassan's 2009 shooting rampage at the army base of Fort Hood, Texas. Just six months before that, a gunman had entered an immigration services center in Binghamton, New York, killing thirteen, wounding four others, and killing himself. Days after the Tucson tragedy, MSNBC host Rachel Maddow traced these events and others when outlining what she called "Jared Loughner's American History"—a timeline of U.S. gun massacres, beginning with a lone gunman's slaughter of twenty-two in Killeen, Texas, in October 1991, when Loughner was only three years old; followed by a raid on a law office in San Francisco and the death of eight when Loughner was five; and the Westside Middle School killings, carried out when Loughner was only nine, by those who were just a few years older than he was. Columbine, the Amish schoolhouse in Nickel Mines, Pennsylvania, then Virginia Tech, Northern Illinois University, and many others all followed. After each event, the words "unimaginable" and "unbelievable" were uttered over and over by many in mourning, but it is perhaps becoming more and more difficult to say and to believe that we cannot imagine such events happening again.

Rachel Maddow's version of "Jared Loughner's American History" gives credence to Malcolm X's analysis four decades earlier. Malcolm X argued that the type of violence that has long been visited on African Americans was broader than that confronting this one population. Rather, an ethos of violence in America catalyzes diverse expressions of violence, of which gun violence constitutes one especially visible form. From Malcolm X's perspective, the firebombings against African churches and the murders of Civil Rights workers in the South were fundamentally linked to the violence that had assassinated a great president. Might other seemingly discrepant events be similarly linked? In 1995, white supremacist Timothy McVeigh blew up a federal building in Oklahoma City, killing children attending a day care center inside. Six years later, Muslim extremists hijacked four commercial airlines and flew them into the World Trade Center and the Pentagon, killing thousands. What connections might there be between these expressions of terrorism? How do the tragic shootings at Virginia Tech fit into a pattern of school-based violence that may not end in death? Moreover, how might the disproportionately high murder rate of young Black men that is no longer newsworthy in some urban markets fit into the ethos of violence that characterizes U.S. society?

What we need are new explanations about the shape and effects of violence on American society, the ways in which violence shapes American interpretations of democracy and justice. "Ground Zero" is the term applied to the New York City site where the twin towers of the World Trade Center once stood. It's sobering to go there and see the vastness of the crater, to imagine the horror of that day. But we must also envision other, more hidden ground zeros that have not yet broken through the surface of the seeming calm of normality. Understanding how an ethos of violence constitutes a deep structural root of U.S. society requires viewing violence as a necessary and ever-present feature of oppression. Oppression in the U.S. context has been organized through specific systems of racism, sexism, class exploitation, heterosexism, age, and citizenship status. Despite being organized differently across varying historical periods, major social institutions of the United States have favored some groups over others and have used varying forms of violence to ensure that women, native peoples, Latinos, Asian immigrants, poor people, LGBT people, and many others stay in their assigned place. Violence has been part of those structural relations of social inequality.

In this context, viewing the very definition of violence as lying *outside* intersecting oppressions of race, class, gender, sexuality, age, and citizenship ignores how the power to define what counts as violence simultaneously constructs these systems of oppression and erases the importance of violence in maintaining them. Given its socially constructed nature, surprisingly little attention has been focused on how power relations shape definitions of violence. The *Oxford English Dictionary*'s definition of violence is fairly standard: Violence is defined as "the exercise of physical force so as to inflict injury on, or cause damage to persons or property; action or conduct characterized by this; treatment or usage tending to cause bodily injury or forcibly interfering with personal freedom" (1989, 654). Everyday understandings of violence see it as being an intentional act of causing physical pain or injury to another person.

Definitions of violence that take power relations into account refute these formal, abstract definitions. Racism, sexism, class exploitation, heterosexism, age, and citizenship status each have distinctive organizational patterns across their domains of power whereby violence takes a specific form. For example, the gendered violence that women encounter takes the form of rape and sexual assault that often goes unpunished by the state. The violence associated with class exploitation may not involve this kind of bodily violation, but rather is more likely to be hidden within public policies that contribute to differential rates of infant mortality or that send poor and working-class kids off to war. Moreover, seeing power relations as intersecting and mutually constructing elevates violence to a characteristic that not only exists within race, class, gender, sexuality, age, and citizenship status as separate systems of power but also joins these systems of power.

Violence can be better imagined as a more dynamic concept whose complexity lies not just in its socially embedded nature in contemporary power relations but also in its ability to shape those same power relations. Violence may be such a naturalized or taken-for-granted dimension of U.S. society that it operates as a saturated site of intersectionality. In other words, violence operates as a form of conceptual glue that enables racism, sexism, class exploitation, and heterosexism to function as they do. Thinking about violence within the context of intersecting power relations suggests three distinguishing features of violence that might help us develop a more nuanced and contextualized definition: (1) the power to define violence; (2) the symbiotic relationship between violent acts and speech; and (3) the routine nature of violence. Armed with more critical definitions of violence, we may be able to imagine new ways of challenging the ethos of violence that permeates U.S. society.

The Power to Define Violence

First, the interpretation of any given act as "violent" lies not within the act itself but in how powerful groups conceptualize it. In the United States, structural power relations grant wealthy, white, heterosexual, Christian, male U.S. citizens greater power to legitimate what counts as violence than everyone else. As a result, the closer individuals and groups come to approximating this social ideal, the more say they get in defining what counts as violence. The actual harm done by a given act remains less salient than how elites use their authority to legitimate or censure it. For example, the differing treatment of young white women, young African American female sex workers, and young, white heterosexual male prisoners as rape victims speaks to differences in what counts as rape. Young white women get varying levels of protection, based on their relationship with the rapist. African American female sex workers receive no such protection because they are seen as being impossible to rape, a perception that spills over to African American women as a group. Similarly, young, white heterosexual male prisoners who are rape victims are stigmatized as less manly if their status as rape survivor becomes known.

In the United States, intersecting oppressions create very different interpretive frameworks for evaluating the actions of individuals who "inflict injury" and those who are its victims. One would think that killing another human being constitutes an inherently violent act. Yet, in actual social contexts, definitions are rarely used so uncritically. Historically, many African American men have been beaten and killed by police officers, and this pattern borders on business as usual unless it is especially egregious. Reminiscent of the rioting in Los Angeles following the Rodney King verdict in 1992, African Americans in Cincinnati, Ohio, in 2001 erupted in several days of community protests in response to the absence of sanctions against police for killing *fifteen* Black men. These two incidents, which are drawn from many more examples, illustrate how patterns of urban uprisings reflect not only the violent acts of rioters but also how police violence targeted at Blacks and Latinos often goes unpunished, if it is recognized as violence at all. In contrast, African American men accused of killing police receive much harsher treatment than that routinely meted out to African American youth who challenge police authority. Take, for example, the case of Mumia Abu-Jamal, an African American journalist who was convicted in 1981 of murdering a white police officer and received the death penalty. Tried before a judge holding the national record for sending the most people to death row, Abu-Jamal's trial was allegedly compromised by coerced eyewitness testimony, fabricated evidence, and clearly inadequate legal counsel. Currently on death row and the subject of an international protest, Abu-Jamal's incarceration has been described by one journalist as a "legal lynching."

The same violent act of killing another human being, whether accusations facing police for killing young Black men or those confronting Abu-Jamal for killing a police officer, becomes legitimated or censured not exclusively in reference to some external moral, ethical code. Instead, the violence of killing becomes defined in relation to power relations of race, gender, class, age, and sexual orientation, as mediated through the legal system, government agencies, media images, and other social institutions. Social institutions routinely endorse their own violence as legal and authoritative, yet sanction violence committed by less powerful individuals and groups as being illegal or immoral. Whether government or religious organization, when it comes to the power to define what counts as violence, the type of social institution matters less than the power of the institution to sanction or censure, and that power reflects systems of inequality.

Social institutions regulate behavior via sanction and censure and also advance interpretive frames for analyzing it. These frameworks encourage the public to interpret violence in ways that support the vested interests of more powerful groups. In other words, these frames help the public interpret what often is identical behavior differently, depending on who is engaging in it. Race, class, gender, sexuality, age, and citizenship status determine the perpetrators and victims of violence from one setting to the next. For example, Marion Sims was a slave owner who practiced medical experimentation without anesthesia on enslaved African women. His medical practice reflected his belief that Black women did not experience pain in the same way that white women did. Sims interpreted his medical experiments as being neither abusive nor violent. The power differential between slave owner and slave was so vast that it eliminated the need to identify perpetrators and victims. Medical experimentation in that setting was not seen as violent at all. Because Black women were defined as chattel and not persons with personal freedom, the bodily injury inflicted on them fell outside the very definition of violence. Ironically, Sims is still celebrated as the father of modern gynecology.

Symbiotic Relationship between
Violent Actions and Speech

The significance of frames for determining what counts as violence leads to a second distinguishing feature of a more contextualized and nuanced definition of violence, namely, the symbiotic relationship linking violent actions and violent speech. In the U.S. legal system, rape is a crime of violence, but the threat of force that accompanies it, the verbal violence that is designed to belittle, humiliate, and strip the rape victim of a sense of self-worth, typically falls outside the purview of the very definition of violence. This division between speech and actions is also part of the ethos of violence.

Most people would classify *acts* such as hitting, slapping, pinching, beating, waterboarding, strangling, mutilating, and killing as violent acts. Whether any given violent act is seen as justified or not, the action itself would still be deemed violent. Yet, in a framing context that severs acts from ideas, speech can *never* be violent. Speech can only provoke violence and cannot itself *be* violent. American constitutional protections for free speech aggravate this division between speech and acts to the point where violent acts are typically seen as the *only* expressions of violence. This division fails to recognize that acts of physical violence require the climate of fear and terror created and maintained by verbal violence and hate speech.

Because speech and action are typically classified into two mutually exclusive categories, hate speech typically falls outside of definitions of violence. The hate speech of men against women, of whites against people of color, of heterosexuals against gays and lesbians, and of adults against children remains largely invisible as part of violence unless it erupts into a recognizable violent act. However, the violent acts in everyday life targeted against individuals from these and other less powerful groups are typically accompanied by verbal violence. Belittling children, humiliating them, and telling them that they are worthless and will never amount to anything—the benchmarks of what child advocates now identify as emotional abuse—is hate speech. Hate speech against children is highly effective because children have substantially less power than the adults who abuse them. The emotional abuse caused by verbal violence is often deemed to be of lesser importance than visible, quantifiable, and therefore more easily legitimated physical or sexual acts of violence. Its effects, however, can be equally, if not more, devastating to its victims.

Constitutional protections for "free" speech minimize the harm done by such speech to its victims. Engaging in hate speech is not just expressing one's opinion. Such speech is designed to belittle, humiliate, and tell women, African Americans, Latinos, Native Americans, Asian Americans, and undocumented immigrants that they are worthless and will never amount to anything, or to keep them in their place. As feminist legal theorist Patricia Williams suggests, "The attempt to split bias from violence has been this society's most enduring and fatal rationalization. Prejudice does hurt, however, just as absence of it can nourish and shelter. Discrimination can repel and vilify, ostracize, and alienate. Any white person who doesn't believe it should spend a week telling everyone she meets that one of her parents or grandparents was black" (Williams 1991, 61).

The ways in which speech and acts interconnect on a societal level are especially apparent in violence against women. Women in abusive relationships often know that their boyfriends and husbands intend to harm them. It's no secret—the men threaten them repeatedly and make their intentions clear. Yet, the police and courts can do little to protect women in this situation other than issuing restraining orders telling the men to stay away from the women. Like the prevalence of gun violence, women are murdered by their boyfriends and husbands, often in front of co-workers, friends, and their own children. Many of these men take their own lives. In hindsight, often everyone "saw it coming," primarily because the boyfriend or husband said that he was going to kill. The message to women seems to be a promise of protection when the boyfriend or husband actually takes action. Yet, by then, it's often too late.

The growth of mass media has brought with it a more expansive conception of speech that includes not just words but also a range of images, lyrics, gestures, and other forms of communication that collectively contribute to an ethos of violence. Representations of Black women and men within mass media sites of entertainment, news, and advertising come awfully close to being the kind of hate speech that fuels an ethos of violence. Within Black popular culture, for example, Black women appear as targets of violence. This depiction works to desensitize viewers to the type of violence visited on countless African American women and to encourage African American men (and those who emulate them) that it is their right to engage in such conduct. In the same way that pornography against women is recognizable because it links sexuality to violence, persistent media images of women as sexualized body parts and women being called "b-tch in the street" create a climate of hate speech that fosters Black women's abuse. Many African American women not only recognize this symbiotic relationship between hate speech associated with various forms of oppression and the treatment that they encounter in everyday life but also see how grappling with an ethos of violence affects their ability to resist. As one woman in Tracy West's study of Black women and male violence recounts:

> It feels the same. Being called nigger, being called nigger b-tch in the street and having to deal with a racist white professor at my college. I feel powerless. It feels the same as having my father do what he did to me. I start to regress. I implode. I feel the same, as if it doesn't matter what I do or say, or what I think is wrong. There is nothing that I can do. (West 1999, 43)

Racial/ethnic groups, feminists, and lesbian, gay, bisexual, and transgendered (LGBT) people often vehemently protest media stereotypes because groups who are targets of such speech often experience it as hate speech. In contrast, individuals and groups who are privileged within systems of race, gender, class, and sexuality as singular or intersecting systems of power often perceive all speech as free speech that does no harm. Those who suffer from the consequences of hate speech are encouraged to lighten up, laugh it off, and see speech as opinion. Violent acts thus become explained by the damaged psyche of the individual, and not by the institutional structures that organized and condoned the ensuring violence.

Violence as Routine

Violence has become so routine across an array of social institutions that most people fail to notice it, and if they do, they do not complain. Major events, such as the terrorism of Oklahoma City and 9/11 or the long string of events associated with gun violence, garner public attention because they are unusual. Yet, the routineness of violent acts and violent speech can be so pervasive that it barely gets noticed at all.

Within power relations of race, class, gender, sexuality, age, and citizenship status that organize violence, the daily, micro-assaults that we all experience are far more important in shaping our encounters than the big events that do not personally concern us. For example, I have been driving for decades, but have only been pulled over by the police twice, once for running a red light and once for going ten miles an hour over the speed limit in a twenty-five-mile-per-hour zone. I experienced neither encounter as abusive or violent. Yet, when I talk with my African American male students, they are routinely pulled over by the police and many experience the pattern of being stopped as abusive and violent. Some see being harassed and arrested by the police as a Black male "rite of passage." Just as getting a driver's license might serve as a rite of passage for white suburban youth, getting hassled by the police serves the same function for inner-city Black youth. In 1994, this rite was deemed to be so universal that a majority Black public high school just outside Washington, D.C., decided to offer courses that were designed to teach kids how to handle themselves if stopped by the police. Sponsored by the county police, educators, the local chapter of the NAACP, and the Black Lawyers Association, through discussion and role-playing, the course advised students on how to respond to personal searches by police, as well as the immobilizing techniques of standard police procedure. As a local reporter described the course, "Three male students are lined up in front of the stage, with their legs spread apart and their hands on the stage floor. A young officer, Cpl. Diane Salen, is patting them down. Minutes later, Cpl. Salen demonstrates on one of the students how an officer attempting to handcuff a suspect maintains control by holding the suspect's thumbs" (Miller 1996, 100–101).

Events such as these demonstrate how micro-assaults have become so routine within American society that the victims typically try to accommodate them. Because the violence targeted toward less powerful groups is so wide-spread across a range of social institutions, its visibility limits our ability to see it as violence at all. How else can we explain the participation of the NAACP and the Black Lawyers Association as co-sponsors of a course for Black students on how to get arrested?

Micro-assaults also characterize public speech. Within a good deal of American popular culture, violence against women gets redefined as entertainment. Seeing images of women as victims of violence is an old trope within American culture. For example, in American films, African American women and men are often brutally murdered, yet theater audiences can be heard cheering at their demise. An especially gruesome scene in the film *Wild at Heart* comes to mind. When I saw the footage of a Black man getting his brains smashed on a marble staircase, I was disgusted. Yet, the audience around me seemed to enjoy this murder as spectacle. A group of young Black men who attended the matinee performance of Spike Lee's film *School Daze* expressed similar pleasure at the gang-rape scene of a young Black coed. They actually cheered.

Hidden in plain sight, the everyday violence joining speech and action in the workplace, government, media, streets, and other social institutions remains so prevalent and racially and gender encoded that, like the *Wild at Heart* audience or the Black adolescent boys watching *School Daze,* most people have difficulty identifying such violence as violence at all until something unusual occurs to rupture its routine. For example, African American motorist Rodney King's 1992 beating by members of the Los Angeles police department became newsworthy not because of the violent act itself. Instead, this rather ordinary police beating merited attention because it was videotaped by an onlooker and televised. While subsequent court decisions censured the police, the beating of Rodney King highlighted the legitimated, routine, and public nature of the beating of African American men by police or their representatives. Similarly, television footage of the beating of Reginald Denny, a white motorist, by African American youth during the Los Angeles uprisings that ensued also became newsworthy due to its extraordinary nature. Because African American mobs do not routinely assault white men simply because they are white, Denny's beating highlighted an unusual and thereby newsworthy event. Subsequent news media coverage treated both videotaped events as if they were equivalent, yet the placement of King and Denny within U.S. racial politics meant that these virtually identical acts of "damage to persons" were interpreted quite differently.

The routine nature of violence is highly significant in maintaining the social control needed for social inequalities to be seen as natural, normal, and inevitable. The significance of violence goes much deeper than the small number of visible violent acts that actually occur in relation to the size of the American population as well as the interpretive climate needed to define it. Rather, the *threat* of violence constitutes a powerful tool of social control. For example, women who monitor what they wear, where they walk and with whom, and the time of day they appear in public places adjust their behavior in response to the fear of violence against them. Women do not have total access to the streets because these spaces remain coded as male spaces, at least most of the time. A particular woman need not be raped to know that some streets are always dangerous or that all streets are sometimes dangerous. The fear of physical and sexual assault is sufficient to keep her in her place. Similarly, young Black men often find themselves up against a wall or a car or face down on the ground, assuming the position of a suspected criminal. In some cases, guns are drawn. The fact that police have killed African American men and have not been prosecuted serves as a chilling example that Black men should neither run from the police nor try to fight back. In these cases, the speech community that shapes perceptions of public space as one where African American women are potential rape victims and African American men are potential criminals is just as important in constructing violence as the acts of specific individuals.

Just Say No? Social Injustice and the Ethos of Violence

America has long declared war on the least powerful people within its borders. This state of "normalized war" predicated on the acceptability of violence targeted toward select groups remains unrecognized because it too is routine. Warfare against people of color was sanctioned in the past, an unfortunate phase when the U.S. government declared war on sovereign native populations, stood by while Southern mobs planned lynching parties for uppity Negroes, or refused to define rape as violence, preferring instead to blame the skirt length of the victim or prevailing conceptions of masculinity suggested by the phrase "boys will be boys." The historical effects of an ethos of violence have been recognized, if not redressed. The Japanese Americans whose property was stolen and who were interned in response to anti-Asian bias during World War II have received an apology. A monument to Reverend Martin Luther King, Jr., now stands on the National Mall in Washington, D.C. Without a more expansive understanding of violence that examines how power inequities shape the ability to define what counts as violence, how violent speech and acts depend on one another, and how to see violence within routine, it is reasonable to assume that the ethos of violence described here does not apply to now.

With this focus on the past, we may misread both the nature of the violence of the present as well as its broadening reach beyond its traditional victims. What if this ethos of violence that has been routinely visited on segments of the American population has come to affect more than historically derogated groups? What is the effect on U.S. society if warfare constitutes less a break from a normal peace than a new normal? What might the effects of a normalized ethos of violence be on citizens as well as on American democracy itself?

Warfare is no longer big and obvious, engaged in by armies. Instead, the "normalized war" of contemporary society may be far more muted, permeating the very fabric of society itself. Past domination relied on strategies such as segregating or quarantining people into ghettos, Bantustans, reservations, homelands, or colonies for reasons of control. Contemporary forms of domination are successful when the powerful can "reduce" violence to such an extent that domination of a targeted population is possible precisely because there *is* no target and therefore no violence. The shrinking global context has made it increasingly unsuitable to wage war on others who are far away without somehow doing damage to the self. People go willingly, not grudgingly, to their assigned place. Violence is still used as a tool of domination, but not in the old way of engaging in visible warfare and manufacturing visible enemies. In contemporary forms of institutionalized racism and sexism that are organized via desegregation, violence is covered up and victims/survivors are rendered invisible. In this context, the constellation of practices that comprise institutionalized rape gain in importance. As a tool of control, the hate speech that condones violent practices against women, children, and similar vulnerable populations—practices that are typically directed toward individuals and that may occur in private—grows in significance. Visible and unsanctioned violent acts, such as police action against unarmed citizens, are censured.

In a context of normalized war, where violence is a pervasive feature of society, a simple "just say no to violence" approach won't work. What exactly would we be saying "no" to? Superficial interpretations of nonviolence as a social justice strategy seem based on formal definitions of violence. If America is characterized by an ethos of violence, there is no way to just say no to it, other than leaving. Instead, the beginnings of a comprehensive anti-violence project must go hand in hand with a commitment to social justice, broadly defined. Violence will continue, changing shape and tactics, as long as the power relations it relies on remain unchallenged.

ADDITIONAL RESOURCES

Kapsalis, Terri. 1997. *Public Privates: Performing Gynecology from Both Ends of the Speculum*. Durham, N.C.: Duke University Press.

Matsuda, Mari J., Charles Lawrence III, Richard Delgado, and Kimberle Crenshaw. 1993. *Words That Wound: Critical Race Theory, Assaultive Speech, and the First Amendment*. Boulder, Colo.: Westview Press.

Miller, Jerome G. 1996. *Search and Destroy: African-American Males in the Criminal Justice System*. New York: Cambridge University Press.

Oxford English Dictionary. 2nd ed., vol. XIX. 1989. London: Clarendon Press.

West, Traci C. 1999. *Wounds of the Spirit: Black Women, Violence, and Resistance Ethics*. New York: New York University Press.

Williams, Patricia J. 1991. *The Alchemy of Race and Rights*. Cambridge, Mass.: Harvard University Press.

Who's Right? What's Left?

Family Values and U.S. Politics

REFLEXIVE ESSAY: *In my work, I conceptualize family as an important site for examining intersecting systems of power. For over two decades, my scholarship has examined how the construct of family constitutes a saturated site of intersectionality, namely, a set of ideas and practices that provides conceptual glue and organizes race, class, gender, sexuality, ethnicity, and national identity. Within U.S. society, understandings of family had long influenced public policy. By 2005, I saw a significant shift in public discourse about family. At that time, the United States was involved in two prolonged wars in Iraq and Afghanistan, and socially conservative agendas seemed hegemonic. Part of the Right's effectiveness lay in its ability to speak to issues of family values that resonated with public concerns. By casting themselves as pro-family, the Right painted dissenters from their point of view as anti-family and anti-American. By 2008, times had changed. Barack Obama won the presidency, but how had he done it? How did he navigate the family values discourse that had played such an important role in the resurgence of social conservatism? This essay investigates these issues.*

I delivered an earlier version of this talk as a panelist in a 2005 American Sociological Association plenary session under the title "Some Family Matters: Exploring the Rightward Shift within American Politics." I returned to these themes in a 2009 panel discussion on families as part of the Humanities Council series at the Graduate Center in New York. This essay constitutes a fusion of these two prior talks, edited to reflect contemporary social issues.

I HAVE LONG BEEN curious about how wealthy families manage to convince the American people that American public interest is best served by saddling senior citizens with sky-high prescription drug costs, providing corporate welfare for oil companies and defense contractors, sending poor and working-class kids off to war, and allowing hard-working middle-class families to lose their homes to foreclosures.

Two decades of living in Ohio sheds light on domestic American politics. Ohio, a state whose state motto is "Ohio, the heart of it all," is a microcosm of American society. On the one hand, despite the pressing bread-and-butter issues the majority of Ohio citizens face, many faithfully continue to vote for politicians who fail to deliver jobs, housing, good roads, and schools. Instead, gun rights, gay marriage, regulating contraception, and similar issues raised by social conservatives take center stage. Are people in Ohio so mesmerized by the smoke and mirrors of right-wing Republican morality that the combination of fundamentalist preachers and Fox TV constitutes the new opiate of the people? Do Ohioans really believe that team prayer on the public school gridiron will convince God to favor their football team over those who wear different team colors? How will criminalizing abortion deter women who have been raped by family members or who simply do not have the money to raise a child from making that choice? Will demonizing homosexuality promote stable heterosexual marriages, abolish domestic abuse, or get more deadbeat dads to pay child support? Is Ohio a heartland without a heart?

On the other hand, as a storied state with a long American history, Ohio has deep-seated populist traditions that are quintessentially American. People in Ohio take principled stances, eschewing the nihilism that can run rampant in academic circles. Currently, the Freedom Center Museum, part of the Smithsonian complex, stands on the banks of the Ohio River in downtown Cincinnati as a symbol of global aspirations for freedom. Abolitionist activities under slavery catalyzed the specifics of the museum—Cincinnati's role in the Underground Railroad; the Taft house in Cincinnati, where Harriet Beecher Stowe wrote *Uncle Tom's Cabin,* the book that helped create a groundswell of antipathy toward slavery—yet the Freedom Center itself is bigger than the African American freedom story. Within Ohio, one uncovers all sorts of freedom stories, then and now, that breathe life into American democracy.

For those of you who are located on either coast, the tensions that characterize Ohio politics may seem ideologically driven and therefore irrational (or rational, depending on the ideology used to make the judgment—one's own ideological positions always seem far more rational than those of one's opponent). Many of you may think that people in Ohio are incredibly naïve or stupid or committed or heroic. You are welcome to think this and to continue to position Ohio within the binary framework of being a "swing state" that moves back and forth between two clearly defined choices that are obviously right or wrong. In the context of national elections, Ohio is indeed a bona fide swing state. The world is far more nuanced than this, however, and when it comes to contemporary U.S. politics, something else may be at play.

All of us must come to terms with the challenges of living in a vastly different world than that of our parents and grandparents. Academics lack a good language to describe these changes and encourage us to conceptualize the present in terms of the past. They resort to attaching the prefix "post-" to all sorts of things. Look at the language—post-colonialism, post-nationalism, postmodernism, post-Civil Rights, post-family, post-religion—extreme social constructionists suggest that we live in a hyper-real world that is essentially post-reality. Many people would gladly trade in the ambiguities of the contemporary "post" period for the imagined certainties of the past. Then, everybody seemingly understood, accepted, and went willingly to his or her assigned place, whether good or bad. In our current times of economic, political, and social instability, the imagined past offers comfort: Negroes knew to lower their eyes when talking to whites, women loved to stay home and have babies, no one knew any gay people because such people simply did not exist, and every Christian could trumpet with great certainty, "My religion is number one!" The imagined and idealized past provides an illusory comfort that promises purpose, direction, and meaning in times of extraordinary change.

The future offers no such guarantees. The farther along the "post" path that we travel, the rockier and more unfamiliar the road appears to be. To live in this uncertain present, we imagine future prospects, new visions of society that draw from the past but emerge within our active imaginations. Democracy itself is such an imagined entity—a set of ideas always in the making and never actually finished. For this reason, democracy cannot be installed in another country by substituting its form of rule with one that more closely resembles our own. The United States is committed to becoming a democracy, with its fiber measured not solely by the distance it has traveled in moving along this path but also by its commitment to taking democratic principles into its own future.

When it comes to democracy, the choice either to retreat to the past or to move into an unknowable future faces individuals and the nation alike. Moreover, these choices reflect very different orientations about what America was, is, and might be. Both of these frameworks for understanding America require a situated imagination. Our contentious present is characterized by the tensions linking the imagined certainties of the past and the imagined possibilities of the future. The fundamental moment of reality is now.

Politicians, business elites, scholars, and grassroots organizers alike who recognize this need and know how to speak to it can, in fact, and with great success, exploit it. The Right attacks the recent past that it rejects, aiming to reinstall a male-dominated, heterosexual, white, middle-class America that existed primarily in the imaginations of the more powerful. Backed into the corner of protecting what it assumed were stable past victories, the Left seems too timid or perhaps too tired to imagine new futures. In this context, the Right has done a far better job than the Left of speaking convincingly to the uncertainties that affect all people in the United States. Stated differently, the messages of the Right resonate with people's lives. But why, and how?

In his groundbreaking work on sexuality and power, *The History of Sexuality, Volume I: An Introduction,* Michel Foucault argues that heterosexism as a system of power penetrates into each individual to annex the power of the erotic. Through this process of annexation and being disciplined by the social institutions that are organized to accomplish it, we learn to regulate ourselves and watch one another to ensure that no one is breaking the rules. This is a new model of power, not one solely of the domination of brute force, where the state oppresses people through laws, armies, and police forces. Rather, this modern form of power relies on a deeply entrenched self-surveillance where we learn not only to watch each other but also to censor ourselves. In this context of surveillance and fear, all strangers are potential foes until we figure out ways to tell who belongs to our ever-shrinking circle of friends.

Foucault's scholarship suggests that certain core ideas might be very important within these new power relations, especially during today's period of immense social change. To be such a powerful idea, the concept would need to have the ability to transverse the biological borders of our individual bodies as well as the borders of our social institutions. Unchallenged through its ubiquity, such a powerful idea would be hidden in plain sight, a tool that can be annexed to a range of political and/or personal agendas.

The concept of *family* may operate in just this fashion. Ideas about family tap our deepest emotions and travel to the highest levels of society. The power of the concept of *family* lies in its dual function as both an ideological construction and a fundamental principle of social organization. As ideology, family rhetoric provides a flexible, interpretive framework that accommodates a range of meanings. Relying on the rhetoric of family for their own political agendas has been a common strategy for conservative movements of all types, building on a recognition of the importance of family in people's actual and imagined lives. The religious right's censure of abortion and of gay marriage that has animated a sustained anti-abortion social movement and the willingness of low-wage Latino workers to send money home to family members in Mexico, Guatemala, and El Salvador *both* invoke ideas about family to advance very different political agendas.

Moving Right: Focus on the Family and the Politics of Family

One reason why the Right has been so successful stems from its masterful manipulation of both the rhetoric of family and social policies that draw on family rhetoric to give them meaning. Politicians routinely invoke ideas about family to motivate all types of behavior. In the United States, people are expected to sacrifice for their own biological families. Many feel so personally responsible for their families that they work jobs that leave them little time to spend with those same families. Family values are everywhere, motivating behaviors concerning race, class, and national priorities. For example, whites are told that the decision to move into a white neighborhood is not about upholding racism, but rather constitutes a personal choice to protect the interests of their children and provide them with a "good" education. Frowning on interracial marriage upholds the integrity of racially homogeneous families, even if one's best friend on the job is African American. Many citizens now believe that the decline of the United States is directly tied to the erosion of so-called family values. "The broken families of black welfare mothers," citizens decry, "are the problem—parasites on the state." Military service in defense of one's nation is cast as duty to family in which the nation itself is seen as one large family unit. Some must sacrifice their lives in Afghanistan and Iraq so that the American national family can endure. Such is the power of the idea of family.

Examining how family rhetoric operates on the Right sheds light on contemporary political phenomena. Some years back, I toured the Colorado Springs headquarters of Focus on the Family, a socially conservative group whose radio stations, publications, curricular products for home-based schooling, and other outreach efforts have a global reach. Focus on the Family is not a church and does not advance a particular religion, but it does have a clear moral agenda. Nor was Focus on the Family an all-white organization. Pictures of families from diverse racial and ethnic backgrounds hung on its walls, letting visitors know that the organization was trying to be responsive to diversity. During my visit, I had an extended conversation with an African American woman who was shopping in the Focus on the Family gift shop. She pointed me to pamphlets that would help families deal with social problems, in her case, how to be a good mother if your man is gone. Lesbian, gay, bisexual, and transgendered (LGBT) families were not endorsed, but I was surprised to see a pamphlet advising parents what to say to their child if he or she claimed to be gay.

Of the many memorable experiences of the tour, one stood out: my reaction to an enormous room that looked to me to be the size of a soccer field, filled with computer terminals. The task of workers at the terminals was to answer each and every one of the large volume of letters that people sent to Focus on the Family. The letter writers did not contact this organization as Democrats, Republicans, or Independents seeking political changes; they wrote as individuals with problems that social institutions around them failed to address. Our tour guide told us that people wrote letters about everything—losing jobs, losing their houses, their worry about their kids on drugs, their loss of faith, violent spouses and boyfriends, a parent with Alzheimer's, for example—all issues that were tied in some way to their specific family situations. Many were simply worried about whether their families would survive and thought that Focus on the Family might be a sympathetic listener to their problems. Apparently, Focus on the Family received few letters about world peace, global warming, the evils of racism and sexism, or the need to pass major pieces of legislation regarding health care, education, the economy, or Social Security.

The list of problems would be familiar to most sociologists. Apparently, the letter writers were concerned about the very same social problems that sociologists have been engaging so diligently for so long. The letter writers turned neither to scholars nor to government officials for help—they turned to an organization named Focus on the Family because of its seeming concern for families. The job of the workers at the computer terminals was to write a personal response to each and every letter. If the letter writers had written instead to government officials or even to sociologists who might be studying the social problem that most concerned them, I doubt that they would have gotten a personal response, if they got a response at all.

How Focus on the Family responded to the heterogeneity of requests was eye-opening. To prepare their responses, the Focus on the Family workers were required to look up James Dodson's teachings on the problem in question and compose a letter by stitching together prewritten, boilerplate text. Problems that could not be handled in this fashion were referred to on-staff social workers, who composed a more personal letter, and who, depending on the seriousness of the problem, contacted these people through other means. What appeared to be a personal response from a caring organization was in actuality a form letter and stock response. Relying on technology, Focus on the Family found a way to provide empathy and help during times of uncertainty and social change. It is no accident that the organization is named Focus on the Family. If you were one of those letter writers, what kind of politician would get your vote?

Focus on the Family and similar organizations have come to claim ownership over the moral capital of family rhetoric, leaving those who oppose organizations such as this stigmatized as being anti-family. The Right claims the high ground on morality, yet its sustained opposition to social policies that would help poor children and their families belies its own beliefs. The Right now has the moral high ground because it seems to care about "family." But what does this really mean? The Right may claim that it is protecting the children of America; yet, it does so only by putting large numbers of poor and working-class American children in harm's way. Before the War in Iraq wound down in 2010 and the War in Afghanistan became increasingly unpopular, television viewers in Ohio experienced a steady diet of nightly news recounting poignant stories of the latest Ohio casualties. The decade-long "War on Terror" was fought by poor and working-class American youth, disproportionately from states like Ohio. They were the ones sacrificed to keep the sanctity of our national family in place. The heart-wrenching coverage of how each individual family grappled with the death of their loved one makes it more difficult to claim that each casualty was in vain. Better to find meaning in that death through maintaining the fiction that war is heroic, and that the person died protecting his or her homeland, family, and the American way of life, than to acknowledge the hypocrisy of family rhetoric.

Ownership of the moral high ground of the language of family has encouraged the Right to castigate those whose family rhetoric does not match its own.

This is apparent in both domestic and foreign policy. Domestic policies on affir-mative action, immigration, equal rights for women, and gay marriage certainly reflect the Right's conception of the worth of various members of the Ameri-can national family. Take, for example, the striking resemblance between the language used for adoption and that describing how so-called aliens become American citizens. Children who lack biological ties to parents are screened for their suitability for adoption, with factors such as their racial, religious, and ethnic background occupying a prominent place in their placement. Younger children who allegedly have received less socialization in a different family cul-ture are typically preferred over older ones. When adoptions are finalized, such children become "naturalized," receive new birth certificates, and are consid-ered legally indistinguishable from children biologically born into the national family unit. In a similar fashion, immigration policies screen potential citi-zens in terms of how well they match the biological and economic needs of the American national family. Russian immigrants are favored over Haitian ones, and the willingness of undocumented Latino immigrants to work in the worst jobs pressures immigration officials to overlook their ethnic difference. Chang-ing immigration policies have reflected the perceived racial, ethnic, and labor needs of the "domestic" political economy. Those who become adopted citizens undergo some sort of conversion experience. This naturalization process trans-forms so-called aliens into bona fide American citizens.

Foreign policy shows a similar predilection for drawing on and repackag-ing the Right's rhetoric of family drawn from an imagined past. Obtaining and/ or protecting a people's "homeland" or national territory has long been central to definitions of nation and to nationalist aspirations. After its successful anti-colonial struggle against England and its formation as a new nation-state, the United States pursued a sustained imperialist policy in acquiring much of the land that defines its contemporary borders. More recently, its imperialistic ex-pansion as the sole remaining superpower, most notably, the War in Iraq, speaks to a continuation of this belief in American manifest destiny, not a new direc-tion. Since the United States has operated as a dominant world power, shield-ing its own home soil from intruders has been equally important as protecting both American individuals and businesses that occupy foreign soil. These in-dividuals and businesses on foreign soil become extensions of American terri-tory, representatives of the American family, who must be defended at all costs.

Moving Left: Barack Obama and the Politics of Family

Given this context, how did Barack Obama manage to get elected President of the United States? I am sure that there are many reasons, but I want to ex-amine how family might have had some effect. So much about Barack Obama seems antithetical to the unquestioned logic of family advanced by social con-servatives. Barack Obama's election not only shakes up the present but also forces a reexamination of both the imagined past and what can be imagined for the future.

Barack Obama's election as the first African American President of the United States illustrates a similar use of family rhetoric as that of the Right, but strategically deployed toward quite different political ends. The Right uses ideas about family as a code for a constellation of conservative values about the seeming homogeneity of American national identity. In contrast, Barack Obama's use of family rhetoric, primarily through representations of his own family, provides alternative views of family.

Throughout his campaign, Senator Obama was especially candid in presenting his personal family stories as quintessentially American. He routinely incorporated personal family stories into his speeches and used family stories to explain his vision of the American Dream. For example, his "A More Perfect Union" speech about race affirmed his faith in the decency and generosity of a diverse American public: "I am the son of a black man from Kenya and a white woman from Kansas. I was raised with the help of a white grandfather who survived a Depression to serve in Patton's army during World War II and a white grandmother who worked on a bomber assembly line . . . I am married to a black American who carries within her the blood of slaves and slave owners—an inheritance we pass on to our two precious daughters. I have brothers, sisters, nieces, nephews, uncles and cousins, of every race and every hue, scattered across three continents."

Here Mr. Obama invokes the multicultural face of America, past and present, within his own family. In his 2008 speech, "A World That Stands as One," delivered to a large, enthusiastic outdoor rally in Berlin, Germany, he shared another version of the same tale that recasts the American story as a multicultural story: "I know that I don't look like the Americans who've previously spoken in this great city. The journey that led me here is improbable. My mother was born in the heartland of America, but my father grew up herding goats in Kenya." Here he stresses the promise of upward social mobility, even for someone as improbable as himself. Whether speaking to an audience grappling with the contradictions of race or a global audience enthralled by the candidacy of an African American person, Barack Obama was consistent about his narrative being an American story: "For as long as I live, I will never forget that in no other country on Earth is my story even possible," he proclaimed.

Barack Obama's stories of himself as a family man illustrate how family rhetoric can be used to express connections between the status of American families, economic security, and racial politics. All three of these themes are difficult to engage without drawing the censure of the Right. By using family rhetoric, he embedded ideas about the future of America, especially its democratic future of inclusivity, within themes that the public could understand. In essence, Barack Obama began to reclaim the moral space associated with family that had so long been ceded to the Right.

By sharing his own personal story of how his *past* upbringing was central to his current economic prosperity and political success, Barack Obama valorized nontraditional family structures, namely, blended families with stepfathers and half-siblings, families maintained by single mothers, extended families that include grandparents as primary caretakers, and families formed across racial and ethnic boundaries. The values he learned within these diverse family forms seemingly override their nontraditional structures and signal a new politics of race (and family) that more closely resembles the multi-racial, multi-ethnic, and multi-cultural fabric of American society. If strong families are the foundation of American society, then showcasing family diversity expands notions of American national identity.

Michelle Obama's family story contains different details, but serves a similar function. In telling her *past* family story, Michelle Obama focuses on growing up in her intact, working-class African American family in Chicago. For example, she opens her speech introducing Barack Obama at the 2008 Democratic National Convention by focusing on family ties—as a sister to her brother who is her "protector and lifelong friend," as a wife to a husband who will make "an extraordinary president," as a mom whose "girls are the heart of my heart and the center of my world," and as a daughter. Michelle Obama pays special attention to the intact African American family of her childhood: "I come here as a daughter—raised on the South Side of Chicago by a father who was a blue-collar city worker and a mother who stayed at home with my brother and me."

Here Michelle Obama uses her brother's success as well as her own to highlight the significance of family to economic security. She thanks her parents for their contributions: "Thanks to their faith and hard work, we both were able to go on to college. So I know firsthand from their lives—and mine—that the American dream endures." As U.S. President, Barack Obama's *current* family experiences within the first-ever Black First Family, namely, as a devoted husband and father in a racially homogeneous, married, heterosexual nuclear family with legitimate children, signal more traditional conceptions of the links between family and economic success. Barack and Michelle Obama may have followed different paths to their current family status, but their shared values enabled them to create one family. For example, Michelle Obama explains how the family values that she gained growing up in an intact African American family resembled those of her spouse, despite his less traditional lineage: "What struck me when I first met Barack was that even though he had this funny name, even though he'd grown up all the way across the continent in Hawaii, his family was so much like mine . . . Barack and I were raised with so many of the same values: that you work hard for what you want in life; that your word is your bond and you do what you say you're going to do; that you treat people with dignity and respect, even if you don't know them, and even if you don't agree with them."

The family values that are associated with the Obama family's nuclear structure, such as teaching their children the importance of education, hard work, exercise, healthy food consumption, and service to the less fortunate, uphold traditional ideas about the family that ostensibly foster the American Dream.

Barack and Michelle Obama's reliance on family stories has at least three possible effects that may signal a revitalized use of family rhetoric that better represents a broader American public. First, ideas about family permeate two major changes of the early twenty-first century, namely, challenges to the economic security long promised by holding fast to the American Dream and the emergence of a new colorblind racial formation, where talking openly of race can be interpreted as creating and fostering racism. In this context, Barack and Michelle Obama's reliance on family stories signals a new way of presenting broader social issues, primarily class-based, economic concerns, by using family rhetoric to build unity across differences (in this case, racial differences) for specific policies (such as work–family balance). In a context of colorblindness, where talking of race is seen by many as promoting racism, family stories provide a zone of tolerance, where race is recognized yet is not seen as the definitive factor that shapes economic security.

Second, *how* Barack and Michelle Obama rely on family stories is also significant. The multiple and often competing narratives from the campaign as well as those about the first Black First Family reflect intentional and/or media-generated ambiguities concerning connections among marriage, family, and economic security. As illustrated by President Obama's support of responsible fatherhood initiatives, observers with widely diverging political sympathies seemingly find comfort in various dimensions of President Obama's hopeful messages about how strengthening family fosters economic security. When read selectively, the past and present strands of President Obama's family narratives speak to quite diverse political programs concerning the centrality of family to economic prosperity. Without due diligence on the part of the Obama administration, economic security policies honed within these unresolved tensions concerning family might suggest that the path to economic success for nonstandard families, for example, those headed by single African American mothers or those maintained by LGBT people, lies in embracing the new Black First Family's model of marriage and parenting. Barack Obama's impressive accomplishments could easily be recast as yet another role model for how one might overcome a nontraditional past to achieve economic security through marriage. "Be like Barack and the First Family," we may be told, "and you too will find wealth, fame, and fortune." As indicated by documents produced by the Obama campaign and presidency, notably, the detailed plan and signature speeches assembled in *Change We Can Believe In,* and the plethora of documents available on the official website, this does not seen to be the kind of change that President Obama had in mind. Yet, in a highly partisan political context, when it comes to issues of gender, work, and family, this could be the kind of change that the first Black First Family comes to represent.

Third, the family drama surrounding the first Black First Family serves as a template for a new multi-racial, multi-cultural American national identity.

Barack Obama's heterogeneous family ties, the family that raised him, the family that he formed through marriage, and Michelle Obama's heritage all enable him to make some legitimate claims about racial/ethnic diversity and how to overcome the legacy of slavery that has been central to American society. Although he identifies as African American, Barack Obama notes that individuals of diverse racial backgrounds are all members of his family. Barack Obama demonstrates that his family background, especially its diversity, allows him to see and respect the individuals of different backgrounds that make up the larger American family. The repeated references to Barack Obama's family tree, both by the media and by Barack Obama himself, seem preoccupied with figuring out the blood lineages that have made the Obama family, often framing the Obama family as products of their diverse genealogical records. Rather than rejecting his mixed-race, multi-ethnic heritage, Barack Obama proudly claims it. Significantly, claiming family diversity enables Barack Obama to tap into the diversity of the American national family and to ask others to expand participation in the American Dream along diverse lines. Developing a new understanding of race and of racial families enables a recasting of the American story, now predicated on a new multi-cultural racial family, which in turn has real implications for understanding American democracy and for actual policies that might foster economic security for families.

The Emancipatory Possibilities of Family?

Socially conservative discourses of the Right and Barack Obama's use of family rhetoric both draw on the idea of family as a unifying mechanism for race, class, gender, sexuality, and nationality. Yet this shared family construct fosters quite different understandings of American national identity, the American Dream, and the significance of families. Family rhetoric occupies such a prominent place in the language of public discourse that rejecting it outright may be counterproductive for groups from all places along the political spectrum. Because the power of the idea of family lies in its ability to harness energy to all sorts of political projects, ceding this powerful social construct to the Right seems shortsighted. The Right's own ethical contradictions concerning its use of family rhetoric, let alone its actual family policies, constitute its Achilles heel.

However, merely criticizing the foibles of the Right is unlikely to yield much relief. A long list of sociologists and advocacy organizations has tried this approach, measuring, evaluating, and criticizing the inconsistencies between the rhetoric and the status of children in the United States. Data are invaluable, but rationality and facts by themselves are unlikely to topple power of this magnitude. Through its analysis of political campaigns, Drew Westen's book, *The Political Brain: The Role of Emotion in Deciding the Fate of the Nation,* shows how the Left has ceded power to the Right by relying solely on facts and reason to sway voters. Westen argues that the Right's use of emotion successfully lent them the moral superiority of major political debates on a variety of issues, including that of family. In this context, the annexation of the concept of family goes too deep into each person and functions too pervasively as a principle of social organization to be stopped by a graph or a sociological factoid.

In a context where many American citizens nostalgically hope that restoring the traditional American family will catalyze economic security, and where global processes have made the family wage, the stay-at-home-mom, ownership of a single-family home, if not marriage and family themselves, less attainable, the media attention afforded the Obama family as the first Black First Family is important. The family stories of the Obama First Family lend valor to the kinds of families that people actually have, and are likely to have into the future. Eschewing a moral agenda concerning the necessary form that a good family should take, the Obama family counsels the nation to hold fast to the American Dream during a period of economic transformation and colorblind racism. Yet, looking ahead, it is apparent that there are no easy answers. In this context, perhaps is it sufficient to have more people at the table who argue in defense of families without proscribing their point of view as natural, normal, or ideal.

ADDITIONAL RESOURCES

Collins, Patricia Hill. 2012. "Just Another American Family? The First Black First Family." *Qualitative Sociology*, 35 (2):123–141.

Coontz, Stephanie. 1992. *The Way We Never Were: American Families and the Nostalgia Trap.* New York: Basic Books.

Gerson, Kathleen. 2010. *The Unfinished Revolution: How a New Generation Is Reshaping Family, Work, and Gender in America.* New York: Oxford University Press.

Lakoff, G. 2008. *The Political Mind: Why You Can't Understand 21st Century Politics with a 19th Century Brain.* New York: Viking Adult.

Obama, Barack. 2006. *The Audacity of Hope: Thoughts on Reclaiming the American Dream.* New York: Crown.

———. 2008. *Change We Can Believe In: Barack Obama's Plan to Renew America's Promise.* New York: Three Rivers Press.

V

Intellectual Activism
Revisited

Toward a New Vision

Race, Class, and Gender as Categories of Analysis and Connection

REFLEXIVE ESSAY: *I originally presented this essay in 1989 as a keynote address at the Workshop on Integrating Race and Gender into the College Curriculum, sponsored by the Center for Research on Women at Memphis State University. "Toward a New Vision" outlines some of the core ideas that have framed much of my intellectual activism. Working from African American women's ideas and experiences, I focus on the ideas and experiences of historically oppressed groups and point out how taking on multiple points of view fosters empathy. I also introduce the basic ideas of intersectionality as a paradigm for conceptualizing social reality. Before this talk, I had been working with issues of race, class, and gender as separate concerns. Yet, like others during the 1980s, I saw the limitations of this monocategorical approach. I conclude with a call for political resistance, by developing coalitional politics that are attentive to power differences and grounded in empathy. Because it is a touchstone for my work, I have not updated this speech.*

In keeping with other essays in *On Intellectual Activism*, and because this essay has been widely reprinted, I have omitted the original endnotes and substituted a brief reading list from the original essay. This talk reflects the collective effort of the Center and all of the people who attended its workshops in the late 1980s and early 1990s. I have also retained the original capitalization of "black" and "white" used in this volume.

The true focus of revolutionary change is never merely the
oppressive situations which we seek to escape, but that piece
of the oppressor which is planted deep within each of us.
                              —AUDRE LORDE, from *Sister Outsider* (123)

A UDRE LORDE'S STATEMENT raises a troublesome issue for scholars
and activists working for social change. While many of us have little
difficulty assessing our own victimization within some major system
of oppression, whether it be by race, social class, religion, sexual orientation,
ethnicity, age, or gender, we typically fail to see how our thoughts and actions
uphold someone else's subordination. Thus, White feminists routinely point
with confidence to their oppression as women but resist seeing how much their
white skin privileges them. African Americans who possess eloquent analyses of racism often persist in viewing poor White women as symbols of white
power. The radical Left fares little better. "If only people of color and women
could see their true class interests," they argue, "class solidarity would eliminate racism and sexism." In essence, each group identifies the type of oppression with which it feels most comfortable as being fundamental and classifies
all other types as being of lesser importance.

Oppression is full of such contradictions. Errors in political judgment that
we make concerning how we teach our courses, what we tell our children, and
which organizations are worthy of our time, talents, and financial support flow
smoothly from errors in theoretical analysis about the nature of oppression and
activism. Once we realize that there are few pure victims or oppressors, and
that each one of us derives varying amounts of penalty and privilege from the
multiple systems of oppression that frame our lives, then we will be in a position to see the need for new ways of thought and action.

To get at that "piece of the oppressor which is planted deep within each
of us," we need at least two things. First, we need new visions of what oppression is, new categories of analysis that are inclusive of race, class, and gender as
distinctive yet interlocking structures of oppression. Adhering to a stance of
comparing and ranking oppressions—the proverbial "I'm more oppressed than
you"—locks us all into a dangerous dance of competing for attention, resources,
and theoretical supremacy. Instead, I suggest that we examine our different experiences within the more fundamental relationship of domination and subordination. To focus on the particular arrangements that race or class or gender
take in our time and place without seeing these structures as sometimes parallel and sometimes interlocking dimensions of the more fundamental relationship of domination and subordination may temporarily ease our consciences.
But while such thinking may lead to short-term social reforms, it is simply inadequate for the task of bringing about long-term social transformation.

While race, class, and gender as categories of analysis are essential in helping us understand the structural bases of domination and subordination, new
ways of thinking that are not accompanied by new ways of acting offer incom-

plete prospects for change. To get at that "piece of the oppressor which is planted deep within each of us," we also need to change our daily behavior. Currently, we are all enmeshed in a complex web of problematic relationships that grant our mirror images full human subjectivity while stereotyping and objectifying those most different from ourselves. We often assume that the people we work with, teach, send our children to school with, and sit next to in conferences such as this will act and feel in prescribed ways because they belong to given race, social class, or gender categories. These judgments by category must be replaced with fully human relationships that transcend the legitimate differences created by race, class, and gender as categories of analysis. We require new categories of connection, new visions of what our relationships with one another can be.

Our task is immense. We must first recognize race, class, and gender as interlocking categories of analysis that together cultivate profound differences in our personal biographies. But then we must transcend those very differences by reconceptualizing race, class, and gender to create new categories of connection.

My presentation today addresses this need for new patterns of thought and action. I focus on two basic questions. First, how can we reconceptualize race, class, and gender as categories of analysis? Second, how can we transcend the barriers created by our experiences with race, class, and gender oppression to build the types of coalitions essential for social change? To address these questions, I contend that we must acquire new theories of how race, class, and gender have shaped the experiences not just of women of color but also of all groups. Moreover, we must see the connections between these categories of analysis and the personal issues in our everyday lives, particularly our scholarship, our teaching, and our relationships with our colleagues and students. As Audre Lorde points out, change starts with self, and relationships that we have with those around us must always be the primary site for social change.

How Can We Reconceptualize Race, Class, and Gender as Categories of Analysis?

To me, we must shift our discourse away from additive analyses of oppression. Such approaches are typically based on two key premises. First, they depend on either/or, dichotomous thinking. Persons, things, and ideas are conceptualized in terms of their opposites. For example, Black/White, man/woman, thought/ feeling, and fact/opinion are defined in oppositional terms. Thought and feeling are not seen as two different and interconnected ways of approaching truth that can coexist in scholarship and teaching. Instead, feeling is defined as antithetical to reason, as its opposite. Despite the fact that we all have "both/and" identities (I am both a college professor and a mother—I don't stop being a mother when I drop my child off at school, or forget everything I learned while scrubbing the toilet), we persist in trying to classify each other in either/or categories. I live each day as an African American woman, a race/gender-specific experience. And I am not alone. Everyone in this room has a race/gender/class-specific identity. Either/or, dichotomous thinking is especially troublesome when applied to theories of oppression because every individual must be classified as being either oppressed or not oppressed. The both/and position of simultaneously being oppressed and oppressor becomes conceptually impossible.

A second premise of additive analyses of oppression is that these dichotomous differences must be ranked. One side of the dichotomy is typically labeled "dominant" and the other "subordinate." Thus, Whites rule Blacks, men are deemed superior to women, and reason is seen as being preferable to emotion. Applying this premise to discussions of oppression leads to the assumption that oppression can be quantified, and that some groups are oppressed more than others. I am frequently asked, "Which has been most oppressive to you, your status as a Black person or your status as a woman?" What I am really being asked to do is divide myself into little boxes and rank my various statuses. If I experience oppression as a both/and phenomenon, why should I analyze it any differently?

Additive analyses of oppression rest squarely on the twin pillars of either/or thinking and the necessity to quantify and rank all relationships to know where one stands. Such approaches typically see African American women as being more oppressed than everyone else because the majority of Black women experience the negative effects of race, class, and gender oppression simultaneously. In essence, if you add together separate oppressions, you are left with a grand oppression greater than the sum of its parts.

I am not denying that specific groups experience oppression more harshly than others—lynching is certainly objectively worse than being held up as a sex object. But we must be careful not to confuse this issue of the saliency of one type of oppression in people's lives with a theoretical stance positing the interlocking nature of oppression. Race, class, and gender may all structure a situation but may not be equally visible and/or important in people's self-definitions. In certain contexts, such as the antebellum American South and contemporary South Africa, racial oppression is more visibly salient, while in other contexts, such as Haiti, El Salvador, and Nicaragua, social class oppression may be more apparent. For middle-class White women, gender may assume experiential primacy unavailable to poor Hispanic women struggling with the ongoing issues of low-paid jobs and the frustrations of the welfare bureaucracy. This recognition that one category may have salience over another in a given time and place does not minimize the theoretical importance of assuming that race, class, and gender as categories of analysis structure all relationships.

To move toward new visions of what oppression is, I think that we need to ask new questions. How are relationships of domination and subordination structured and maintained in the American political economy? How do race, class, and gender function as parallel and interlocking systems that shape this basic relationship of domination and subordination? Questions such as these promise to move us away from futile theoretical struggles concerned with ranking oppressions and toward analyses that assume race, class, and gender are all present in any given setting, even if one appears more visible and salient than the others. Our task becomes redefined as one of reconceptualizing oppression by uncovering the connections among race, class, and gender as categories of analysis.

Institutional Dimension of Oppression

Sandra Harding's contention that gender oppression is structured along three main dimensions—the institutional, the symbolic, and the individual—offers a useful model for a more comprehensive analysis encompassing race, class, and gender oppression. Systemic relationships of domination and subordination structured through social institutions such as schools, businesses, hospitals, the workplace, and government agencies represent the institutional dimension of oppression. Racism, sexism, and elitism all have concrete institutional locations. Even though the workings of the institutional dimension of oppression are often obscured with ideologies claiming equality of opportunity, in actuality, race, class, and gender place Asian American women, Native American men, White men, African American women, and other groups in distinct institutional niches, with varying degrees of penalty and privilege.

Even though I realize that many in the current administration would not share this assumption, let us assume that the institutions of American society discriminate, whether by design or by accident. While many of us are familiar with how race, gender, and class operate separately to structure inequality, I want to focus on how these three systems interlock in structuring the institutional dimension of oppression. To get at the interlocking nature of race, class, and gender, I want you to think about the antebellum plantation as a guiding metaphor for a variety of American social institutions. Even though slavery is typically analyzed as a racist institution, and occasionally as a class institution, I suggest that slavery was a race-, class-, and gender-specific institution. Removing any one piece from our analysis diminishes our understanding of the true nature of relations of domination and subordination under slavery.

Slavery was a profoundly patriarchal institution. It rested on the dual tenets of White male authority and White male property, a joining of the political and the economic within the institution of the family. Heterosexism was assumed, and all Whites were expected to marry. Control over affluent White women's sexuality remained key to slavery's survival because property was to be passed on to the legitimate heirs of the slave owner. Ensuring affluent White women's virginity and chastity was deeply intertwined with maintenance of property relations.

Under slavery, we see varying levels of institutional protection given to affluent White women, working-class and poor White women, and enslaved African women. Poor White women enjoyed few of the protections held out to their upper-class sisters. Moreover, the devalued status of Black women was key in keeping all White women in their assigned places. Controlling Black women's fertility was also vital to the continuation of slavery, for children born to slave mothers themselves were slaves.

African American women shared the devalued status of chattel with their husbands, fathers, and sons. Racism stripped Blacks, as a group, of legal rights, education, and control over their own persons. African American women could be whipped, branded, sold, or killed, not because they were poor, or because they were women, but because they were Black. Racism ensured that Blacks would continue to serve Whites and suffer economic exploitation at the hands of all Whites.

So we have a very interesting chain of command on the plantation—the affluent White master as the reigning patriarch; his White wife helpmate to serve him, help him manage his property, and bring up his heirs; his faithful servants, whose production and reproduction were tied to the requirements of the capitalist political economy; and largely property-less, working-class White men and women watching from afar. In essence, the foundations for the contemporary roles of elite White women, poor Black women, working-class White men, and a series of other groups can be seen in stark relief in this fundamental American social institution. While Blacks experienced the harshest treatment under slavery, and thus made slavery clearly visible as a racist institution, race, class, and gender interlocked in structuring slavery's systemic organization of domination and subordination.

Even today, the plantation remains a compelling metaphor for institutional oppression. Certainly, the actual conditions of oppression are not as severe now as they were then. To argue, as some do, that things have not changed all that much denigrates the achievements of those who struggled for social change before us. However, the basic relationships among Black men, Black women, elite White women, elite White men, working-class White men, and working-class White women as groups remain essentially intact.

A brief analysis of important American social institutions mostly controlled by elite White men should convince us of the interlocking nature of race, class, and gender in structuring the institutional dimension of oppression. For example, if you are from an American college or university, is your campus a modern plantation? Who controls your university's political economy? Are elite White men over-represented among the upper administrators and trustees controlling your university's finances and policies? Are elite White men being joined by growing numbers of elite White women helpmates? What kinds of people are in your classrooms grooming the next generation who will occupy these and other decision-making positions? Who are the members of the support staff who produce the mass mailings, order the supplies, fix the leaky pipes? Do African Americans, Hispanics, or other people of color form the majority of the invisible workers who feed you, wash your dishes, and clean up your offices and libraries after everyone else has gone home?

If your college is anything like mine, you know the answers to these questions. You may be affiliated with an institution that has Hispanic women as vice-presidents for finance, or substantial numbers of Black men among the faculty. If so, you are fortunate. Much more typical are colleges where a modified version of the plantation as a metaphor for the institutional dimension of oppression survives.

The Symbolic Dimension of Oppression

Widespread, societally sanctioned ideologies used to justify relations of domination and subordination comprise the symbolic dimension of oppression. Central to this process is the use of stereotypical or controlling images of diverse race, class, and gender groups. To assess the power of this dimension of oppression, I want you to make a list, either on paper or in your head, of "masculine" and "feminine" characteristics. If your list is anything like that compiled by most people, it reflects some variation of the following:

Masculine	*Feminine*
Aggressive	Passive
Leader	Follower
Rational	Emotional
Strong	Weak
Intellectual	Physical

Not only does this list reflect either/or dichotomous thinking and the need to rank both sides of the dichotomy but it also makes you ask yourself exactly which men and women you had in mind when compiling these characteristics. This list applies almost exclusively to middle-class White men and women. The allegedly "masculine" qualities that you probably listed are only acceptable when exhibited by elite White men, or when used by Black and Hispanic men against each other or against women of color. Aggressive Black and Hispanic men are seen as dangerous, not powerful, and are often penalized when they exhibit any of the allegedly "masculine" characteristics. Working-class and poor White men fare slightly better and are also denied the allegedly "masculine" symbols of leadership, intellectual competence, and human rationality. Women of color and working-class and poor White women also are not represented on this list because they have never had the luxury of being "ladies." What appear to be universal categories representing all men and women instead are unmasked as being applicable to only a small group.

It is important to see how the symbolic images applied to different race, class, and gender groups interact in maintaining systems of domination and subordination. If I were to ask you to repeat the same assignment, but this time, to make separate lists for Black men, Black women, Hispanic women, and Hispanic men, I suspect that your gender symbolism would be quite different. In comparing all of the lists, you might begin to see the interdependence of symbols applied to all groups. For example, the elevated images of White womanhood need devalued images of Black womanhood to maintain credibility.

While this exercise illustrates the interlocking nature of race, class, and gender in structuring the symbolic dimension of oppression, part of its importance lies in demonstrating how race, class, and gender pervade a wide range of what appears to be universal language. Attending to diversity in our scholarship, our teaching, and our daily lives provides a new angle of vision on interpretations of reality thought to be natural, normal, and "true." Moreover, viewing images of masculinity and femininity as universal gender symbolism, rather than as symbolic images that are race-, class-, and gender-specific, renders the experiences of people of color and of nonprivileged White women and men invisible. One way to dehumanize an individual or a group is to deny the reality of their experiences. So when we refuse to deal with race or class because they do not appear to be directly relevant to gender, we are actually becoming part of someone else's problem.

Assuming that the same interlocking set of symbolic images affects everyone differently allows us to move forward toward new analyses. Women of color and White women have different relationships to White male authority, and this difference explains the distinct gender symbolism applied to both groups. Black women encounter controlling images such as the mammy, the matriarch, the mule, and the whore, images that encourage others to reject us as fully human people. Ironically, the negative nature of these images simultaneously encourages us to reject them. In contrast, White women are offered seductive images, those that promise to reward them for supporting the status quo. And yet seductive images can be equally controlling. Consider, for example the views of Nancy White, a 73-year old Black woman, concerning images of rejection and seduction:

> My mother used to say that the black woman is the white man's mule and the white woman is his dog. Now, she said that to say this: we do the heavy work and get beat whether we do it well or not. But the white woman is closer to the master and he pats them on the head and lets them sleep in the house, but he ain't gon' treat neither one like he was dealing with a person. (Gwaltney, 148)

Both sets of images stimulate particular political stances. By broadening the analysis beyond the confines of race, we can see the varying levels of rejection and seduction available to each of us due to our race, class, and gender identity. Each of us lives with an allotted portion of institutional privilege and penalty, and with varying levels of rejection and seduction inherent in the symbolic images applied to us. This is the context in which we make our choices.

Taken together, the institutional and symbolic dimensions of oppression create a structural backdrop against which all of us live our lives.

The Individual Dimension of Oppression

Whether we benefit or not, we all live within institutions that reproduce race, class, and gender oppression. Even if we never have any contact with members of other race, class, or gender groups, we all encounter images of these groups and are exposed to the symbolic meanings attached to those images. On this dimension of oppression, our individual biographies vary tremendously. As a result of our institutional and symbolic statuses, all of our choices become political acts.

All of us must come to terms with the multiple ways in which race, class, and gender as categories of analysis frame our individual biographies. I have lived my entire life as an African American woman from a working-class family, and this basic fact has had a profound impact on my personal biography. Imagine how different your life might be if you had been born Black, or White, or poor, or of a different race/class/gender group than the one with which you are most familiar. The institutional treatment you would have received and the symbolic meanings attached to your very existence might differ dramatically from what you now consider to be natural, normal, and part of everyday life. You might be the same, but your personal biography might have been quite different.

I believe that we carry around the cumulative effect of our lives within multiple structures of oppression. If you want to see how much this has affected you, I ask you one simple question: Who are your close friends? Who are the people with whom you can share your hopes, dreams, vulnerabilities, fears, and victories? Do they look like you? If they are all the same, circumstance may be the cause. For the first seven years of my life, I saw only low-income Black people. My friends from those years reflected the composition of my community. But now that I am an adult, can the defense of circumstance explain the patterns of people I trust as my friends and colleagues? When given other alternatives, if my friends and colleagues reflect the homogeneity of one race, class, and gender group, then these categories of analysis have indeed become barriers to connection.

I am not suggesting that people are doomed to follow the paths laid out for them by race, class, and gender as categories of analysis. While these three structures certainly frame my opportunity structure, as an individual, I always have the choice of accepting things as they are or trying to change them. As Nikki Giovanni points out, "We've got to live in the real world. If we don't like the world we're living in, change it. And if we can't change it, we change ourselves. We can do something" (quoted in Tate, 68).While a piece of the oppressor may be planted deep within each of us, we each have the choice of accepting that piece or challenging it as part of the "true focus of revolutionary change."

How Can We Transcend the Barriers Created by Our Experiences with Race, Class, and Gender Oppression to Build the Types of Coalitions Essential for Social Change?

Reconceptualizing oppression and seeing the barriers created by race, class, and gender as interlocking categories of analysis is a vital first step. But we must transcend these barriers by moving toward race, class, and gender as categories of connection, by building relationships and coalitions that will bring about social change. What are some of the issues involved in doing this?

Differences in Power and Privilege

First, we must recognize that our differing experiences with oppression create problems in the relationships among us. Each of us lives within a system that offers varying levels of power and privilege. These differences in power, whether structured along axes of race, class, gender, age, or sexual orientation, frame our relationships. African American writer June Jordan describes her discomfort on a Caribbean vacation with Olive, the Black woman who cleaned her room:

> Even though both "Olive" and "I" live inside a conflict neither one of us created, and even though both of us therefore hurt inside that conflict, I may be one of the monsters she needs to eliminate from her universe and, in a sense, she may be one of the monsters in mine. (Jordan, 47)

Differences in power constrain our ability to connect with one another, even when we think we are engaged in dialogue across differences. Let me give you an example. One year, the students in my course "Sociology of the Black Community" got into a heated discussion about the reasons for the increase in racial incidents on college campuses. Black students complained vehemently about the apathy and resistance they felt most White students expressed about examining their own racism. Mark, a White male student, found these comments particularly unsettling. After claiming that all the Black people he had ever known had expressed no such beliefs to him, he questioned how representative the viewpoints of his fellow students actually were. When pushed further, Mark revealed that he had participated in conversations over the years with the Black domestic worker employed by his family. Since she had never expressed such strong feelings about White racism, Mark was genuinely shocked by class discussions. Ask yourselves whether that domestic worker was in a position to speak freely. Would it have been wise for her to do so in a situation where the power between the two parties was so unequal?

In extreme cases, members of privileged groups can erase the very presence of the less privileged. When I first moved to Cincinnati, my family and

I went on a picnic at a local park. Picnicking next to us was a family of White Appalachians. When I went to push my daughter on the swings, several of the children came over. They had missing, yellowed, and broken teeth, they wore old clothing—their poverty was evident. I was shocked. Growing up in a large eastern city, I had never seen such awful poverty among Whites. The segregated neighborhoods in which I grew up made White poverty all but invisible. More importantly, the privileges attached to my newly acquired social class position allowed me to ignore and minimize the poverty among Whites that I did encounter. My reactions to those children made me realize how confining phrases such as "Well, at least they're not Black" had become for me. In learning to grant human subjectivity to the Black victims of poverty, I had simultaneously learned to demean White victims of poverty. By applying categories of race to the objective conditions confronting me, I was quantifying and ranking oppressions and missing the very real suffering that, in fact, is the real issue.

One common pattern of relationships across differences in power is one that I label "voyeurism." From the perspective of the privileged, the lives of people of color, of the poor, and of women are interesting for their entertainment value. The privileged become voyeurs, passive onlookers who do not relate to the less powerful but are interested in seeing how the "different" live. Over the years, I have heard numerous African American students complain about professors who never call on them except when a so-called Black issue is being discussed. The students' interest in discussing race or their qualifications for doing so appear unimportant to the professor's efforts to use Black students' experiences as stories to make the material come alive for the White student audience. Asking Black students to perform on cue and provide a Black experience for their White classmates can be seen as voyeurism at its worst.

Most members of subordinate groups do not willingly participate in such exchanges, but often do so because members of dominant groups control the institutional and symbolic apparatuses of oppression. Racial/ethnic groups, women, and the poor have never had the luxury of being voyeurs of the lives of the privileged. Our ability to survive in hostile settings has hinged on our capacity to learn intricate details about the behaviors and worldview of the powerful and adjust our behaviors accordingly. I need only point to the difference in perception of those men and women in abusive relationships. Where men can view their girlfriends and wives as sex objects, helpmates, and a collection of stereotypes—categories of voyeurism—women must be attuned to every nuance of their partners' behavior. Are women "naturally" better at relating to people with more power than themselves, or have circumstances mandated that men and women develop different skills?

Another pattern in relationships among people of unequal power concerns a different form of exploitation. In scholarly enterprises, relationships among students and teachers, among researchers and their subjects, and even among us as colleagues in teaching and scholarship can contain elements of academic colonialism. Years ago, a Black co-worker of mine in the Roxbury section of

Boston described the academic colonialism he saw among the teachers and scholars in that African American community: "The people with notebooks from Harvard come around here and study us. They don't get to know us because they really don't want to and we don't want to let them. They see what they want to see, go back and write their books and get famous off of our problems." Under academic colonialism, more powerful groups see their subordinates as people whom they perceive as subordinate to them, not as sources of entertainment, as in voyeurism, but as a resource to be benignly exploited for their own purposes.

The longstanding effort to "colorize" feminist theory by inserting the experiences of women of color represents at best genuine efforts to reduce bias in Women's Studies. But at its worst, colorization also contains elements of both voyeurism and academic colonialism. As a result of new technologies and perceived profitability, we can now watch black-and-white movie classics in color. While the tinted images we are offered may be more palatable to the modern viewer, we are still watching the same old movie that was offered to us before. Movie colorization adds little of substance—its contributions remain cosmetic. Similarly, women of color allegedly can teach White feminists nothing about feminism, but must confine ourselves to "colorizing" preexisting feminist theory. Rather than seeing women of color as fully human individuals, we are treated as the additive sum of our categories.

In the academy, patterns of relationships among those of unequal power, such as voyeurism and academic colonialism, foster reformist postures toward social change. While reformists may aim to make the movie more fun to watch by colorizing their scholarship and teaching via paying increased lip service to diversity, reformists typically insist on retaining their power to determine what is seen and by whom. In contrast, transformation involves rethinking these differences in power and privilege through dialogues among individuals from diverse groups.

Coming from a tradition where most relationships across difference are squarely rooted in relations of domination and subordination, we have much less experience relating to people as different but equal. The classroom is potentially one powerful and safe space where dialogues among individuals of unequal power relationships can occur. The relationship between Mark, the student in my class, and the domestic worker is typical of a whole series of relationships that people have when they relate across differences in power and privilege. The relationship among Mark and his classmates represents the power of the classroom to minimize those differences so that people of different levels of power can use race, class, and gender as categories of analysis to generate meaningful dialogues. In this case, the classroom equalized racial difference so that Black students who normally felt silenced spoke out. White students like Mark, who are generally unaware of how they had been privileged by their whiteness, lost that privilege in the classroom and thus became open to genuine dialogue.

Reconceptualizing course syllabi represents a comparable process of determining which groups are privileged by our current research and pedagogical techniques and which groups are penalized. Reforming these existing techniques can be a critical first step in moving toward a transformed curriculum reflecting race, class, and gender as interlocking categories of analysis. However, while reform may be effective as a short-term strategy, it is unlikely to bring about fundamental transformation in the long term. To me, social transformations, whether of college curricula or of the communities in which we live and work, require moving outside our areas of specialization and groups of interest to build coalitions across differences.

Coalitions around Common Causes

A second issue in building relationships and coalitions essential for social change is to identity the real reasons for engaging in a coalition. Just what brings people together? The presence of a common enemy is one powerful catalyst that fosters group solidarity. African American, Hispanic, Asian American, and Women's Studies share the common intellectual heritage of challenging what passes for certified knowledge in the academy. But politically expedient relationships and coalitions like these are fragile because, as June Jordan points out, "It occurs to me that much organizational grief could be avoided if people understood that partnership in misery does not necessarily provide for partnership for change: When we get the monsters off our backs all of us may want to run in very different directions" (47).

Sharing a common cause assists individuals and groups in maintaining relationships that transcend their differences. Building effective coalitions involves struggling to hear one another and developing empathy for the other points of view. The coalitions that I have been involved in that lasted and that worked have been those where commitment to a specific issue mandated collaboration as the best strategy for addressing the issue at hand.

Several years ago, master's degree in hand, I chose to teach in an inner-city parochial school in danger of closing. The money was awful, the conditions were poor, but the need was great. In my job, I had to work with a range of individuals who, on the surface, had very little in common. We had White nuns, Black middle-class graduate students, and Blacks from the "community," some of whom had been incarcerated and/or were affiliated with a range of federal anti-poverty programs. Parents formed another part of this community, Harvard faculty another, and a few well-meaning White liberals from Colorado were sprinkled in for good measure.

As you might imagine, tension was high. Initially, our differences seemed insurmountable. But as time passed, we found a common bond. In spite of profound differences in our personal biographies, differences that, in other settings, would have hampered our ability to relate to one another, we found that we were all deeply committed to the education of Black children. By learning to value each other's commitment and by recognizing that we each had different skills that were essential to actualizing that commitment, we built an effective coalition around a common cause. Our school was successful, and the children we taught benefited from the diversity we offered them.

I think that the process of curriculum transformation will require a process comparable to that of political organizing around common causes. None of us alone has a comprehensive vision of how race, class, and gender operate as categories of analysis or how they might be used as categories of connection. Our personal biographies offer us partial views. Few of us can manage to study race, class, and gender simultaneously. Instead, we each know more about some dimensions of this larger story and less about others. While we each may be committed to an inclusive, transformed curriculum, the task of building one is necessarily a collective effort. Just as the members of the school had special skills to offer to the task of building the school, we all have areas of specialization and expertise, whether scholarly, theoretical, or pedagogical, or within areas of race, class, or gender. We do not all have to do the same thing in the same way. Instead, we must support each other's efforts, realizing that they are all part of the larger enterprise of bringing about social change.

Building Empathy

A third issue involved in building the types of relationships and coalitions essential for social change concerns the issue of individual accountability. Issues of race, class, and gender oppression form the structural backdrop against which we frame our relationships—these are the forces that encourage us to substitute voyeurism and academic colonialism for fully human relationships. But while we may not have created this situation, we are each responsible for making individual, personal choices concerning which elements race, class, and gender oppression we will accept and which we will work to change.

One essential component of this accountability involves developing empathy for the experiences of individuals and groups different from ourselves. Empathy begins with taking an interest in the facts of other people's lives, both as individuals and as groups. If you care about me, you should want to know not only the details of my personal biography but also a sense of how race, class, and gender as categories of analysis created the institutional and symbolic backdrop for my personal biography. How can you hope to assess my character without knowing the details of the circumstances I face?

Moreover, by taking a theoretical stance that we have all been affected by race, class, and gender as categories of analysis that have structured our treatment, we open up possibilities for using those same constructs as categories of connection in building empathy. For example, I have a good White woman friend with whom I share common interests and beliefs. Yet we know that our racial differences have provided us with different experiences. So we talk about them. We do not assume that, because I am Black, race has only affected me, and not her, or that because I am a Black woman, race neutralizes the effect of gender in my life, while accentuating it in hers. We take those same categories of analysis that have created cleavages in our lives, in this case, categories of race and gender, and use them as categories of connection in building empathy for each other's experiences.

Finding common causes and building empathy is difficult, no matter which side of privilege we inhabit. Building empathy from the dominant side of privilege is difficult, simply because individuals from privileged backgrounds are not encouraged to do so. For example, for those of you who are White to develop empathy for the experiences of people of color, you must grapple with how your white skin has privileged you. This is difficult to do because it not only entails the intellectual process of seeing how whiteness is elevated in institutions and symbols but also involves the often painful process of seeing how your whiteness has shaped your personal biography. Intellectual stances against the institutional and symbolic dimensions of racism are generally easier to maintain than sustained self-reflection about how racism has shaped all of our individual biographies. Were and are your fathers, uncles, and grandfathers really more capable than mine, or can their accomplishments be explained in part by the racism that members of my family experienced? Did your mothers stand by silently and watch all this happen? More importantly, how have they passed on the benefits of their whiteness to you?

These are difficult questions, and I have tremendous respect for my colleagues and students who are trying to answer them. Because there is no compelling reason to examine the source and meaning of one's own privilege, I know that those who do so have freely chosen this stance. They are making conscious efforts to root out the piece of the oppressor planted within them. To me, they are entitled to the support of people of color in their efforts. Men who declare themselves feminists, members of the middle class who ally themselves with anti-poverty struggles, and heterosexuals who support gays and lesbians are all trying to grow, and their efforts place them far ahead of the majority who never think of engaging in such important struggles.

Building empathy from the subordinate side of privilege is also difficult, but for different reasons. Members of subordinate groups are understandably reluctant to abandon a basic mistrust of members of powerful groups because this mistrust has traditionally been central to their survival. As a Black woman, it would be foolish for me to assume that White women, Black men, White men, or any other group with a history of exploiting African American women has my best interests at heart. These groups enjoy varying amounts of privilege over me, and therefore I must watch them carefully and be prepared for a relation of domination and subordination.

Like the privileged, members of subordinate groups must also work toward replacing judgments by category with new ways of thinking and acting—refusing to do so stifles prospects for effective coalition and social change. Let me use another example from my own experiences. When I was an undergraduate, I had little time or patience for the theorizing of the privileged. My initial years at a private, elite institution were difficult, not because the coursework was challenging (it was, but that wasn't what distracted me) or because I had to work while my classmates lived on family allowances (I was used to work). The adjustment was difficult because so many people who took their privilege for granted surrounded me. Most of them felt entitled to their wealth. That astounded me.

I remember one incident that occurred while I was watching a White woman who lived down the hall in my dormitory try to pick out which sweater to wear. The sweaters were piled up on her bed in all the colors of the rainbow, sweater after sweater. She asked my advice in a way that let me know that choosing a sweater was one of the most important decisions she had to make on a daily basis. Standing knee-deep in her sweaters, I realized how different our lives were. She did not have to worry about maintaining a solid academic average so that she could receive financial aid. Because she was in the majority, she was not treated as a representative of her race. She did not have to consider how her classroom comments or her basic existence on campus contributed to the treatment her group would receive. Her allowance protected her from having to work, so she was free to spend her time studying, partying, or in her case, worrying about which sweater to wear. The degree of inequality in our lives and her unquestioned sense of entitlement concerning that inequality offended me. For a while, I categorized all affluent White women as being superficial, arrogant, overly concerned with material possessions, and part of my problem. But had I continued to classify people in this way, I would have missed out on making some very good friends whose discomfort with their inherited or acquired social class privileges pushed them to examine their position.

Because I opened with the words of Audre Lorde, it seems appropriate to close with another of her ideas. As we go forth to the remaining activities of this workshop, and beyond this workshop, we might do well to consider Lorde's perspective:

> Each of us is called upon to take a stand. So in these days ahead, as we examine ourselves and each other, our works, our fears, our differences, our sisterhood and survivals, I urge you to tackle what is most difficult for us all, self-scrutiny of our complacencies, the idea that since each of us believes she is on the side of right, she need not examine her position. (Lorde 1985)

I urge you to examine your position.

ADDITIONAL RESOURCES

Bambara, Toni Cade, ed. 1970. *The Black Woman.* New York: Signet.
Davis, Angela. 1981. *Women, Race and Class.* New York: Random House.
Dill, Bonnie Thornton. 1983. "Race, Class, and Gender: Prospects for an All-Inclusive Sisterhood," *Feminist Studies* 9(1):131–150

Gwaltney, John Langston. 1980. *Drylongso: A Self-Portrait of Black America*. New York: Vintage.

Jordan, June. 1985. *On Call: Political Essays*. Boston: South End Press.

Lorde, Audre. 1984. *Sister Outsider*. Trumansberg, N.Y.: Crossing Press.

———. 1985. Keynote Address, "Sisterhood and Survival," Conference on the Black Woman Writer and the Diaspora, Michigan State University.

Tate, Claudia, ed. 1983. *Black Women Writers at Work*. New York: Continuum.

Zinn, Maxine Baca, Lynn Weber Cannon, Elizabeth Higginbotham, and Bonnie Thornton Dill. 1986. "The Cost of Exclusionary Practices in Women's Studies." *SIGNS: Journal of Women and Culture in Society* 11(2):290–303.

Where Do We Go from Here?

REFLEXIVE ESSAY: *In my 1989 article "Toward a New Vision: Race, Class, and Gender as Categories of Analysis and Connection," I discussed a new vision for intellectual activism for scholars and activists. Because that essay has been reprinted many times over the last two decades, I began to wonder how "visionary" its ideas are today. In this essay, I replicate the process that I used in "Toward a New Vision," namely, assessing the present to imagine useful directions for thought and action.*

THE IDEAL OF FREEDOM has long been central to American national identity. The vision of freedom is compelling—freedom from religious and other forms of persecution; freedom that promises to treat the rich and poor alike as citizens before the law; and freedom to aim as high as individual desire will take you. Democracy constitutes the mechanism for achieving this ideal of freedom, a process of building community capacity to achieve these ends.

That's the vision. The reality for people living in the United States can be quite different. For most Americans, opportunity remains linked to gender, race, class, sexuality, and citizenship status. Wrapping babies in blue and pink blankets sets them on lifelong, gender-specific trajectories that mask where nature and nurture begin and end. Poor and working-class African American boys living in inner-city neighborhoods nail milk crates to telephone poles for games of street basketball while their female counterparts find few opportunities to play outside at all. White middle-class youth—boys and girls alike—

I delivered an earlier version of this essay as a keynote address at the 2011 spring symposium organized by students of color at Harvard Graduate School of Education.

play soccer on well-manicured green fields in affluent suburban neighborhoods. Poor and working-class white kids living in rural America, with few opportunities for schooling, jobs, or a way to support a family, turn to the military and to meth labs as sources of income and/or solace. In Washington, D.C., a worried Latina second grader raises her hand to ask First Lady Michelle Obama whether the government is going to send her parents away because they don't have papers. In some towns, holding hands with a person of the same gender can get you killed. Practices such as these suggest that the bodies into which we are born, as well as the places where our bodies allegedly belong, determine virtually everything.

I have spent much of my career trying to understand the peculiar combination of change and stasis within American society as it stumbles on, trying to put teeth into its vision of freedom. How is it, in the context of such a powerful vision, that social inequalities of race, class, gender, sexuality, ability, age, and citizenship not only persist but also do so in ways that increasingly erase their characteristic forms of organization and practice? Social inequalities continue, yet we find it increasingly difficult to see them, let alone figure out what to do about them.

More than two decades ago, I delivered a much anthologized speech titled "Toward a New Vision: Race, Class, and Gender as Categories of Analysis and Connection." My speech foreshadowed these seeming contradictions of change and stasis and of freedom and social inequalities. In that talk, I called for confronting cycles of permanent winners and losers, where some Americans routinely enjoy more freedom than others, by developing new patterns of thought and action. I focused on two basic questions. First, *How can we reconceptualize race, class, and gender as categories of analysis?* This question spoke to the need to analyze the oppressive situations in which people so often found themselves. I assumed that if we better understood the social conditions that surround us, we could imagine new ways of seeing the world, being in the world, and changing our worlds. This belief in critical consciousness and in education as fundamental to its actualization led to my second question: *How can we transcend the barriers created by our experiences with race, class, and gender oppression to build the types of coalitions essential for social change?* This question rested on the assumption that critique constitutes a necessary, albeit insufficient, strategy for eliminating social inequalities. No matter how elegant the analysis or how empirically verifiable the argument, ideas without action can leave us feeling more dispirited than ever when we do not see results.

As I revisit my two questions, I see how complicated answering the first one has turned out to be. In the 1980s, it was groundbreaking to analyze race, class, and gender as relational categories of analysis that collectively shaped oppression. Developing theoretical understandings of how race, class, and gender intersect in framing social inequalities, both in the United States and in a global context, have claimed the lion's share of not only my scholarly career but also that of scholars who study a range of topics. At the same time, my second question seems out of reach within early-twenty-first-century U.S. domestic politics. Like many others, I wonder whether the United States remains committed to a vision of freedom that previous generations of immigrants found so compelling and to the coalitional politics that may be needed to bring it about.

Looking back from the perspective of early-twenty-first-century realities helps me to understand how my earlier two questions might have been visionary in the aftermath of the Civil Rights, feminist, and other mid-twentieth-century social movements. However, times have changed. Despite the continued salience of my questions, moving toward freedom now may require new questions. To lay such a foundation, here I revisit my earlier questions, exploring the accomplishments and challenges that confront intersectional scholarship as well as the need to develop a more robust analysis of coalitional politics. Placing the new knowledge of intersectional scholarship in dialogue with a revitalized commitment to coalitional politics might foster new understandings of freedom.

In Search of New Knowledge: Intersectionality

Initially, the question "How can we reconceptualize race, class, and gender as categories of analysis?" seemed straightforward. Yet, grappling with the complexities of intersecting social inequalities has stimulated far more expansive knowledge projects than I initially envisioned. *Intersectionality* is currently the umbrella term that best incorporates this emerging field of study. My initial questions about race, class, and gender are now part of a much larger body of intersectional scholarship that examines multiple connections, for example, how ability and age are interrelated or how sexuality operates within and across ethnic groups.

Within American higher education, the contributions and challenges of intersectional scholarship have become increasingly visible and accepted across several fields of study. Because my work on Black feminism has been necessarily interdisciplinary, I have encountered a broad array of scholars in other disciplines, across varying national settings, and from diverse backgrounds who are also intrigued with how their intellectual projects might be enhanced by a greater emphasis on examining the intersections of race, class, gender, sexuality, age, ability, and citizenship status. In this sense, intersectional frameworks are simultaneously universal and particular. They transcend any one discipline, national setting, or level of analysis (e.g., micro or macro).

Looking back, I see deeper understandings within intersectional scholarship in answering my first question. First, we now know far more about the saliency of race, class, and gender as categories of analysis in varying social contexts. Because these categories are organized differently from one setting to the next, they are not deterministic, master categories that explain all social inequalities. Race, class, and gender are categories that are more salient in the U.S. context than in other national, cultural, and regional settings, where other categories, such as sexuality, age, ability, citizenship status, and religion, may be equally, if not more, prominent. The constellation of all of these categories shifts such that specific combinations become more visible or muted across varying geographic locations, political units, and time periods.

Second, intersectional scholarship has identified an important conceptual shift away from seeing race, class, and gender as discrete phenomena and toward viewing the *relationships* among them as the focus of attention. Power relations of racial and gender segregation as well as those of colonialism rely on categorical thinking that divides the world, and knowledge itself, into separate entities, each having a specific place. Much as the books in a library are shelved with only one number, systems using racism, heterosexism, class exploitation, and sexism also separate and categorize people. In contrast, contemporary relationships of desegregation, decolonization, and recolonization are far more fluid. Just as books can carry multiple keywords, rather than a single number, we now know that individuals have multiple identities; many people hold dual citizenship, for example. When it comes to contemporary power relations in a decolonizing world, intersectional frameworks suggest that there are no pure oppressors or oppressed and that, instead, most social phenomena reflect a tangled set of relationships of privilege and penalty. By replacing "either/or" understandings of the world with a "both/and" lens, intersectional scholarship has focused attention on the processes of relationality.

Third, this shift toward relationality has enabled intersectionality to produce more robust analyses of power. Specifically, we now have a much better sense of how oppressions mutually construct one another within relations of structural power. Many of us have improved our capacity to think outside the boxes of heterosexual-only, or West/North-only, or Christian-only, and similar kinds of thinking that aim to impose a monocategorical, and therefore monocausal, framework on what is obviously a complex and ever-changing set of power relations. Similarly, intersectional analyses have broadened prevailing understandings of identity beyond individual experiences. Instead, focusing on how intersecting systems of power shape a host of constructs, such as personal and group identities, the experiences that accompany such identities, and the social problems faced by people holding those identities, reverses attention from the subjective experience of individual identity to structures of power.

Despite these contributions, intersectional scholarship faces new challenges. Becoming a named discourse has been important for reasons of academic legitimacy, yet the acceptance of intersectionality within the academy raises the question of its connections to its origins in social justice initiatives. The challenges of intersectionality resemble those facing U.S. Black feminism as a social justice project, namely (1) refocusing U.S. Black feminism on the everyday realities of Black women's lives; (2) paying careful attention to how the language of Black feminism is being used, often in ways that are antithetical to Black feminist politics; and (3) developing new standards for evaluating the effectiveness of Black feminism as a social justice project within a greatly changed political environment (for an extended discussion of these points, see Chapter 5). In a similar fashion, the more legitimate that intersectional scholarship becomes in colleges and universities, the more abstract and disengaged it can become from actual social relations. This disengagement may move the discourse away from its origins in social justice projects and their focus on human freedom. Intersectional scholarship may gain legitimacy while losing its very reason for existing.

In Search of New Practice: Coalitional Politics

Despite my excitement at witnessing the explosive growth of scholarly attention to my first question, my second question can seem utopian and unrealistic in the context of early-twenty-first-century political realities. In the U.S. political context, bitter domestic partisan politics suppress efforts toward compromise, making it difficult, if not impossible, to cross party lines. The public suffers with a government that seems increasingly dysfunctional. Coalitions seem like pipe dreams. In the global context, wars, drugs, poverty, HIV/AIDS, and environmental degradation have uprooted people from their communities, producing refugees and migrants in search of political freedom, economic opportunities, and security. A multicultural global elite enjoys wealth without oversight, while the world's poor suffer. What sense does it make to ask my second question in this context? Is it the best question to ask?

My second question, "How can we transcend the barriers created by our experiences with race, class, and gender oppression to build the types of coalitions essential for social change?" may seem unrealistic, but I suggest that it is needed today more than ever. Social movements in the 1960s and 1970s initially drew attention to the barriers to actualizing an American belief in freedom created by racism, class exploitation, sexism, and heterosexism, as well as discrimination based on age, religion, and ability. In a segregated world, the barriers were clear and seemingly impenetrable. Breaking barriers was inherently political. The feminist movement, for example, understood that its success depended on being inclusive of all women. Through strategies such as holding consciousness-raising meetings, where women could organize around common concerns, or building alliances among women's groups that shared common agendas concerning reproductive rights, violence against women, equal pay, and/or similar social issues, feminists aimed to break the barriers that kept women separated and disempowered. In that context, building fully human relations across barriers of race, class, and gender was quite radical. In a similar fashion, many groups worked to remedy the most egregious barriers wrought by the segregation of colonialism.

Despite these accomplishments, my second question may be even more necessary now, precisely because the barriers that separate people are more subtle and many people no longer see the need to practice coalitional politics in their everyday lives. Segregation is not what it once was, but this does not mean that desegregation is complete. For example, because most American children attend K–12 schools that remain segregated by race and/or class, they lack everyday exposure to people outside their own racial/class groups. Black, Latino, and white children attend disproportionately homogeneous schools, but Black and Latino youth pay a far higher price for attending segregated institutions than white youth. All-Black or all-Latino settings with no white children in attendance are tolerated. In contrast, all-white settings can raise red flags for many white parents because such situations challenge widely held beliefs that racial integration has been achieved. Despite the fact that white youth attending overwhelmingly white schools may have limited exposure to youth of color, situations that contain one or two children of color are not seen by most whites as being racially segregated. In this context, middle-class white youth gain exposure to people of color through the media, while their own social circles often include only a few people of color. Ironically, despite the election of Barack Obama, or perhaps because of it, the token inclusivity of a few people of color suggests that America has become a post-racial society (for a discussion of this issue, see Chapters 16 and 18). Yet this imperfect desegregation also masks the continued barriers experienced by racial/ethnic people in accessing opportunities. The language of barriers may seem to be outdated in this world of appearances, where media and web-based virtual realities promise unlimited and unregulated access to others across the barriers of segregated housing, schools, neighborhoods, and national borders. If social media platforms provide us access to one another and to a wealth of information about each other that formerly was rationed by elites, where exactly are the contemporary barriers?

Despite the continued significance of structural barriers in everyday life that are masked by new communication technologies, using the language of barriers as a primary strategy to tackle tough social problems may no longer be effective. The language of breaking barriers is part of a late-twentieth-century "deconstructive" moment when the Berlin Wall fell and the legal walls that upheld South African apartheid were dismantled. What comes after we have broken through? What's left? Deconstructive politics may seem radical in the moment of destroying the walls of segregation that separate people from one another. The pile of rubble left behind holds the promise of a new society, yet it cannot be a new society until we build something new with the pieces.

Rather than focusing on breaking down barriers, the language of community provides fresh avenues of investigation for imagining new ways of organizing social relations that draw from the past yet go beyond the rhetoric of deconstruction. Whether the relationship is within a particular community or among communities, all communities must negotiate the differences in power. As I learned through working in activist and academic communities, a community need not be harmonious; nor are communities necessarily grounded in dynamic, democratic, coalitional politics. Many people who eschew the language of community rightly point out that communities are often places of oppression for many of their members. Gender oppression starts in families, feminists claim. Families in turn naturalize hierarchies of gender and sexuality in ways that render these systems of power virtually invisible. Family practices that uphold gender and sexual hierarchies form a bedrock of intolerance within many religious communities. Many lesbian, gay, bisexual, and transgendered (LGBT) people leave their communities of origin, fearing the intolerance that they experience there. Cases such as these, where communities rely on static social hierarchies, with perpetual winners and losers, reflect only one way of organizing communities.

Communities can also be organized around democratic decision making that ensures all members a fair share of power. As I examine in *Another Kind of Public Education*, this theme of building democratic communities is one of the most important issues confronting American society, both in local communities and on the national level. There is no one best model of crafting democratic communities. Communities that embrace democratic decision making can be organized around a shared identity (which can be fostered by having a common enemy), where members feel a solidarity with one another based on a common history and culture. Democratic communities can also be grounded in a shared vision that attracts a heterogeneous group of people. Neither form of community is superior; some communities may embrace both sets of organizational practices. The bottom line is that democratic communities reject naturalized hierarchies that make members permanent winners and losers from one generation to the next.

For the purposes of this essay, thinking about how communities negotiate the power differences within them points to the significance of coalition building for democratic communities. Because coalition building also requires negotiation of power relations across categories of difference, coalition building might provide an important set of tools both for breaking down barriers and for building communities that can accommodate heterogeneity. Coalition building requires transcending the barriers created by experiences with race, class, and gender oppression. Redefining communities as places of power negotiation suggests that communities constitute the scaffold on which coalitional politics operate. Coalition building focuses on the processes of negotiating these power differentials, with communities as the outcome of negotiation.

Understanding how processes of coalition building shape democratic power relations within and across communities is especially crucial for people of color in the United States. Because racism and anti-racist politics have been so central to American national identity and its commitment to freedom, the kinds of issues that confront racial/ethnic groups in building coalitions might be instructive for understanding coalitional politics writ large. Two features of coalitional politics stand out: (1) coalitional politics *within* racial/ethnic groups, for example, how relationships of gender, sexuality, and class operate within the boundaries of a given racial/ethnic group as it constructs its community; and (2) coalitional politics *among* racial/ethnic groups, specifically, the ways in which the term "people of color" might serve as a political identity that can accommodate the distinctive histories of racial/ethnic groups that are bringing new political communities into being. My analysis is not unique to racial/ethnic groups. Gender, sexuality, and class all lend themselves to a similar approach of examining the coalitional politics within a given group as well as the kinds of coalitions that the group has with others. Yet because racism has been so central to U.S. society, analyzing the experiences of racial/ethnic groups with coalitional politics and communities might prove especially instructive.

Looking Inward: Coalitions within Communities

Analyzing how political coalitions might facilitate racial/ethnic group empowerment requires analyzing relationships that naturalize social inequalities within the communities of native peoples, Asian Americans, Latinos, and African Americans. Often the power hierarchies within racial/ethnic communities remain unexamined, primarily because such communities are imagined to be equally comfortable for all members of a group. Focusing on coalition building within such communities challenges the understanding of communities as static entities. Instead, assuming that communities are not naturally occurring entities that stand outside analysis raises important questions about internal group processes: How might racial/ethnic groups negotiate fair practices within group boundaries that reflect the heterogeneity within that community? How do we move from situations where communities require some members to be oppressed all of the time, some members to be differentially oppressed depending on the context, and still other members to serve routinely as unquestioned spokespersons for the group?

African Americans constitute an important social group for thinking through these questions. I make no claim that African American issues are universal, nor that they are so idiosyncratic that they cannot be found within other groups. Instead, the particularities of African American social organization provide one site for approaching some common themes that affect other groups. Black people have a long and storied history in the U.S. context, one that has enabled this group to form a collective community identity. Unlike immigrant populations, who often migrated voluntarily and built communities that maintained ties to their countries of origin, African Americans crafted communities in response to external factors of racism. Slavery initially pushed individuals together, and over time it produced a collective sense of solidarity based on a shared fate. It has only been in the post–Civil Rights period that African Americans gained sufficient political clout to question this historical sense of community and the internal hierarchies it engendered. In other words, seeing the need for coalition building within Black communities is new.

Several themes that characterize the internal politics within African American communities shed light on broader questions of coalition building. One issue concerns which form of community will prevail among African Americans, namely, historical patterns of naturalized hierarchy or emerging processes of democratic decision making. Black communities have been especially prone to self-define as sites of naturalized hierarchy where there is no need to consider coalitional politics because community members are assumed to share some sort of natural "black" culture. For example, racism ostensibly creates natural alliances between African American women and African American men, making the issue of gender politics moot. Similarly, poor African Americans seemingly have a natural alliance with their more privileged African American counterparts, whose leadership they should naturally accept. Without challenging these assumptions and exploring how relations of race, class, and gender create social inequalities *within* a given community, African American communities run the risk of becoming static and dysfunctional.

A second theme consists of how the absence of intersectional frameworks can foster superficial or incomplete political agendas. Racism has been such an overarching force in shaping the origins of African American communities that there is a tendency to reduce everything to questions of race. Thus, one important dimension of coalition building within African American communities consists of explaining how racism does not shape everyone's experiences in the same way. Many group members see racism as a socially constructed and immoral system of power, one that can be changed (or not) by individual and group-based action. Debates within Black communities then pivot on questions of ideology (integrationist or nationalist) or on tactics that should be used. Yet in the absence of a more robust intersectional analysis of social inequalities within African American communities, the kind I tried to advance in *Black Feminist Thought* and *Black Sexual Politics,* anti-racist politics can be limited.

A third theme concerns the continued significance of internal policing in shaping dynamics within a group. To be effective, internal policing relies on silencing of less powerful group members. When individuals refuse to be silenced about their differential treatment by other group members, they challenge taken-for-granted assumptions about the naturalness of community. Black feminism, for example, not only contests the gender politics within U.S. society overall but also takes aim at gender hierarchies within African American communities. Similarly, Black LGBT people exert considerable leadership within African American communities when they point out how homophobia constitutes a barrier to effective political action. Social class differences within African American communities also foster a rethinking of naturalized hierarchies within Black communities. Rather than assuming a natural leadership role for the Black middle class, the need for cross-class coalitions seems increasingly apparent. No longer can a Black middle class advancing a politics of respectability speak for the entire Black community. As Cathy Cohen explores in *Democracy Remixed: Black Youth and the Future of American Politics,* African American adults cannot speak for Black youth, whose experiences vary dramatically from those of their parents and grandparents. As strategies for internal policing fray within African American communities, and with a growing recognition that communities are continually built and rebuilt, understanding how processes of coalition building might aid in this construction becomes more important.

Looking Outward: Coalitions among Racial/Ethnic Communities

Relationships among racial/ethnic groups that are categorized under the amorphous umbrella of "people of color" constitute another site for analyzing coalitional politics. The political identity "people of color" can have great potential, but African Americans, Latinos, native peoples, Asian Americans, Muslim Americans, and similar racial/ethnic/cultural groups must also recognize the strengths and limitations of this political identification. The category "people of color" is neither a recognized U.S. Census category nor a historically recognized term of self-identification. This category did not emerge from within contemporary grassroots politics of racial/ethnic communities. For example, African Americans constitute an elastic racial/ethnic group, historically incorporating waves of immigrants from the Caribbean and the African continent as well as numerous mixed-race individuals. Puerto Ricans, Mexican Americans, Cuban Americans, Dominicans, and immigrants from Argentina, Venezuela, and other South American countries still grapple with the terms "Hispanic" and "Latino" that are used for this large and culturally and politically heterogeneous population. Pan-Asian identities are comparably complex. Newly arriving Vietnamese immigrants have little in common with well-established Japanese American citizens or affluent immigrants from India, yet they may be classified as Asian all the same. Color has distinctive meanings for these groups, broadly defined. What issues might accompany coalitional politics that are organized under the umbrella of "people of color"?

First, coalition building under the umbrella identity of "people of color" requires taking these specific group histories into account. It is important to stress that racial/ethnic communities are different than chosen associations. They are unlike clubs, workplace collectivities, unions, reading groups, or similar forms of voluntary association. One cannot stop "looking" Black, Latino, or Asian by willing it to be so. Racial/ethnic classifications and the communities they reference have been created within and sustained by race, class, gender, and nation as intersecting systems of power in the U.S. context. These diverse histories reflect their placement within U.S. racial politics. Time of arrival combines with place of origin to shape how a group is treated or even whether it is seen as a group at all. Native peoples, Chicanos, Puerto Ricans, Chinese Americans, Japanese Americans, and African Africans, all racial/ethnic groups with identifiable histories in the United States, have had time to carve out distinctive racial/ethnic identities within U.S. politics. In contrast, groups arriving in the late twentieth century from Asia, Latin America, the Caribbean, and continental Africa have faced the challenge of figuring out where they fit within an ever-changing system of American racial/ethnic classification.

Given these structural realities of time of arrival, place of origin, and region, as well as the varied class compositions of racial/ethnic groups, the challenge for racial/ethnic communities lies in constructing a broad-based political community that can speak to the different needs of diverse racial/ethnic groups. The heterogeneous groups that might identify under the umbrella term "people of color" confront the daunting task of building a political community from scratch. This task of coalition building will not be easy because coalitional politics among racial/ethnic communities requires an understanding of differential group experiences within a system of white supremacy and of how those experiences reflect differences of power within varying racial formations. More to the point, these different histories are themselves hierarchically arranged in ways that create differential treatment for individuals and groups. Coalition building requires connections across these differences in power among communities that may or may not share common interests.

Second, when it comes to building coalitions among people of color, clarifying what "color" means in a contemporary U.S. and global context is crucial. On the one hand, "color" as a metaphor for racism draws from the important work of William E. B. Du Bois. When Du Bois made his proclamation that the "color line" would be a defining feature of the twentieth century, his understanding of the color line was grounded in a complex historical, sociological, and cross-cultural analysis of global racism. Du Bois knew that racism referenced a historically created, dynamic set of social practices that defended racial hierarchy, with the notion that racism will change form and shape, or "color." Du Bois used the notion of the "color line" as a metaphor for discussing racism as a system of power. On the other hand, ideas about color feature prominently within contemporary ideas of a post-racial, or colorblind, society, where color has little significance beyond a benign cultural difference that can be appreciated, celebrated, and/or tolerated. These two different understandings of the relationship between color and racism foster different political identifications.

People of color can still use the language of color for purposes of coalition building, yet must be extremely clear about the history, limitations, and possibilities that accompany this term. Just as the general public misreads the difference between the ideal of a colorblind society and its actuality, so too might the premature rush to the term "people of color" reflect a similar fusion of a valued ideal with some tough contemporary realities. When it comes to building political coalitions, racial/ethnic groups that are situated under the umbrella of "people of color" need to ask, "Which version of 'color' are we embracing?" Is the version of "color" invoked within the phrase "people of color" a cosmetic coloring in of existing power relations of colorblind racism? Or does "color" invoke Du Bois's historically rich meanings of a flexible, fluid, and ever-changing color line that has been central in upholding racial hierarchy?

Given these two issues, how might members of racial/ethnic groups add some political teeth to this notion of "color," contemporary configurations of the "color line," and self-identification as "people of color" who find themselves in this new racial formation? One way forward lies in developing structures *within* racial/ethnic communities for identifying issues that are of concern to them. These initial agendas can serve as points of contact for conversations among communities. We need a conceptual and political shift from the initial steps of developing group-based standpoints that ostensibly represent the needs of Latinos, Blacks, or immigrant populations—my case study of African Americans was designed to sketch out the difficulties of crafting any group-based position—to see the dynamic interconnections among an array of situated standpoints. A community needs to know where it stands before it can appreciate where other communities stand on similar issues. Moreover, communities cannot determine where they stand without dialogue with other communities that are engaged in a similar process of moving toward democratic decision making within their own borders and reaching out beyond those borders for coalition building.

Where Do We Go from Here?

In this essay, I have sketched out how a revitalized commitment to coalitional politics that is informed by an intersectional understanding of community might suggest new visions and accompanying courses of action. But where do we go from here? Three implications of my argument thus far suggest some future directions.

First, this essay shows the limitations of social change as a vision for coalitional politics. Thus far, I have emphasized themes of barriers and coalition building, the nuts and bolts of moving toward a vision. At the same time, I have neglected the assumption from "Toward a New Vision" that the objective of coalitional politics is "social change." A belief in social change may be a good starting point for coalition building, but this idea cannot sustain coalitional politics. Social change is neither a philosophy nor an ethical position. It is a tool, a technique, a description of variation across time toward or away from some goal. Social change begs the question of what goals are desirable as well as the standards used to move toward them.

The construct of social justice might offer a richer overarching framework that can guide and evaluate the success of coalitional politics. For many of us engaged in intellectual activism, social justice has become a far more useful concept than amorphous notions of social change. A renewed emphasis on social justice might also benefit intersectional scholarship. An ethics of social justice might help to clarify the purpose of intersectional scholarship, its intended audiences, its content, and the forms that such scholarship might take. This shift toward social justice highlights the necessity of principled positions for both coalitional politics and intersectional scholarship. A question more suitable for today might read: *How can we transcend the barriers created by our experiences within intersecting systems of oppression to build coalitions that foster social justice?*

A second implication of this essay concerns the need for more complex analyses of collective action. In "Toward a New Vision," I issued a call to action, suggesting that a changed consciousness within each individual was essential for building coalitions. I ended that earlier essay by charging readers to "examine their own position." Developing an understanding of one's own position is necessary, but it is far from sufficient for social justice projects. Individuals can understand their own positions, yet, if they are disconnected from social justice commitments, they may be ineffective in contesting social inequalities. I now reject the notion that the "revolution" is buried deep within each of us and that all we need to do is "find" it, like a hidden treasure. This may be the case for many people, but when it comes to social inequalities that stem from intersecting systems of power, much more is needed than assessing our own individual consciences.

Refocusing attention on coalitional politics and on the skill set needed to engage in such politics pushes back against a narcissistic individualism that encourages each of us to hunt for our own "private revolutions." We need to develop a more robust understanding of social groups; coalitional politics; and the reasons why some individuals engage in activism, whereas others, armed with the same information and undergoing similar experiences, do not. This essay's discussion of coalition building, both within and among communities of color, suggests that, although individuals are the foundation of any political action, we need better analyses of how social groups are organized and operate. Moreover, intersectional analyses that remain attentive to the social justice implications of scholarship may be positioned to make important contributions to coalitional politics.

Finally, claiming an ethics of social justice and linking it to a more robust understanding of coalitional politics creates space for coalitions of conscience. Such coalitions would be grounded in an ethical framework of the sort suggested by a commitment to social justice. Conscience would be expressed not solely through an individual's consciousness but also via group-based, principled commitments. My earlier discussion of communities and coalitional politics was designed to broaden our thinking about forms of political organization and democratic processes. Building on this analysis, here I suggest that communities might also be sites of "conscience," where group members take principled positions on the social injustices that result from intersecting systems of power. Ethical frameworks that inform such communities need not emerge primarily from *a priori* abstractions about the meaning of social justice. Rather they are constantly reworked within social justice projects that are honed in the crucible of experience. My earlier discussion of coalition building, both within and across communities of color, sketched out some of the issues associated with engaging in this form of robust community politics.

Many of us have had glimpses of coalitions of conscience and may have been members of communities that housed them. We can find many examples of coalitions of conscience in everyday life. Coalitions of conscience do not usually form the focus of scholarship, but when they do, they offer important lessons. For example, in their conversations as recorded in *We Make the Road by Walking,* Paulo Freire and Myles Horton discuss their road into activism and their shared view of literacy as foundational to empowerment. Similarly, Mark Warren does us a real service in his volume *Fire in the Heart,* a nuanced study of how whites who are committed to racial justice initiatives actively chose to engage in coalitions of conscience. Dawne Moon's book *God, Sex and Politics: Homosexuality and Everyday Theologies* thoroughly explores the internal politics of building coalitions of conscience among individuals within faith communities. These examples illustrate how building coalitions of conscience can be exciting, exasperating, and empowering for community members and show that scholarship about coalitions of conscience that reflects intersectional analysis can have a far-reaching effect.

For me, coalitions of conscience do not exist in my imagination—rather, they have taken tangible forms as I have traveled the path of my own intellectual activism. Whether drawn from my engaged scholarship on Black feminism, intersectionality, the sociology of knowledge, or critical education, I have a lifetime of experiences that remind me of the value of coalitions of conscience and the hard work it takes to bring them about. Where do I go from here? I have not yet walked away, so it seems I'll keep on trying. Where do we go from here? The answer to this question is in your hands.

ADDITIONAL RESOURCES

Bell, Brenda, John Gaventa, and John Peters, eds. 1990. *We Make the Road by Walking: Conversations on Education and Social Change,* by Myles Horton and Paulo Freire. Philadelphia: Temple University Press.

Cohen, Cathy J. 2010. *Democracy Remixed: Black Youth and the Future of American Politics.* Chicago: University of Chicago Press.

Collins, Patricia Hill. 1993. "Toward a New Vision: Race, Class, and Gender as Categories of Analysis and Connection." *Race, Sex and Class* 1:25–45.

———. 2009. *Another Kind of Public Education: Race, Schools, the Media and Democratic Possibilities.* Boston: Beacon Press.

———. 2010. "The New Politics of Community." *American Sociological Review* 75(1): 7–30.

Moon, Dawne. 2004. *God, Sex and Politics: Homosexuality and Everyday Theologies.* Chicago: University of Chicago Press.

Warren, Mark R. 2010. *Fire in the Heart: How White Activists Embrace Racial Justice.* New York: Oxford University Press.

Index